VISUAL QUICKSTART GUIDE

PowerPoint
2000/98

FOR WINDOWS AND MACINTOSH

Rebecca Bridges Altman

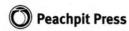 **Peachpit Press**

Visual QuickStart Guide
PowerPoint 2000/98
Rebecca Bridges Altman

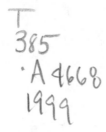

Peachpit Press
1249 Eighth Street
Berkeley, CA 94710
(800) 283-9444
(510) 524-2178
(510) 542-2221 (fax)

Find us on the World Wide Web at
http://www.peachpit.com

Peachpit Press is a division of Addison Wesley Longman

Editor: Lisa Theobald
Copy editor: Margie Bridges
Production coordinator: Lisa Brazieal
Compositor: Lisa Brazieal
Cover design: The Visual Group
Indexer: Carol Burbo

ISBN: 0-201-35441-1

9 8 7 6 5

Dedication

To my two-year-old daughter, Jamie, who
kept me entertained with her frequent visits,
kisses, and hugs as I wrote this book.

Acknowledgments

This book was truly a family affair. I'd like to thank the following family members for their help:

My mother, **Margie Bridges**, for her copy editing skills.

My sister-in-law, **Jan Altman**, for her thorough technical editing.

My brother, **Bruce Bridges**, for his 24-hour Macintosh technical support.

My husband, **Rick Altman**, for his willingness to answer various and sundry computer questions.

I'd also like to thank the staff at Peachpit Press for all their support:

Nancy Ruenzel for publishing this book.

Lisa Theobald for editing and overseeing the project.

Lisa Brazieal for managing the production of the book.

TABLE OF CONTENTS

TABLE OF CONTENTS

Chapter 9: Creating Tables (Mac OS)   133

Chapter 10: Adding Graphical Objects   153

ABLE OF CONTENTS

INTRODUCING POWERPOINT

Visual QuickStart Guides offer a unique way to learn a software package. For the most part, each page is self-contained with a single topic. Each page has concise step-by-step instructions on how to perform a certain task and is accompanied by illustrations and explanatory captions. This type of organization makes it less overwhelming to learn an extensive program such as PowerPoint, and allows you to master just the features you need.

At the end of each topic, you'll find a list of helpful tips. These tips provide you with shortcuts, alternate techniques, additional information, and related topics. Some of these tips are undocumented or buried so deep in the documentation that it's unlikely you would ever find them.

Time permitting, you may want to read the book cover-to-cover, but in all likelihood, you will probably just turn to a specific chapter or topic you want to learn about. And the way this book is organized, you will be able to do so quickly and efficiently.

This first chapter provides you with an introduction to presentation graphics and to PowerPoint's capabilities.

Chapter 2 is a great way to learn the main features of PowerPoint, especially if you have a presentation that needs to be out the door yesterday.

Chapters 3 through 12 explain how to create different types of slides (bulleted lists, charts, tables, and organization charts) and format your presentations.

Chapters 13 and 14 illustrate two additional ways to view and organize presentations: Outline view and Slide Sorter view.

Chapters 15 and 16 show you different ways to output your presentation: onscreen in a slide show, in printed form, and in 35mm slides.

Chapter 17 describes how to show your PowerPoint presentations on the Internet.

INTRODUCING POWERPOINT

PowerPoint on Windows and Mac OS Computers

This book covers the latest versions of PowerPoint for Windows (included with Office 2000) and for the Macintosh (Office 98). The features, menus, and dialog boxes in these two programs are extremely similar in most cases. Any differences will be clearly noted. For example, if a feature is available on only one of the platforms or if the procedure is significantly different in the two versions, the section will be labeled "Windows Only" or "Mac OS Only."

When specific keys or commands are different, the operating system will be noted in parentheses. For instance, "Choose Tools > Preferences (Windows) or Tools > Options (Mac OS)."

PowerPoint on Windows and Mac OS

Presentation Graphics

What exactly can presentation graphics software do? This type of software provides you with tools for creating slides formatted with a variety of different elements, such as bulleted lists, numeric tables, organization charts, and business charts (pies, bars, lines, and more).

You also get tools for adding graphic elements to your slides. For example, you can create designs for the background of your slide using the Rectangle, Oval, and Line tools. But don't worry if you aren't artistically inclined—you can always insert a ready-made drawing from the clip art library, or you can use a professionally designed template (**Figure 1.1**).

There are three good reasons to use a presentation graphics package. First, as its name implies, this type of software *presents graphics*. You can present the graphics in a variety of ways: in an onscreen slide show (complete with special transition effects), on paper (one per page, or several per page for audience handouts), or on 35mm slides.

Second, a presentation graphics package can bring all the components of a presentation together, into a single file. You can use it to create the slides, or, if you prefer, you can import elements from other programs into slides in the presentation graphics program.

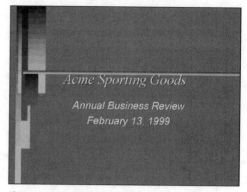

Figure 1.1 The graphical objects on this slide were produced by applying a professionally designed template.

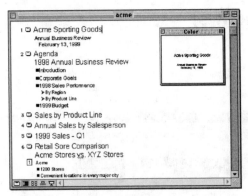

Figure 1.2 Outline view shows the structure of your presentation, letting you easily reorganize the presentation if necessary.

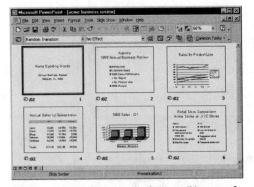

Figure 1.3 Slide Sorter view displays small images of the slides and lets you move them around at will.

Third, the software offers convenient ways to organize the presentation. Using the Outline view (**Figure 1.2**) or Slide Sorter view (**Figure 1.3**), you can see the structure of the presentation and reorganize the slides if necessary.

As you can see, there are quite a few advantages to creating your presentations in a presentation graphics package, and PowerPoint is an excellent choice for these tasks.

PRESENTATION GRAPHICS

The PowerPoint Window (Windows)

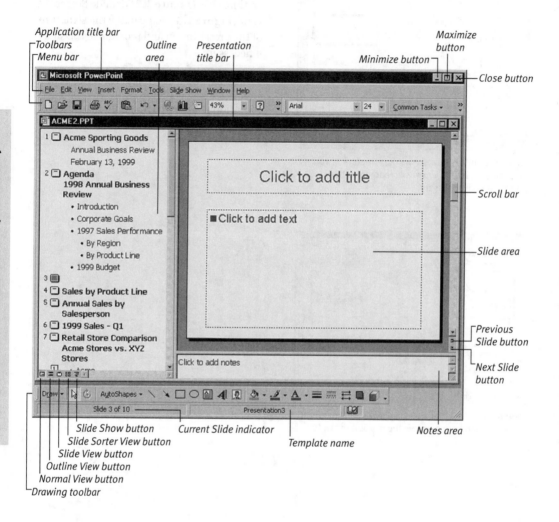

Figure 1.4 Here are the important areas of the PowerPoint window. For further details on any of these areas, refer to the key on the opposite page.

Key to the PowerPoint Window (Windows)

Application title bar
Displays the name of the current application (Microsoft PowerPoint).

Presentation title bar
Shows the name of the current presentation.

Minimize button
Shrinks the application to a button on the taskbar.

Maximize button
Enlarges the window so that it fills the screen. When the window is maximized, the Restore button is displayed; this button restores the window to its previous size.

Close button
Closes the window.

Menu bar
The main menu of choices. Clicking a menu item displays a drop-down menu.

Toolbars
Contain buttons for frequently used tasks, such as opening, saving, and printing.

Outline area
In Normal view, the presentation outline appears in this area.

Drawing toolbar
Contains buttons for drawing and formatting objects.

Normal View button
Simultaneously displays an area in which you can work on a single slide, an outline of your presentation, and an area to enter speaker notes.

Outline View button
Displays an outline of the presentation (slide titles and main text).

Slide View button
Displays a single slide in the presentation window.

Slide Sorter View button
Displays miniature versions of each slide, allowing you to see many slides at once.

Slide Show button
Presents the slides one at a time in an onscreen slide show.

Current Slide indicator
Indicates the number of the slide currently on the screen.

Template name
Name of the current template (design). Double-clicking this area lets you apply another template.

Notes area
An area in Normal view where you can enter speaker notes for the current slide.

Scroll bar
Displays other slides in the presentation.

Slide area
The work area where you create, format, and modify the slide elements.

Previous Slide button
Displays the previous slide in the presentation.

Next Slide button
Displays the next slide in the presentation.

The PowerPoint Window (Mac OS)

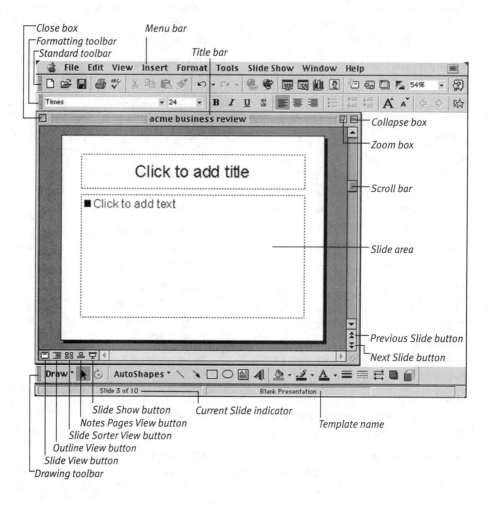

Figure 1.5 Here are the important areas of the PowerPoint window. For further details on any of these areas, refer to the key on the opposite page.

Key to the PowerPoint Window (Mac OS)

Menu bar
The main menu of choices. Clicking a menu item displays a drop-down menu.

Standard toolbar
Contains buttons for frequently used tasks, such as opening, saving, and printing.

Formatting toolbar
Contains buttons for formatting text.

Close box
Closes the window.

Drawing toolbar
Contains buttons for drawing and formatting objects.

Collapse box
Collapses the window. (This box is available in Mac OS 8.0 or higher.)

Zoom box
Enlarges the window as much as possible, or restores the window to its previous size.

Title bar
Shows the name of the current presentation.

Scroll bar
Displays other slides in the presentation.

Slide area
The work area where you create, format, and modify the slide elements.

Previous Slide button
Displays the previous slide in the presentation.

Next Slide button
Displays the next slide in the presentation.

Current Slide indicator
Indicates the number of the slide currently on the screen.

Slide View button
Displays a single slide in the presentation window.

Outline View button
Displays an outline of the presentation (slide titles and main text).

Slide Sorter View button
Displays miniature versions of each slide, allowing you to see many slides at once.

Notes Pages View button
Displays speaker notes pages, allowing you to type notes about the slide. These notes can be printed and referred to during a slide show.

Slide Show button
Presents the slides one at a time in an onscreen slide show.

Template name
Name of the current template (design). Double-clicking this area lets you apply another template.

THE POWERPOINT WINDOW (MAC OS)

Using PowerPoint Menus

You can choose options on the PowerPoint menu bar just as you do in other applications. In the Windows version, however, the menus work a little bit differently—they automatically modify themselves as you use them. When you first display a drop-down menu, you see an abbreviated list of the most frequently-used options (**Figure 1.6**). This short menu saves you from having to wade through a list of options that you rarely use.

If you don't see the option you want, just pause for a few seconds and the complete list will appear (**Figure 1.7**). If you then choose one of these secondary commands, it will automatically appear on the initial list in the future (and over time, options you have stopped using will drop off the initial menu).

✔ Tip

- If you prefer giving commands with the keyboard instead of the mouse, you'll want to use the many shortcut keys that are available. For example, instead of choosing Edit > Select All, you can press Ctrl+A (Windows) or Command+A (Mac OS). The shortcut keys are listed next to the menu options (**Figure 1.8**).

Indicates that some commands are hidden

Figure 1.6 Use the initial abbreviated menu for frequently-used options.

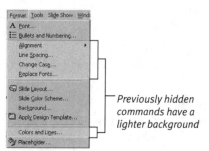

Previously hidden commands have a lighter background

Figure 1.7 You can choose more options from the expanded menu.

Figure 1.8 The shortcut keys appear next to the menu options. (A Mac OS menu is shown here.)

USING POWERPOINT MENUS

Click here...

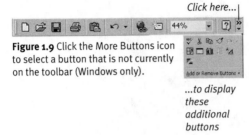

Figure 1.9 Click the More Buttons icon to select a button that is not currently on the toolbar (Windows only).

...to display these additional buttons

Formatting toolbar
Standard toolbar

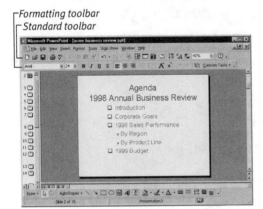

Figure 1.10 After you drag it down, the Formatting toolbar appears on its own line.

Using Toolbars

PowerPoint has toolbars for drawing, outlining, creating tables, formatting text, formatting pictures, adding animation effects, and more. You can turn these toolbars on and off, depending on your needs.

To display or hide a particular toolbar:

1. Choose View > Toolbars.

2. Select the toolbar you want to display or hide.

PowerPoint offers dynamic toolbars that automatically update to reflect the buttons you use most often (Windows only).

To use the dynamic toolbars:

1. Click the More Buttons icon to see additional buttons (**Figure 1.9**).

2. Select the button you want to use. It will automatically be added to the toolbar.

✔ Tip

■ In Windows, the Standard and Formatting toolbars are combined onto one line. If you like, you can click an empty area at the end of the toolbar (not on a button) and drag down until the Formatting toolbar jumps down onto a line of its own (**Figure 1.10**).

USING TOOLBARS

Using Shortcut Menus

A shortcut menu lists the most common commands pertaining to a selected object (**Figure 1.10**). Options on a shortcut menu vary depending on what is selected. If nothing is selected, a menu with options for formatting your presentation will appear.

To display the shortcut menu:

1. Point to the object.

2. Press the right mouse button (Windows).

   or

   Hold down the Control key as you press the mouse button (Mac OS).

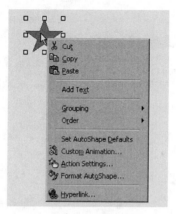

Figure 1.10 Use the shortcut menu to choose commands that affect the selected object.

Using the Office Assistant

The Office Assistant can be your right-hand man when you're using PowerPoint. Whenever you have a question, just type it in the Assistant's question box. The Assistant comes in a variety of forms, such as Clipit or Max the computer man (**Figure 1.12**).

To use the Office Assistant:

1. If you don't see your Assistant, click the Help button on the toolbar. ⌗

   or

   If you do see your Assistant, click on it.

2. Type your question or just enter the key words you want to look up (**Figure 1.13**).

3. Click Search.

4. Click a topic in the list that appears (**Figure 1.14**). You will see a Help window with the answer to your question.

✔ Tips

- To print a help topic, click the Print icon on the toolbar (Windows) or choose File > Print (Mac OS).

- To set Office Assistant options, click on your Assistant and choose Options. By selecting the Gallery tab, you can choose a different type of Assistant (such as a dog or a cat).

- If you would like your F1 or Help key to bring up the standard Help window, click the Options button in Office Assistant and unselect the checkbox Respond To F1 Key (Windows) or Respond To Help Key (Mac OS).

Figure 1.12 The Office Assistant can appear as Clipit or Max the computer man.

Figure 1.13 This window appears when you click the Office Assistant.

Figure 1.14 If the Office Assistant lists the topic you want, just click the topic to view a help window.

USING THE OFFICE ASSISTANT

A QUICK TOUR OF POWERPOINT

2

Suppose you need to create a set of charts by the end of the day, but you have never used PowerPoint. What will you do? Don't panic—just read this chapter. We understand that in today's busy world, people may not have time to read an entire book before they dive into a real-life project. But by reading this chapter, you'll learn the most important things you need to know about creating a presentation in PowerPoint.

After reading this chapter, you'll be able to create bullet lists and charts, format the slides, print the slides, view an onscreen slide show, and use Outline and Slide Sorter views to reorganize the presentation. This chapter gives you the bare bones information; for details, turn to the referenced chapters.

Launching PowerPoint

You can launch PowerPoint in a number of ways, depending on how your system is set up. Some possibilities are listed below.

To launch PowerPoint in Windows:

◆ Click the Start button, point to Programs, and click Microsoft PowerPoint (**Figure 2.1**). The opening dialog box appears (**Figure 2.2**).

To launch PowerPoint in Mac OS:

◆ Open the Microsoft Office 98 folder on your hard disk, and double-click the Microsoft PowerPoint icon (**Figure 2.3**).

Figure 2.1 Choose Microsoft PowerPoint from the Programs menu (Windows).

Figure 2.2 After PowerPoint for Windows is launched, this dialog box opens.

Figure 2.3 To start PowerPoint, first open Microsoft Office 98 folder (Mac OS).

Select the Design Templates tab to see the template names — Click a filename to preview the template — List button

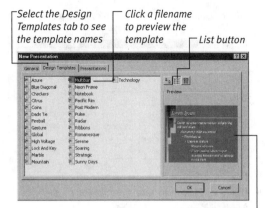

Preview box

Figure 2.4 Choose a template for a new presentation (Windows) from the New Presentation window.

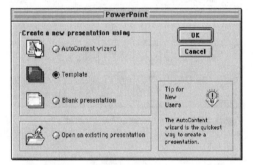

Figure 2.5 This opening dialog box is displayed after launching PowerPoint (Mac OS).

Select the Presentation Designs tab to see the template names

Click a filename to preview the template — View field

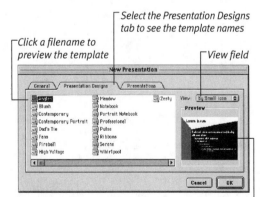

Figure 2.6 Choose a template for a new presentation (Mac OS). — Preview box

Choosing a Template

A template controls the look of your presentation—the colors, the format, graphics placed on each slide, and so forth. PowerPoint comes loaded with dozens of templates.

To choose a template (Windows):

1. If the opening dialog box (**Figure 2.2**) is displayed, choose Design Templates and click OK.

   or

   If the opening box is not displayed, choose File > New.

2. Select the Design Templates tab (**Figure 2.4**).

3. Click the List button to see more template names at once.

4. Click a template name and look at the preview box to see this design.

5. When you find a template you like, click OK.

To choose a template (Mac OS):

1. If the opening dialog box (**Figure 2.5**) is displayed, choose Template and click OK.

   or

   If the opening box is not displayed, choose File > New.

2. Select the Presentation Designs tab (**Figure 2.6**).

3. In the View field, choose By Small Icon to see more template names at once.

4. Click a template name and look at the preview box to see this design.

5. When you find a template you like, click OK.

To learn more about templates, see Chapter 12.

Choosing a Layout

PowerPoint offers 24 different AutoLayouts to help you define the elements you want on a slide, such as a bulleted list, a chart, a table, and an organization chart.

You choose a layout from the New Slide dialog box shown in **Figure 2.7**. This dialog box automatically displays when you create a new presentation or add a new slide.

To choose a layout:

1. Click the desired layout (scroll to see more choices). **Figure 2.7** shows the first set of layouts; **Figure 2.8** shows the second set.

2. Click OK.

On the following pages you will see examples of two types of layouts: Bulleted List and Chart.

✔ Tips

■ When you click a layout in the New Slide dialog box, a description of the layout displays in the box (**Figure 2.7**).

■ Instead of clicking the layout and clicking OK, you can double-click the layout in the New Slide dialog box.

■ To select a different layout for an existing slide, choose Format > Slide Layout.

Click a layout...⌐   ...to display a description of ⌐
                            the layout here

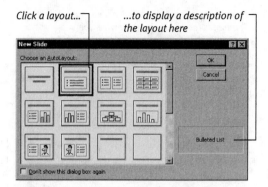

Figure 2.7 Choose an AutoLayout as you create a new slide.

⌐Scroll bar

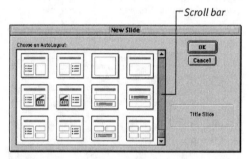

Figure 2.8 By using the scroll bar, you can see additional layouts.

Title placeholder ⌐　　　　　*Text placeholder* ⌐

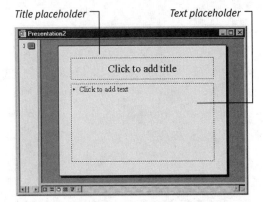

Figure 2.9 A new Bulleted List slide appears before any text has been added.

Press Tab to indent

Press Shift+Tab to unindent

Figure 2.10 This list shows two levels of bullets.

Creating a Bulleted List

Bulleted lists are one of the most common types of slide used in presentations.

To create a bulleted list:

1. If the New Slide dialog box is not displayed, click the text "Click to add first slide" or click the New Slide button on the toolbar.

2. In the New Slide dialog box, choose the Bulleted List layout.

3. Click the *title placeholder* (**Figure 2.9**), and type the title of your bulleted list.

4. Click the *text placeholder* (**Figure 2.9**), and type your bulleted text. Follow these simple rules:

   ◆ Press Enter to type another bullet.

   ◆ Press Tab to indent the current line (**Figure 2.10**).

   ◆ Press Shift+Tab to decrease the indent on the current line.

✔ Tip

■ To change the bullet shape, use the Format > Bullets & Numbering command (Windows) or the Format > Bullet command (Mac OS).

   See Chapter 3 for additional information on creating text charts.

Creating a Chart

Instead of showing your audience columns and rows of numbers, use a chart to illustrate your data graphically. PowerPoint offers a wide variety of chart types—line, column, area, and pies are a few examples.

When you create charts in PowerPoint, you actually use the Microsoft Graph program.

To create a chart:

1. If the New Slide dialog box is not displayed, click the New Slide button on the toolbar.

2. In the New Slide dialog box, choose the Chart layout.

3. Click the *title placeholder* (**Figure 2.11**), and type the title of your chart.

4. Double-click the *chart placeholder* to launch Microsoft Graph. A datasheet with sample data appears.

5. To erase the sample data, click the Select All button (**Figure 2.12**) and press the Delete key (Windows) or the Del key (Mac OS).

6. Enter your chart data (**Figure 2.12**).

7. To close the datasheet and view the chart, click the View Datasheet button on the toolbar.

   Figure 2.13 shows a column chart of the data in Figure 2.12.

✔ Tip

■ To redisplay the datasheet, click the View Datasheet button again.

   See Chapter 4 for more information on inserting charts that have axes.

   See Chapter 6 for information on creating pie charts.

Title placeholder ⌐   Chart placeholder ⌐

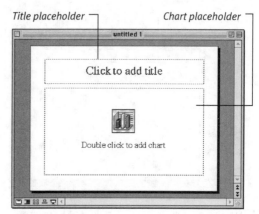

Figure 2.11 Double-click the chart placeholder to launch Microsoft Graph.

Labels in this row will be the x-axis labels ⌐

⌐Select All button

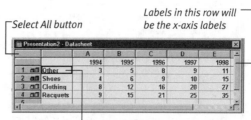

Labels in this column will be part of the legend

Figure 2.12 Enter your chart data in the datasheet.

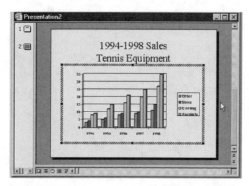

Figure 2.13 You can create column charts like this one.

Border ⌐

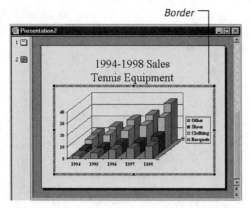

Figure 2.14 When a chart has a border around it, you are in Microsoft Graph (Windows).

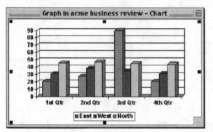

Figure 2.15 When a chart appears in its own window, you are in Microsoft Graph (Mac OS).

⌐Select a chart type...   ⌐...then choose
                                 a sub-type

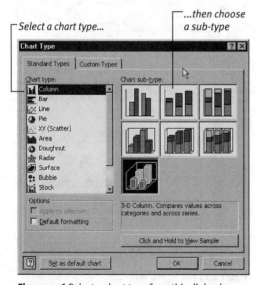

Figure 2.16 Select a chart type from this dialog box.

Choosing a Chart Type

To format a chart, you must still be in Microsoft Graph. To determine whether you are in Graph, look for a border around the chart (**Figure 2.14**) or a chart window (**Figure 2.15**). If you aren't in Microsoft Graph, double-click the chart placeholder.

To change the chart type:

1. Choose Chart > Chart Type.

   The Chart Type dialog box appears (**Figure 2.16**).

2. Select the desired chart type.

3. Choose a sub-type, and click OK.

✔ Tip

■ You can select the chart type before you fill in the datasheet.

Formatting a Chart

To format an element on a chart, just double-click the item you want to format. The appropriate Format dialog box will then appear. For example, suppose you want to place the legend at the bottom of the chart.

To format the legend:

1. Point to the legend; you will see a bubble that says "Legend" (**Figure 2.17**).

2. Double-click the legend to display the Format Legend dialog box.

3. Select the Placement tab (**Figure 2.18**).

4. Choose Bottom.

5. Click OK.

   Figure 2.19 shows the legend after it was placed at the bottom of the chart.

✔ Tips

- Because some of the chart elements are very close together, read the bubble that appears when you point to an element to make sure you have selected the one you intended.

- To exit from Microsoft Graph in the Windows environment, click the slide outside of the chart placeholder. To exit Microsoft Graph in the Mac OS, choose File > Quit & Return.

- To reload Microsoft Graph, double-click the chart.

  See Chapter 5 for additional information on formatting charts and Chapter 6 for information on formatting pie charts.

Object name

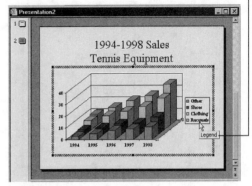

Figure 2.17 When you point to an object, a bubble appears with the name of the object.

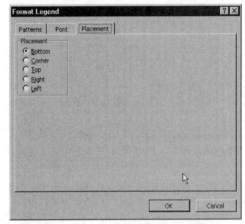

Figure 2.18 Choose a placement option from the Pacement tab of the Format Legend dialog box.

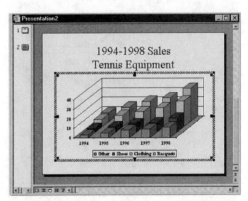

Figure 2.19 The legend now appears at the bottom of the chart.

Slide numbers and titles appear as you drag the scroll box ——— *Scroll box*

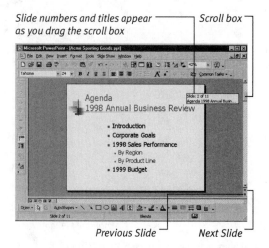

Previous Slide ——— *Next Slide*

Figure 2.20 Use the scroll bar to go to other slides in the presentation.

Navigating a Presentation

The status line at the bottom of the PowerPoint window indicates the current slide number. The slide numbers and titles also appear as you drag the vertical scroll box (**Figure 2.20**). In Slide or Normal view, you can use the keyboard commands listed in **Table 2.1** to display other slides in the presentation:

Table 2.1

Navigation Keys	
TO MOVE TO...	PRESS...
Next Slide	Page Down
Previous Slide	Page Up
First Slide	Ctrl+Home (Windows) Command+Home (Mac)
Last Slide	Ctrl+End (Windows) Command+End (Mac)

You can also use the Next Slide and Previous Slide buttons in the scroll bar. Use the following guidelines when navigating with the scroll bar:

◆ Drag the scroll box to the top of the scroll bar to go to the first slide.

◆ Drag the scroll box to the bottom of the scroll bar to go to the last slide.

◆ Drag the scroll box up or down to go to a specific slide.

✔ Tip

■ In Normal view, you can scroll through the outline and click the slide title you want to see (Windows only).

Saving, Opening, and Closing Presentations

The commands for saving, opening, and closing presentations are on the File menu.

To save a new presentation:

1. Choose File > Save As.

   The Windows dialog box is shown in **Figure 2.21**; the Mac OS dialog box is shown in **Figure 2.22**.

2. Type a descriptive name.

3. Choose a different disk or folder, if necessary.

4. Click Save.

To open an existing presentation:

1. Choose File > Open.

2. Choose a different disk or folder, if necessary.

3. Click the name in the list and click Open.

To close the current presentation:

◆ Choose File > Close or click the close button in the presentation window.

✔ Tips

■ The shortcuts for saving are Ctrl+S (Windows) or Command+S (Mac OS). You can also click the Save button on the toolbar. 🖫

■ The shortcuts for opening are Ctrl+O (Windows) or Command+O (Mac OS). You can also click the Open button on the toolbar. 📂

■ The names of recently-opened presentations appear at the bottom of the File menu. To open one of these files, just click the name.

The current folder ⌐

The Up One Level button displays the previous folder

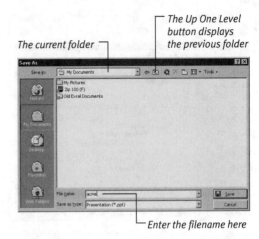

└ Enter the filename here

Figure 2.21 Saving a presentation (Windows).

⌐Enter the filename here   ⌐ Click here to choose a different drive or folder

The current folder ⌐

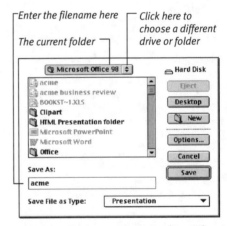

Figure 2.22 Saving a presentation (Mac OS).

Current printer

Click here to select a different printer

Be sure to select a print range

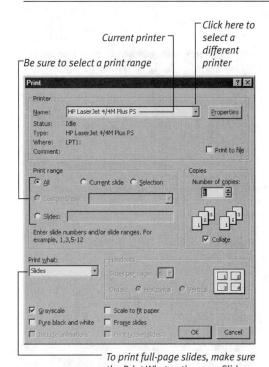

To print full-page slides, make sure the Print What option says Slides

Figure 2.23 Select options from the Print dialog box (Windows).

To print full-page slides, make sure the Print What option says Slides

Be sure to select a page range

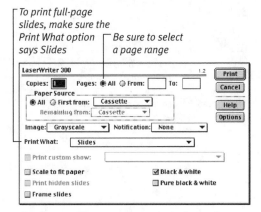

Figure 2.24 Select a page range and other options from the Print dialog box (Mac OS).

Printing a Presentation

Before showing your final presentation to an audience, you may want to print the slides on paper so you can see and correct any mistakes.

To print a presentation:

1. Choose File > Print.

   Figure 2.23 shows the Windows Print dialog box and **Figure 2.24** shows the Mac OS printer dialog box.

2. Select the range to print.

3. In the Print What list box, make sure Slides is selected.

4. Click OK (Windows) or Print (Mac OS).

✔ Tips

- The keyboard shortcut for printing is Ctrl+P (Windows) or Command+P (Mac OS).

- You can also print by choosing the Print button on the toolbar. However, this button does not display the Print dialog box—it prints the range last specified in the Print dialog box. It doesn't give you a chance to specify a print range. 🖨

  See Chapter 16 for more information on printing a presentation.

Using Normal View (Windows Only)

The new Normal view is offered only in the Windows version of PowerPoint 2000. Normal view lets you simultaneously see the presentation outline, the current slide, and the notes page for the current slide. **Figure 2.25** points out the three panes of Normal view.

To use Normal view:

1. Click the Normal View button at the bottom of the window. ■

2. Build and/or modify the current slide in the slide pane.

3. Click the notes pane and type any speaker notes pertinent to the current slide.

4. To display a different slide, click its title in the outline pane.

   The slide you clicked then appears in the slide pane.

✔ Tips

■ To control the amount of space devoted to the outline and notes panes, drag their borders (**Figure 2.26**).

■ All Outline view commands are applicable to the outline pane in Normal view.

■ If the Outlining toolbar is not displayed, choose View > Toolbars > Outlining.

   See Chapter 13 for more information about Outline view.

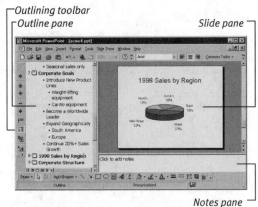

Outlining toolbar
Outline pane
Slide pane
Notes pane

Figure 2.25 Use Normal view to display three window panes.

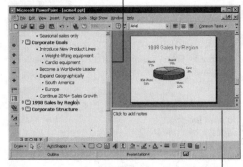

Drag this border left or right to change the width of the outline pane

Drag this border up to change the height of the notes pane

Figure 2.26 You can resize panes by dragging their borders.

Outlining toolbar

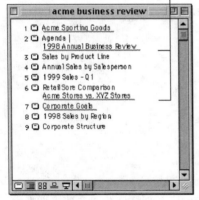

Figure 2.27 Use Outline view to see an outline of your presentation.

The lines indicate that text is hidden

Figure 2.28 This outline shows only the titles (no body text) and does not display the text formatting.

Using Outline View

Outline view (**Figure 2.27**) displays an outline of your presentation that includes the slide titles and any main text, such as bulleted items. Optionally, you can hide or *collapse* part of the outline so that you see only the slide titles. Outline view is ideal for seeing the structure of your presentation and for reordering slides.

To use Outline view:

1. Click the Outline View button at the bottom of the window. ▣

2. If the Outlining toolbar is not displayed, choose View > Toolbars > Outlining.

3. To display only the slide titles, click the Collapse All button on the Outlining toolbar. ▭

4. To redisplay the entire outline, click the Expand All button. ▪

5. To display or hide text formatting, click the Show Formatting button. ↳

   Compare **Figures 2.27** and **2.28**. **Figure 2.27** displays the text formatting; **Figure 2.28** does not.

✔ Tips

■ To move a slide, first click the icon in front of the slide title. Then click the Move Up or Move Down button ⬆ until the slide is in its new position. ⬇

■ You can use the outline pane in Normal view in the same way you use Outline view (Windows only).

See Chapter 13 for more information about Outline view.

USING OUTLINE VIEW

Using Slide Sorter View

Slide Sorter view (**Figure 2.29**) gives you the best of both worlds. As in Outline view, you can see the big picture of your presentation and you can reorder the slides. As in Slide (or Normal) view, you can actually see the charts on the slides, albeit in miniature form. The size of the slides in Slide Sorter view can be controlled in the Zoom field, shown in **Figure 2.30**.

To use Slide Sorter view:

1. Click the Slide Sorter View button. ⊞

2. To see more slides, choose a smaller percentage in the Zoom field. (The slides in **Figure 2.30** are zoomed out to 50%.)

3. To see fewer slides but more detail, choose a higher zoom percentage in the Zoom field. (In **Figure 2.31**, the slides are zoomed in to 100%.)

✔ Tip

■ To move a slide, drag it to a new location.

See Chapter 14 for more information on Slide Sorter view.

Click in the Zoom box and type a number...   ...or click the arrow and choose a percentage

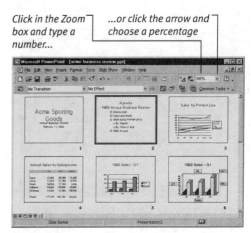

Figure 2.29 You can see miniatures of your slides in Slide Sorter view.

Zoom field

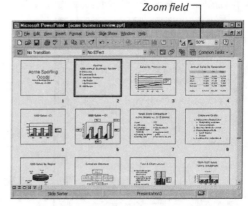

Figure 2.30 These slides are zoomed out to show more slides.

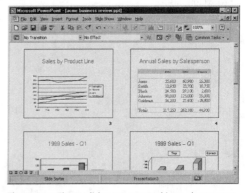

Figure 2.31 These slides are zoomed in to show more detail.

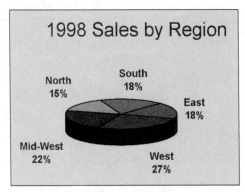

Figure 2.32 Click the Slide Show button and the current slide, a pie chart, shows full screen.

Viewing a Slide Show

A *slide show* displays each of the slides in the presentation, one after another, full screen. To show slides to a large audience, you can project the slide show onto a large screen, saving you the time, cost, and trouble of producing 35mm slides.

To view a slide show:

1. Press Ctrl+Home (Windows) or press Command+Home (Mac OS) to go to the first slide.

   The current slide displays full screen (**Figure 2.32**).

2. Click the Slide Show button. 🖵

3. To view the next slide, press Page Down.

   See Chapter 15 for additional information on slide shows.

✔ Tips

■ To view the previous slide in a slide show, press Page Up.

■ To cancel the slide show, press Esc.

■ You can run a slide show directly from Windows Explorer or My Computer, without having to launch PowerPoint. Just right-click the presentation filename and choose Show from the shortcut menu (Windows only).

VIEWING A SLIDE SHOW

CREATING
TEXT SLIDES

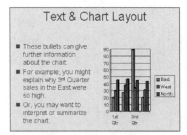

Figure 3.1 A Bulleted List slide.

Figure 3.2 A 2 Column Text slide.

Figure 3.3 A slide that combines text with a chart.

In this chapter you'll learn how to create slides that contain text, and how to edit and format the text. The types of slides that consist primarily of text are Title slides, Bulleted Lists (**Figure 3.1**), and 2 Column Text (**Figure 3.2**).

Other slide types combine text with elements such as clip art, charts (**Figure 3.3**), or media clips.

Choosing a Text Layout

When you insert a slide into the presentation, you are given the opportunity to choose a layout for the new slide. Of the 24 layouts for new slides, most have a text placeholder. (A *text placeholder* is simply a container for text.) **Figure 3.4** points out some of the layouts that have placeholders for body text.

To create a slide with a text layout:

1. In Slide or Normal view, click the New Slide button. □

   The New Slide dialog box (**Figure 3.5**) shows the first set of AutoLayouts.

2. Use the scroll bar to see additional layouts, if necessary.

3. Click the desired layout and click OK.

   or

   Double-click the desired layout.

   See also Choosing a Layout in Chapter 2.

✔ Tips

- If you don't find an AutoLayout that fits your needs perfectly, don't despair; you can add, move, or delete placeholders.

   See Manipulating Text Placeholders later in this chapter.

- To create a new slide with the same layout as the current slide, hold down Shift as you click the New Slide button. This action bypasses the New Slide dialog box.

- To select a different layout for an existing slide, choose Format > Slide Layout.

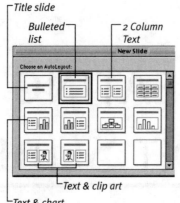

Figure 3.4 In the first set of layouts, the indicated layouts have body text placeholders.

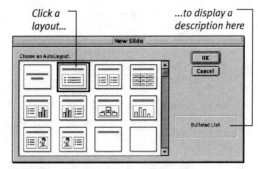

Figure 3.5 Choose a layout in the New Slide dialog box.

Dotted lines surround empty AutoLayout text placeholders; these lines disappear as soon as you enter text into the placeholder

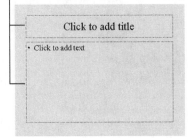

Click to add title

• Click to add text

Figure 3.6 Choosing the Bulleted List layout creates two text placeholders: one for the title and one for the bulleted text.

Entering Text into a Placeholder

Text placeholders that are created with an AutoLayout have a dotted-line boundary (**Figure 3.6**). They tell you exactly what to do to enter text in them: *Click to add title* or *Click to add text.*

To enter text into a placeholder:

1. Click inside the placeholder.

2. Start typing. Refer to **Table 3.1** for ways to edit your text.

3. Click outside the placeholder when you're finished.

✔ Tip

■ If you start typing on a new slide without clicking a placeholder, the text is placed in the title placeholder.

Table 3.1

Editing Text Within a Placeholder		
To move cursor to...	**In Windows...**	**In Mac OS...**
Beginning of line	Press Home	Press Home
End of line	Press End	Press End
Next word	Press Ctrl+right arrow	Press Command+right arrow
Previous word	Press Ctrl+left arrow	Press Command+left arrow
To delete...	**In Windows...**	**In Mac OS...**
Character to the right	Press Delete	Press Del
Character to the left	Press Backspace	Press Delete
Any amount of text	Select text and press Delete	Select text and press Del
To select...	**In Windows...**	**In Mac OS...**
Word	Double-click word	Double-click word
Paragraph	Triple-click paragraph	Triple-click paragraph
All text in placeholder	Click text and press Ctrl+A	Click text and press Command+A
Any amount of text	Click and drag across characters	Click and drag across characters

Creating a Text Box

Sometimes you'll need to add your own text boxes—for example, to annotate a chart (**Figure 3.7**) or to insert a footnote on a Title slide (**Figure 3.8**).

To create a text box:

1. Click the Text Box tool on the Drawing toolbar at the bottom of the window. 🖼

2. To insert a single line, just click where the text should go and start typing. **Figure 3.9** shows a text box that was inserted this way.

   or

   To create a word-wrapped text box, drag a box to the desired size. When you type, text will word-wrap inside the box. The text box in **Figure 3.10** was created with this technique.

✔ Tip

■ If you don't see the Drawing toolbar, choose View > Toolbars > Drawing.

Figure 3.7 The *Record Sales* annotation is inside a text box that was added to the slide.

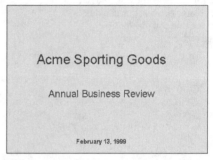

Figure 3.8 The date appears at the bottom of the slide is in a text box.

To create this text box, click the Text Box tool and then click the slide

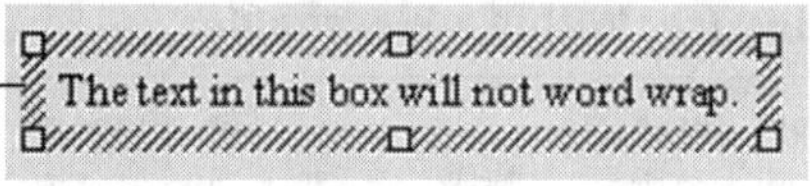

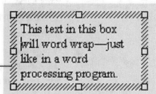

The text in this box will not word wrap.

Figure 3.9 This type of text box is ideal for single-line labels. The box grows wider as you type.

To create this text box, click the Text Box tool and then click and drag a box

This text in this box will word wrap—just like in a word processing program.

Figure 3.10 This type of text box will word-wrap text within the box.

Selection handles ─── Selection box

Acme Sporting Goods|

Annual Business Review
February 13, 1999

Figure 3.11 A selection box with selection handles appears around the text placeholder when you click inside.

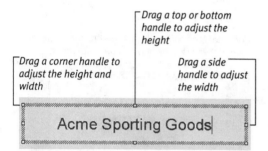

┌ Drag a top or bottom
  handle to adjust the
  height

┌ Drag a corner handle to   Drag a side ───
  adjust the height and   handle to adjust
  width   the width

Acme Sporting Goods|

Figure 3.12 You can use selection handles to resize a text box.

Manipulating Text Placeholders

Text placeholders and boxes can be moved, copied, resized, and deleted.

To move a text placeholder:

1. Click the text. You will see a selection box around the placeholder (**Figure 3.11**).

2. Place the pointer on the selection box (but not on a selection handle).The pointer becomes a four-headed arrow.

3. Drag the placeholder to the desired location on the slide.

To copy a text placeholder:

1. Click the text.

2. Place the pointer on the selection box (but not on a selection handle). The pointer becomes a four-headed arrow.

3. Hold down Ctrl as you drag to a new location (Windows).

   or

   Hold down the Option key as you drag to a new location (Mac OS).

To resize a text placeholder:

1. Click the text.

2. Place the pointer on a selection handle. The pointer becomes a double-headed arrow.

3. Drag the selection handle until the placeholder is the desired size (**Figure 3.12**).

✔ Tip

■ To delete a text placeholder, click the text, click the selection box, and then press Delete.

Moving Text

One way of moving text is using the *cut-and-paste* technique (**Figure 3.13**). An alternate method for moving text is called *drag and drop* (**Figure 3.14**).

To cut and paste text:

1. Select the text that you want to move (**Figure 3.15**).

2. Choose Edit > Cut.

3. Place the cursor where you want to insert the text.

4. Choose Edit > Paste.

To drag and drop text:

1. Select the text to be moved.

2. Place the pointer in the selection.

3. Hold down the mouse button and begin dragging. A vertical line indicates the insertion point.

4. Release the mouse button when the vertical line is positioned where you want to insert the text. The text will then drop into place.

✔ Tips

■ The Standard toolbar contains buttons for cutting, copying, and pasting (**Figure 3.16**).

■ To select a bullet item and all its sub-bullets, click the main bullet (Windows) or triple-click the first bullet line (Mac OS).

■ The keyboard shortcuts for cutting text are Ctrl+X (Windows) and Command+X (Mac OS). The shortcuts for pasting are Ctrl+V (Windows) and Command+V (Mac OS).

See Chapter 13 for information on moving bullet items in Outline view.

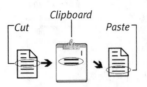

Figure 3.13 The cut-and-paste technique is a way of moving text. The Clipboard is a temporary storage area for objects that are cut or copied.

Figure 3.14 The drag-and-drop technique is another way to move text.

Notice that the bullets themselves are not highlighted (although they will be moved along with the text)

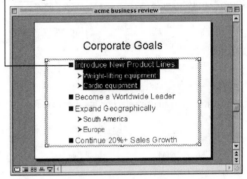

Figure 3.15 The selected text can be moved by using either cut and paste or drag and drop.

Figure 3.16 Part of the Standard toolbar.

MOVING TEXT

Figure 3.17 Select the correct spelling from the list.

If the correct spelling isn't on the list, you can make the correction here and then click Change

The "suspect" word

These options skip over the word

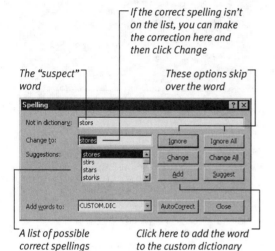

A list of possible correct spellings

Click here to add the word to the custom dictionary

Figure 3.18 Choose Tools > Spelling to display the Spelling dialog box.

Using the Spelling Checker

The spelling checker searches all text placeholders in the presentation and stops at words that aren't in the dictionary. You can either spell check the entire presentation or correct misspellings of single words.

To correct a misspelled word:

1. Place the mouse pointer on a word that has a red wavy line underneath it.

2. Right-click the word (Windows) or hold down the Control key and click the word (Mac OS).

3. Select the correct spelling from the list (**Figure 3.17**).

To spell check the presentation:

1. Choose Tools > Spelling.
   The Spelling dialog box appears (**Figure 3.18**).

2. If the word is spelled correctly, choose Ignore or Ignore All. Or, if you'll use the word frequently, choose Add to add it to the custom dictionary.

3. For misspelled words, choose the correct spelling from the Suggestions list. Or, edit the Change To field and then choose Change or Change All.

4. Repeat steps 2 and 3 for all "suspect" words.

✔ Tips

- The Spelling button is on the Standard toolbar.

- If the mistyped word is an actual word, the spelling checker isn't smart enough to consider the word suspect. Therefore, it's important that you still proofread the text yourself.

Correcting Mistakes Automatically

AutoCorrect automatically corrects mistakes as you type. It will correct capitalization errors, common misspellings, and transpositions (**Figure 3.19**). If AutoCorrect is turned on, mistakes are corrected when you press the spacebar after the word.

The AutoCorrect feature is turned on by default when you enter the program. If you want to turn off this feature or customize the replacement list, you will need to go to the AutoCorrect dialog box (**Figure 3.20**).

To correct mistakes automatically:

1. Choose Tools > AutoCorrect.

2. Select or unselect options, as desired.

3. To add your own replacement item, click the Replace field, and type the word you want replaced. Click the With field, type the replacement word or phrase, then click Add.

4. Click OK when finished.

✔ Tips

- Another way to use the AutoCorrect feature is to automatically replace abbreviations with their longer counterparts. For instance, you can have AutoCorrect replace a code for your company name (such as *asg*) with the full company name (*Acme Sporting Goods*). You'll find this to be a big time saver for words or phrases that you use frequently.

- Another way to add entries to the AutoCorrect replacement list is in the Spelling dialog box.

Mistake or Abbreviation	Correction
ANnual	Annual
wednesday	Wednesday
seperate	separate
adn	and
(c)	©
insted	instead

Figure 3.19 These are examples of the types of corrections the Auto-Correct feature makes.

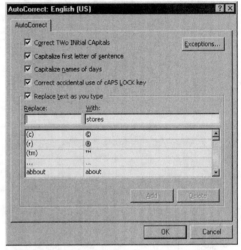

Figure 3.20 You can customize the replacement list in the AutoCorrect dialog box.

Each option shows how the selected text will be formatted

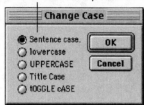

Figure 3.21
Change the capitalization of selected text in the Change Case dialog box.

Changing Case

The Change Case command lets you choose different combinations of uppercase and lowercase for selected text.

To change the case of selected text:

1. Select the text you want to change.

2. Choose Format > Change Case.

3. Select one of the case options (**Figure 3.21**).

4. Click OK.

✔ Tips

- Toggle Case is handy when you have mistakenly typed text with Caps Lock on—it turns lowercase letters into uppercase and vice versa.

- Title Case capitalizes each word in the selected text, except for small words such as *the, and, or, of, at.*

- Use Shift+F3 to toggle between UPPERCASE, lowercase, and Title Case.

- Use PowerPoint's style checker to make sure you have consistently used the same uppercase and lowercase throughout your presentation (Windows only).

  See Correcting Style Inconsistencies on the next page.

CHANGING CASE

Correcting Style Inconsistencies (Windows Only)

PowerPoint makes sure you have consistently capitalized and punctuated your slide titles and body text throughout the presentation. It can also check for visual clarity: it makes sure you haven't used too many fonts (or made them too small), placed too many bullet items in a list, or used too many words in a title or bullet item.

When PowerPoint finds a style inconsistency, a yellow light bulb appears on the slide. Note that to use this feature, the Office Assistant must be turned on.

To correct style inconsistencies:

1. If you have turned off the Assistant, choose Help > Show the Office Assistant.

2. Click the light bulb.

3. Choose the appropriate option on the list (**Figure 3.22**).

To set your style preferences:

1. Click the light bulb.

2. Click Change Style Checker Options for All Presentations.

3. In the Case And End Punctuation tab (**Figure 3.23**), specify the case and end punctuation style for titles and body text.

4. Select the Visual Clarity tab, and change any of the fonts and legibility options.

5. Click OK.

6. Click OK again.

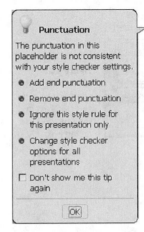

Figure 3.22 When you click the light bulb, a list similar to this one appears.

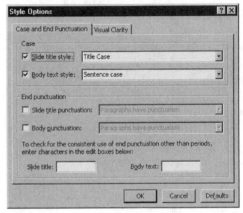

Figure 3.23 Set your style preferences in the Style Options dialog box.

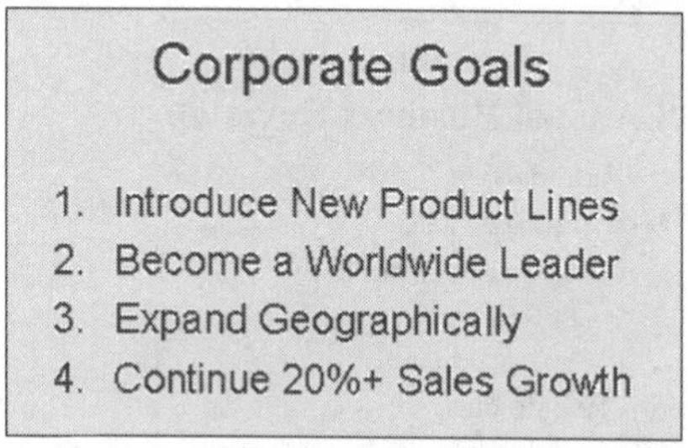

Corporate Goals

1. Introduce New Product Lines
2. Become a Worldwide Leader
3. Expand Geographically
4. Continue 20%+ Sales Growth

Figure 3.24 This list was numbered automatically.

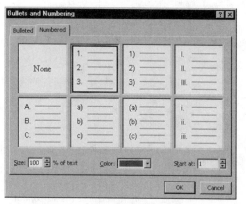

Figure 3.25 Choose a numbering style in the Numbered tab of the Bullets and Numbering dialog box.

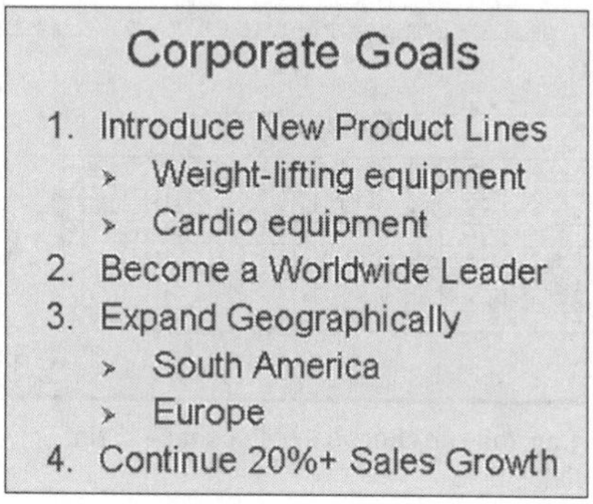

Corporate Goals

1. Introduce New Product Lines
   > Weight-lifting equipment
   > Cardio equipment
2. Become a Worldwide Leader
3. Expand Geographically
   > South America
   > Europe
4. Continue 20%+ Sales Growth

Figure 3.26 This numbered list has sub-bullets.

Numbering a List Automatically (Windows Only)

The list in **Figure 3.24** was automatically numbered with the Format > Bullets and Numbering command.

To number a list automatically:

1. Select the text in the list you want to number.

2. Choose Format > Bullets and Numbering.

3. Select the Numbered tab (**Figure 3.25**).

4. Click the desired numbering style.

5. Change the number's color or size, if you like.

6. Click OK.

✔ Tip

- If there are second-level bullets in between the numbered items (**Figure 3.26**), you cannot select all the text (because the sub-bullets would be numbered, also). Here's a quick way to number this type of list:

  1. Use the Format > Bullets and Numbering command to number the first line.

  2. Click each line that you want numbered and press Ctrl+Y to repeat the command.

Choosing Bullet Shapes

Figure 3.27 shows a Bulleted List slide that uses the default bullets. **Figure 3.28** shows this same list with different bullets selected for the two levels.

To choose a different bullet shape (Mac OS):

1. Click anywhere on the line whose bullet you want to change. To change the bullets in several consecutive lines, select them by clicking and dragging.

2. Choose Format > Bullet.
   The Bullet dialog box appears (**Figure 3.29**).

3. In the Bullets From field, click the arrows to display a list of typefaces.

4. Choose the desired typeface. Wingdings and Zapf Dingbats are two typefaces that contain many symbols appropriate for bullets.

5. Click the desired symbol.

6. Change the bullet's color or size, if you like.

7. Click OK.

✔ Tips

- To remove a bullet from a line, click the Bullets button on the Formatting toolbar. ☰

- To change the bullets for all slides, edit the Slide Master.

  See Changing the Default Format for Text in Chapter 12.

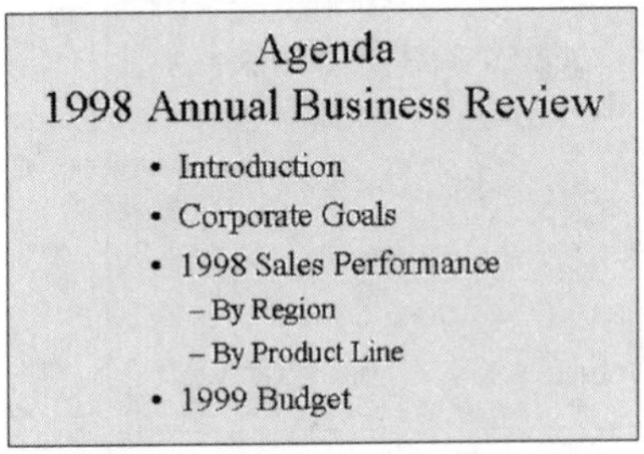

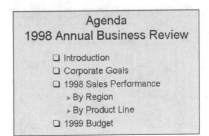

Figure 3.27 This slide uses default bullets.

Figure 3.28 The bullets in this slide were modified.

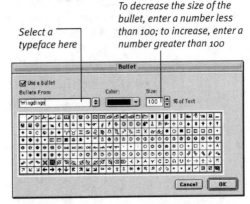

Select a typeface here

To decrease the size of the bullet, enter a number less than 100; to increase, enter a number greater than 100

Figure 3.29 You can choose a bullet shape in the Bullet dialog box.

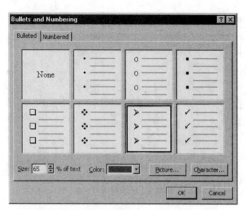

Figure 3.30 The Bullets and Numbering dialog box offers several bullet shapes.

Select a typeface here

To decrease the size of the bullet, enter a number less than 100; to increase, enter a number greater than 100

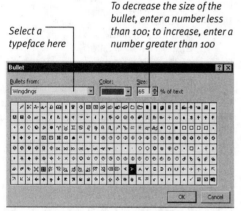

Figure 3.31 You can choose a bullet shape in the Bullet dialog box.

To choose a different bullet shape (Windows):

1. Click anywhere on the line whose bullet you want to change. To change the bullets in several consecutive lines, select them by clicking and dragging.

2. Choose Format > Bullets and Numbering. The Bullets and Numbering dialog box appears (**Figure 3.30**).

3. Click one of the bullets shown and then skip to step 7.

   or

   Click Character.

   The Bullet dialog box appears (**Figure 3.31**).

4. In the Bullets From field, click the arrow to display a list of typefaces.

5. Choose the desired typeface. Wingdings and Zapf Dingbats are two typefaces that contain many symbols appropriate for bullets.

6. Click the desired symbol.

7. Change the bullet's color and size, if you like.

8. Click OK.

✔ Tips

- To remove a bullet from a line, click the Bullets button on the Formatting toolbar. ▤

- The Picture option in the Bullets and Numbering dialog box allows you to use any graphic file as a bullet.

- To change the bullets for all slides, edit the Slide Master.

  See Changing the Default Format for Text in Chapter 12.

Adjusting Bullet Placement

To change the horizontal spacing between the bullet and the text that follows it, you need to display the rulers (**Figure 3.32**) and drag the appropriate markers. **Figure 3.33** shows a Bulleted List slide before any spacing change; **Figure 3.34** shows the same list after a bit of space has been added between the bullet and text.

To adjust the placement of bullets:

1. If the ruler isn't already displayed, choose View > Ruler.

2. Click anywhere on the text.

   For each bullet level, the horizontal ruler shows a set of indent markers that can be individually adjusted. For example, if there are two bullet levels, the ruler displays two sets of indent markers.

3. Drag the left-indent marker in the ruler (**Figure 3.35**) to change the spacing between the bullet and the text.

4. To adjust the position of the bullet, drag the first-line indent marker in the ruler.

   or

   To adjust the position of the bullet *without* changing the spacing between the bullet and the text, drag the square marker in the ruler. (All markers will move together.)

✔ Tips

- You don't need to select all the text in the placeholder before adjusting the indents—the ruler automatically controls the entire placeholder.

- To hide the ruler, choose View > Ruler again.

Vertical ruler　　　　Horizontal ruler

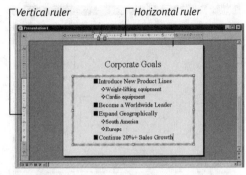

Figure 3.32 To display the rulers, choose View > Ruler.

Figure 3.33 A Bulleted List slide before any adjustment of indents.

Figure 3.34 The same list after the indents have been increased slightly.

First-line indent marker
Left indent marker

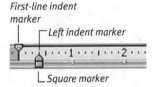

Square marker

Figure 3.35 Move the indent markers in the horizontal ruler to adjust the bullet placement.

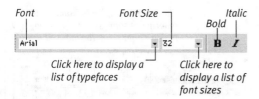

Font   Font Size   *Italic*
            Bold

Click here to display a | *Click here to*
list of typefaces | *display a list of*
font sizes

Figure 3.36 You can format text with the Formatting toolbar.

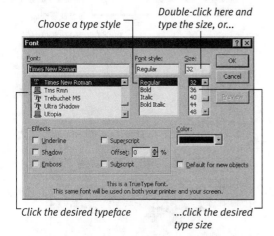

Choose a type style | *Double-click here and*
type the size, or...

Click the desired typeface | *...click the desired*
type size

Figure 3.37 Choose Format > Font to display the Font dialog box.

Changing the Font

You can format text by using either the Formatting toolbar (**Figure 3.36**) or the Font dialog box (**Figure 3.37**).

To change the font:

1. Select the text by dragging across the characters.

   or

   To select an entire text placeholder, first click the text and then click the selection box border.

2. In the Formatting toolbar, use the Font and Font Size fields to change the font. Turn on the Bold or Italic buttons, if desired (**Figure 3.36**).

   or

   Choose Format > Font. In the Font dialog box (**Figure 3.37**), choose a Font, Font Style, and Size, and click OK.

   See the next page for more information on the Font dialog box.

✔ Tips

- If the toolbar doesn't display one of the formatting buttons you want to use, click the More Buttons button and select the formatting button you want (Windows only).

- The Font dialog box contains a Preview button so that you can see how the formatted text looks without closing the dialog box. (You may need to drag the dialog box to the side so you can see the formatted text.)

Adding Text Effects and Color

In addition to options for typeface, size, and style of text, the Font dialog box has options for special effects (such as Underline, Shadow, and Emboss) and Color.

To add effects and color to your text:

1. Select the text by dragging across the characters.

   or

   To select an entire text placeholder, first click the text and then click the selection box border.

2. Choose Format > Font.

   The Font dialog box appears (**Figure 3.38**).

3. Choose an effect.

4. To choose a color, see **Figures 3.38** and **3.39**.

5. Click OK.

✔ Tips

- Use the Superscript effect to raise text above the baseline (e.g., x^2). Use the Subscript effect to lower text below the baseline (e.g., H_2O).

- Instead of using the Underline effect, you can draw a line with the Line tool on the Drawing toolbar. (Do this if you need to control the spacing between the text and the line.)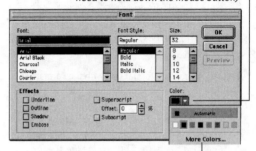

   See Drawing Lines in Chapter 10.

Click here to display the small color palette (on some systems you may need to hold down the mouse button)

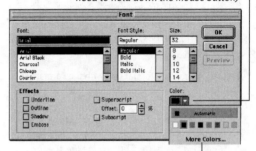

Click here to display the large color palette

Figure 3.38 The Font dialog box contains options for adding special effects to your text.

Click any circle here...   *...and the new color is shown here*

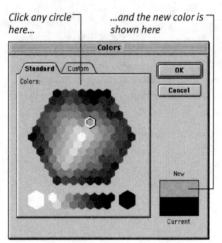

Figure 3.39 Choose a color in the large color palette.

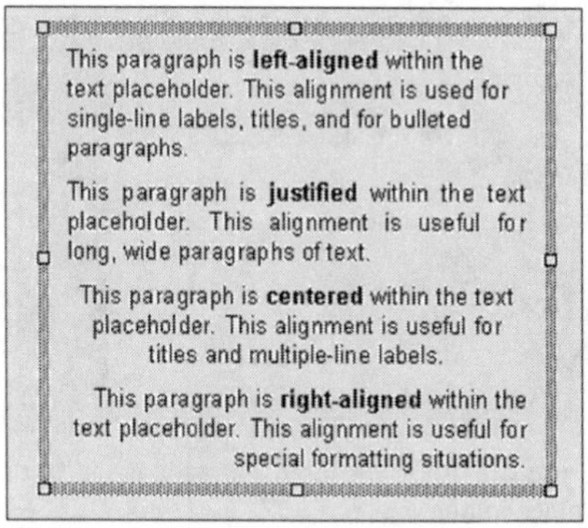

This paragraph is **left-aligned** within the text placeholder. This alignment is used for single-line labels, titles, and for bulleted paragraphs.

This paragraph is **justified** within the text placeholder. This alignment is useful for long, wide paragraphs of text.

This paragraph is **centered** within the text placeholder. This alignment is useful for titles and multiple-line labels.

This paragraph is **right-aligned** within the text placeholder. This alignment is useful for special formatting situations.

Figure 3.40 These paragraphs illustrate the four types of alignment.

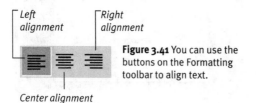

Left alignment

Right alignment

Center alignment

Figure 3.41 You can use the buttons on the Formatting toolbar to align text.

Aligning Paragraphs

Figure 3.40 shows examples of the four types of paragraph alignment.

To align paragraphs:

1. Select the paragraphs to be aligned.

2. Choose Format > Alignment.

3. **Windows:** Choose Align Left, Center, Align Right, or Justify.

   or

   Mac OS: Choose Left, Center, Right, or Justify.

✔ Tips

- The Formatting toolbar contains buttons for left-aligning, right-aligning, and centering text (**Figure 3.41**).

- To select a single paragraph, just click inside it—you don't need to select any text.

- To select all the text in the placeholder, first click the text and then click the selection box border. When you give an alignment command, all text will be aligned.

- Text is aligned within the text placeholder. If the text isn't positioned quite where you want it, try adjusting the size or position of the placeholder.

  See the next page to see how to align text on a particular point within a placeholder.

ALIGNING PARAGRAPHS

Formatting a Text Placeholder

To control the horizontal and vertical placement of a block of text within a placeholder, you set a *text anchor*. Compare Figures 3.42 and 3.43. In **Figure 3.42**, the list is anchored on the top left side of the placeholder; in **Figure 3.43**, the list is anchored along the top center. While the Alignment command centers each paragraph separately, the text anchor controls the position of the text as a whole unit. This command also lets you align text vertically.

To format a text placeholder:

1. Click anywhere in the text placeholder.

2. Choose Format > Placeholder (Windows) or Format > AutoShape (Mac OS).

3. Select the Text Box tab (**Figure 3.44**).

4. Click in the Text Anchor Point field, and choose where you want the text anchored in the placeholder:

    ◆ Top
    ◆ Middle
    ◆ Bottom
    ◆ Top Centered
    ◆ Middle Centered
    ◆ Bottom Centered

5. Click OK.

✔ Tips

■ If the title has center alignment, bulleted lists often look good when you choose one of the centered text anchor points.

■ The Top, Middle, and Bottom anchor points are all anchored to the left side of the placeholder.

■ To add extra space between the placeholder boundary and the text, adjust the internal margin settings.

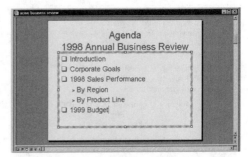

Figure 3.42 The list is anchored along the top left side of the placeholder.

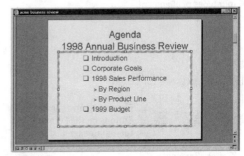

Figure 3.43 The list is anchored in the top center of the placeholder.

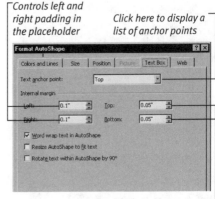

Controls left and right padding in the placeholder

Click here to display a list of anchor points

Controls top and bottom padding in the placeholder

Figure 3.44 Use the Text Box tab to control the horizontal and vertical positioning of all the text in a placeholder.

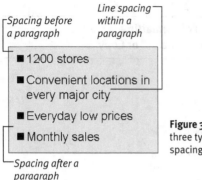

Spacing before a paragraph

Line spacing within a paragraph

- ■ 1200 stores
- ■ Convenient locations in every major city
- ■ Everyday low prices
- ■ Monthly sales

Spacing after a paragraph

Figure 3.45 The three types of spacing.

Double-click in the box and enter a new value, or...

...click here to increase (or decrease) the value in 0.05 increments

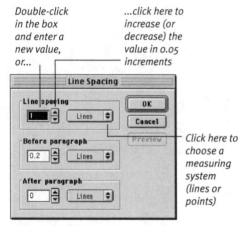

Click here to choose a measuring system (lines or points)

Figure 3.46 Choose Format > Line Spacing to display this dialog box.

Controlling Line and Paragraph Spacing

PowerPoint helps you control spacing between lines in a paragraph as well as between each paragraph. **Figure 3.45** illustrates these types of spacing.

To adjust line and paragraph spacing:

1. Select the paragraphs to be formatted.

2. Choose Format > Line Spacing (**Figure 3.46**).

3. Enter the new values for Line Spacing, Before Paragraph, and/or After Paragraph.

4. Click OK.

✔ Tips

- You won't usually want to choose both Before Paragraph and After Paragraph spacing. If you choose both, the two spacing values will be added together.

- Do not use the Enter or Return key to get extra space between paragraphs. The Line Spacing dialog box gives you more precise control over the spacing.

- To select a single paragraph, just click inside it—you don't need to select any text.

- To select all the text in the placeholder, click the text and then the border of the selection box. Then, when you give a spacing command, all text will be formatted.

- The Line Spacing dialog box contains a Preview button so that you can see how the formatted text looks without closing the dialog box. (You may need to drag the dialog box to the side so you can see the formatted text.)

Copying Formatting Attributes

If you want the text in one placeholder to be formatted exactly like another, you can do so by "painting" the format. **Table 3.2** lists the types of formatting you can paint.

To copy formatting attributes:

1. Click the text placeholder whose format you want to copy, and then click the border of the selection box.

2. Click the Format Painter button on the Formatting toolbar. 🖌

3. Place the pointer (which now includes a paintbrush) on the text to which you want to apply the format, and click.

✔ Tips

- You can use the Format Painter to "paint" the format of other types of objects (such as boxes, circles, and arrows).

- If the Formatting toolbar isn't displayed, choose View > Toolbars > Formatting.

- If you don't see the Format Painter button on the Formatting toolbar, click the More Buttons button to see other formatting buttons (Windows only). »

Table 3.2

Types of Formatting You Can "Paint" or Copy
Font
Style
Size
Effects
Color
Alignment
Line spacing
Paragraph spacing
Bullets

INSERTING
CHARTS

You can create a wide variety of two- and three-dimensional charts in PowerPoint such as Area, Bar, Column, Line, Pie, Doughnut, Stock, and Cone. This chapter concentrates on the types that have axes. Chapter 6 covers pie and doughnut charts.

When you create charts in PowerPoint, you actually use the Microsoft Graph program.

In Graph, you'll notice that the toolbar offers buttons specific to graphing, and the menu bar contains two new options—Data and Chart.

Launching Graph

You can open Microsoft Graph from within PowerPoint. Here's how.

To launch Microsoft Graph:

◆ Double-click a chart placeholder or an existing chart.

In Windows, you'll see a thick border around the chart (**Figure 4.1**). On the Mac, the chart appears in its own window (**Figure 4.2**).

✔ Tip:

■ To return to PowerPoint, click anywhere on the slide outside of the chart border (Windows), or choose File > Quit & Return (Mac OS).

Chart Terminology

Figure 4.3 points out the key areas of a column chart; many chart types have these same areas.

The *y-axis* is known as the *value axis* since it always displays values on its scale. The *x-axis* is known as the *category axis* because it displays categories of data (such as quarters, months, years, names).

Tick marks appear next to each value on the y-axis and between categories on the x-axis. *Gridlines* may extend from the tickmarks to help you interpret the values at each *data point*. A set of data points makes up a *data series*.

When a chart has more than one data series (**Figure 4.3** has two series—Sales and Expenses), you can use a *legend* to identify each series.

✔ Tip

■ On a three-dimensional chart, the value axis is called the *z-axis* and the series axis running along the depth of the chart is called the *y-axis*.

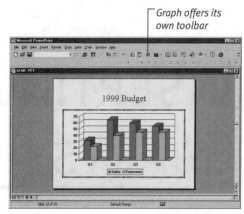

Graph offers its own toolbar

Figure 4.1 The border around the chart indicates you're working in Microsoft Graph (Windows).

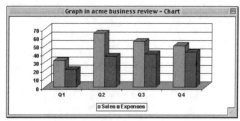

Figure 4.2 On the Macintosh, the chart appears in a new window.

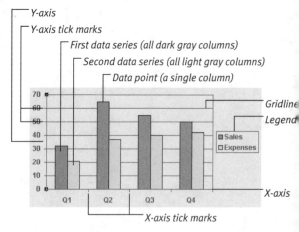

Y-axis
Y-axis tick marks
First data series (all dark gray columns)
Second data series (all light gray columns)
Data point (a single column)
Gridline
Legend
X-axis
X-axis tick marks

Figure 4.3 It's helpful to understand the terminology used for charts.

Layouts that combine text and charts

Chart layout

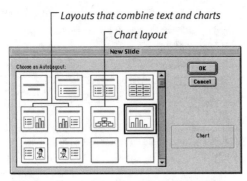

Figure 4.4 Choose a chart layout in the New Slide dialog box.

Figure 4.5 This slide uses the Text & Chart AutoLayout.

Figure 4.6 This new slide uses the Chart layout.

Inserting a Chart Slide

PowerPoint offers three AutoLayouts that include charts (**Figure 4.4**). An example of a slide that combines a bulleted list with a chart is shown in **Figure 4.5**.

To insert a chart slide:

1. Click the New Slide button on the toolbar.

2. In the New Slide dialog box, choose one of the chart layouts (**Figure 4.4**).

3. Click OK.

   The slide appears with title, chart, and perhaps text placeholders (**Figure 4.6**).

4. Click the title placeholder and type the title of your chart.

5. If the slide has a text placeholder, click it and type the text.

6. Double-click the chart placeholder to create your chart.

✔ Tip

■ In the text placeholder of a Text & Chart or Chart & Text layout, you can provide details about the chart, such as an interpretation of the data or a conclusion that can be drawn from the data.

   For information on creating multiple charts on a slide, see Creating Two Charts on a Slide later in this chapter.

Entering Data

You enter your chart data in the datasheet window (**Figure 4.7**). The datasheet initially appears with sample data. Be sure to erase it before entering your own data.

To enter data in the datasheet:

1. If you haven't already done so, double-click the chart placeholder to launch Microsoft Graph.

2. If you don't see the datasheet window, click the View Datasheet button. ▦

3. To erase the sample data, click the Select All button (**Figure 4.7**) and press Delete (Windows) or Del (Mac OS).

4. Enter your chart data (**Figure 4.8**).

5. To view the chart, move the datasheet aside (by dragging the window's title bar) or close the datasheet window (by clicking the View Datasheet button). ▦

✔ Tips

- Be sure to use the Select All button when deleting the sample data. If you just delete a range of cells and your data consumes fewer rows and columns than the sample data, Microsoft Graph still reserves space for this data on the chart (**Figure 4.9**). To fix this problem, use the Exclude Row/Col command on the Data menu. This command tells Graph not to chart the data in the selected row or column.

- Alternatively, you can enter legend labels in the top row and x-axis labels in the first column of the datasheet. But you must use the Data > Series in Columns command to let Graph know that the data series are entered into columns instead of rows.

Drag the borders to resize the datasheet
Drag the title bar to move the datasheet
Select All button

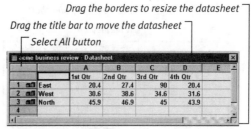

Figure 4.7 The sample data automatically fills the datasheet.

Enter legend labels in this column
Enter x-axis labels in this row

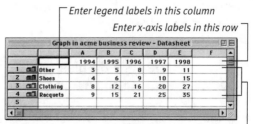

Enter the values for each data series in a different row

Figure 4.8 Enter chart data in the datasheet.

This space is reserved for nonexistent data

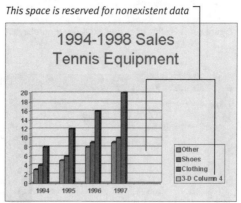

Figure 4.9 The Exclude Row/Col command on the Data menu will fix the problems on this chart.

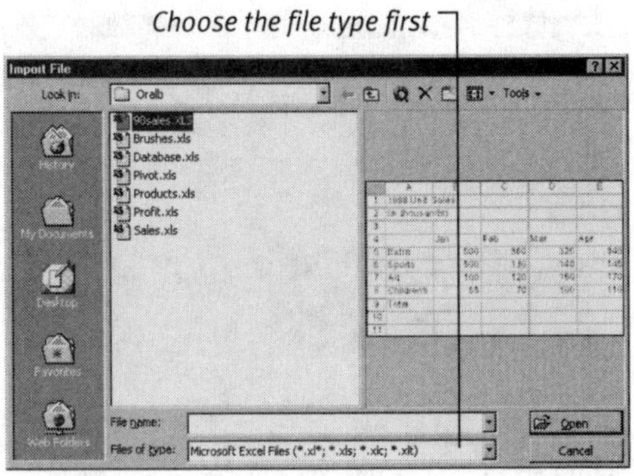

Choose the file type first ⌐

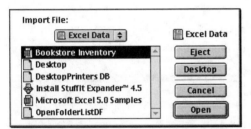

Figure 4.10 Select a file to import from the Import File dialog box (Windows).

Figure 4.11 Select a file to import from the Import File dialog box (Mac OS).

Figure 4.12 Choose whether to import the entire file or a range.

Importing Data

If the chart data already exists in a spreadsheet or text file, you don't need to retype it in the datasheet—you can *import* the data.

To import data from a file:

1. Delete the sample data in the datasheet (see previous page).

2. Click the first cell of the datasheet.

3. Choose Edit > Import File.
   The Import File dialog box appears (**Figures 4.10** and **4.11**).

4. **Windows only**: Click the Files Of Type field, and choose the desired type (such as Microsoft Excel or Lotus 1-2-3).

5. Choose the drive and folder where the file is located.

6. Click the filename.

7. Click Open.
   The Import Data Options dialog box appears (**Figure 4.12**).

8. Select the sheet containing the data you want to import.

9. Choose Entire Sheet.
   or
   Choose Range and type the range of cells (such as *A5:H10*) or enter a range name.

10. Click OK.

✔ Tips

- You can also import data by clicking the Import File button on the toolbar. 📇

- In Windows, you can preview the spreadsheet in the Import File dialog box by clicking the Views button and choosing Preview; you can then write down the range of cells you want to import.

Linking Data

Another way to import data is to *link* it from an existing spreadsheet file. When you link data, changes you make to the source file are automatically reflected in the PowerPoint datasheet and chart.

To link from a file to a datasheet:

1. Launch the application that created the source file, and open the file (**Figure 4.13**).

2. Select the data to be linked, and choose Edit > Copy.

3. Switch back to PowerPoint.

4. Create a new chart slide, double-click the chart placeholder, and then delete the sample data in the datasheet.

5. Click the first cell of the datasheet.

6. Choose Edit > Paste Link, and click OK to continue.

7. Move or close the datasheet to see your new chart.

✔ Tips

- As long as the chart is open in Graph, changes to the source file instantly reflect in the datasheet and chart.

- If you forget the name or location of the source file, choose Edit > Links to display the Link dialog box (**Figure 4.14**).

- A fast way to open your source file is to click Open Source in the Link dialog box.

- Use the Change Source option in the Link dialog box if you have moved or renamed the source file.

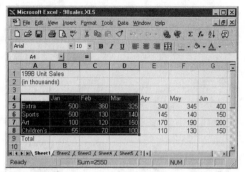

Figure 4.13 The selected range in a Microsoft Excel spreadsheet will be copied and then paste-linked in a PowerPoint datasheet.

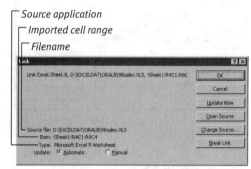

Figure 4.14 While in the datasheet, choose Edit > Links to display the Link dialog box.

Select a chart type   *Click a chart to choose a sub-type*

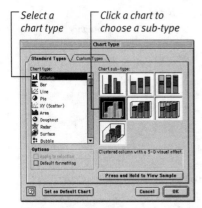

Figure 4.15 Select a chart type from the Chart Type dialog box.

Click here to display a palette of chart types

Chart Type

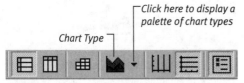

Figure 4.16 Use the Graph toolbar to select a chart type.

Choosing a Chart Type

The default chart type is 3-D clustered column. You can choose a different chart type before or after you enter data in the datasheet. In addition to choosing a chart type, you can choose a *sub-type*. Sub-types are variations of the selected chart type. For example, a column chart has sub-types of clustered bars, stacked bars, 100% stacked bars, and so forth.

To choose a chart type:

1. If necessary, double-click the embedded chart to go into Microsoft Graph.

2. Choose Chart > Chart Type.
   The Chart Type dialog box appears (**Figure 4.15**).

3. Click one of the chart types.

4. Click the desired sub-type.

5. Click OK.

✔ Tips

- Another way to change the chart type is with the Chart Type button on the Graph toolbar (**Figure 4.16**). By clicking the arrow next to the button, you will see a palette of 18 chart types.

- To change the type of just one of the series, select the series before you give the Chart Type command. For example, if you want one of the series in a column chart to be a line, select the series, choose the Chart Type command, and choose one of the Line chart types.

- You can also change the shape of individual series in a 3-D bar or column chart. Select the series, choose the Format > Selected Data Series command, and select the Shape tab. You can then select a shape, such as a cylinder, pyramid, or cone.

Inserting Titles

You can insert titles at the top of the chart or on any of the axes (**Figure 4.17**).

To insert titles on a chart:

1. Choose Chart > Chart Options.

2. Select the Titles tab (**Figure 4.18**).

3. Type the title text in the appropriate box.

4. Click OK.

In Windows, the value axis title is automatically rotated 90 degrees (**Figure 4.19**). In Mac OS, you must choose a command to rotate the title.

To rotate an axis title:

1. Select the axis title—make sure the placeholder has selection handles around it. (If you see the text cursor, click elsewhere on the chart and then again on the title.)

2. Choose Format > Selected Axis Title.

3. Select the Alignment tab (**Figure 4.20**).

4. Type *90* in the Degrees field.

5. Click OK.

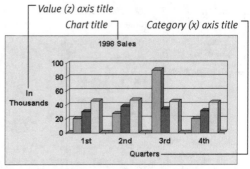

Figure 4.17 Use titles to label charts and axes.

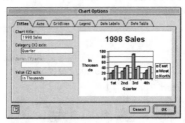

Figure 4.18 Enter the title text.

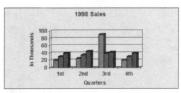

Figure 4.19 The value axis title is rotated 90 degrees.

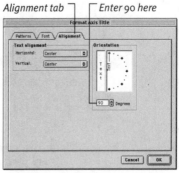

Figure 4.20 Use this dialog box to rotate an axis title.

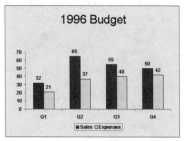

Figure 4.21 Data labels appear above each data point.

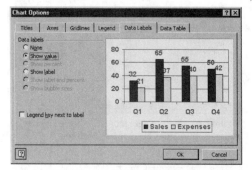

Figure 4.22 Choose Chart > Chart Options and select the Data Labels tab.

Inserting Data Labels

You can place *data labels* on data points to show their exact values (**Figure 4.21**).

To insert data labels:

1. Choose Chart > Chart Options.

2. Select the Data Labels tab (**Figure 4.22**).

3. Choose Show Value.

4. Click OK.

✔ Tips

■ Data labels are not appropriate for all charts. If the chart has many data points or many data series, the chart may look too busy with data labels or the labels will run into one another.

■ To change the number of decimal places displayed in a data label, choose the Format > Selected Data Labels command and select the Number tab.

■ To change the size and color of data labels, choose the Format > Font command.

■ If a label appears above the plot area, you can either move the label or change the upper value on the y-axis scale.

See Repositioning Data Labels on the next page and Scaling the Axis in Chapter 5.

INSERTING DATA LABELS

Repositioning Data Labels

Graph inserts the data labels near the data point but sometimes the labels from one series will overlap the labels from another, or the label may be unreadable in its current position (**Figure 4.23**). Fortunately, you can position the data labels exactly where you want them (**Figure 4.24**).

To reposition data labels automatically (2-D charts only):

1. Select the data labels in a series. (Make sure there are selection handles around each label in the series.)

2. Choose Format > Selected Data Labels.

3. Select the Alignment tab (**Figure 4.25**).

4. In the Label Position field, choose the desired position (such as Inside End).

5. Click OK.

Repeat the above steps for each series you want to reposition.

To move data labels manually (for any chart type):

1. Click the data label you want to move; click until you see selection handles around the one label only (**Figure 4.26**).

2. Drag the border of the selected label to the desired position.

Repeat the above steps for each label to be repositioned.

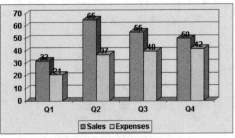

Figure 4.23 With the data labels in the default positions, the values are difficult to read.

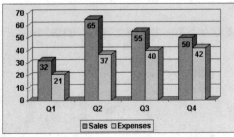

Figure 4.24 After the data labels are moved inside the columns, the values become easier to see.

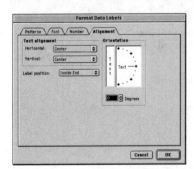

Figure 4.25 For two-dimensional charts, you can reposition the data labels automatically.

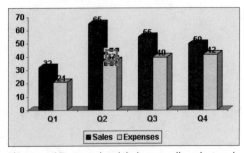

Figure 4.26 To move data labels manually, select each data label and drag it into position.

Double-click the embedded chart

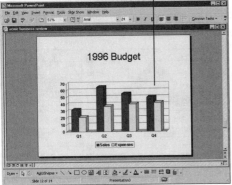

Figure 4.27 Before you can revise a chart, you must open it in Microsoft Graph.

The Graph toolbar is one indication that you are in Graph, not PowerPoint ...

...and this border around the chart is another clue

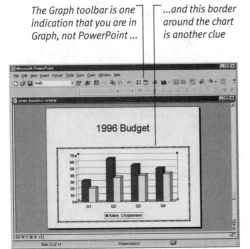

Figure 4.28 The chart is opened in Microsoft Graph (Windows).

Revising a Chart

To revise a previously-created chart, you need to reopen it in Microsoft Graph.

To revise a chart:

1. Double-click the embedded chart (**Figure 4.27**).

2. If you need to update the data and the datasheet is not currently displayed, click the View Datasheet button.

   If you want to change only the formatting, go to step 5.

3. To replace the contents of a cell, click the cell and type the new value. The chart instantly reflects the change to the datasheet.

4. To edit the contents of a cell, double-click the cell. A text cursor appears. Position the cursor where you want to make the change, and then insert or delete characters. Press Enter or Return when you are finished.

5. Make any desired formatting changes to the chart (insert titles, insert data labels, change the chart type, and so forth).

6. To return to PowerPoint:

   ◆ Click the slide outside of the chart (Windows).

   or

   ◆ Choose File > Quit & Return (Mac OS).

✔ Tip

■ **Windows only: Figure 4.28** gives you some clues if you're unsure whether you're in Microsoft Graph or PowerPoint. You can also display the Help menu—the bottom menu choice will be either About Microsoft Graph or About Microsoft PowerPoint.

Creating Two Charts on a Slide

Although PowerPoint doesn't offer a slide layout for two charts, you can easily create one (**Figure 4.29**).

To create two charts on a slide:

1. Use the New Slide button on the toolbar to insert a new slide with the Chart & Text or Text & Chart layout.

2. To delete the text placeholder, click inside the placeholder, click the selection box border, and then press Delete (**Figure 4.30**).

3. Create the first chart.

4. Exit Microsoft Graph.

5. To copy the chart, place the pointer on the embedded chart, and hold down Ctrl (Windows) or Option (Mac OS) as you drag to the other side of the slide (**Figure 4.31**).

6. Revise the second chart.

7. Exit Graph.

✔ Tips

■ To make the two charts align with one another, choose the Align command.

See Aligning Objects in Chapter 11.

■ It's easier to compare data in the two charts when the axes use the same scale.

See Scaling the Axis in Chapter 5.

■ You can title each chart in the Titles tab of the Chart Options dialog box.

See Inserting Titles earlier in this chapter.

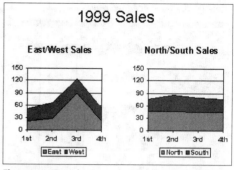

Figure 4.29 Two charts can be shown on one slide.

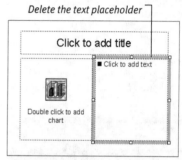

Figure 4.30 To create a slide with two charts, start with the Chart & Text layout.

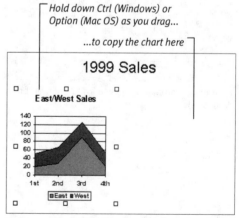

Figure 4.31 You can create a second chart on a slide by dragging the first chart.

FORMATTING CHARTS

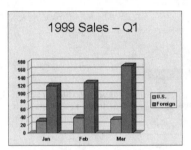

Figure 5.1 This 3-D column chart uses Graph's default settings.

Microsoft Graph offers an abundance of ways to format your charts. You can reposition the legend, add and remove gridlines, change the color of the data series, change the upper and lower limits on the value axis, and more. **Figure 5.1** shows a chart with Graph's default settings, and **Figure 5.2** shows the same chart after formatting.

See Chart Terminology in Chapter 4.

Elevation of 3-D columns changed   *New colors assigned to data series*

Scale units adjusted

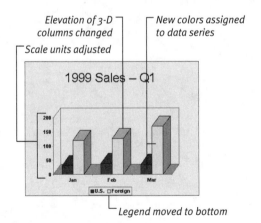

Legend moved to bottom

Figure 5.2 The same 3-D column chart after formatting.

Formatting Charts

No matter what type of chart element you are formatting, the procedure is basically the same.

To format a chart:

1. If you're not already in Microsoft Graph, double-click your embedded chart.

2. Select the area of the chart you want to format—you may need to click more than once. For example, to format the legend, click the legend until you see selection handles around it (**Figure 5.3**).

   When you select an item that's part of a larger group—such as a single point in a data series—the first click selects the group and the second click selects the single item.

3. Choose Format > Selected *xxx* where *xxx* is the name of the selected area. For example, if the legend is selected, the command will be Selected Legend (**Figure 5.4**).

✔ Tips

- A quick way to display the appropriate Format dialog box is to double-click the chart element you want to format.

- To make sure you have selected the object you intended, just point to the object and pause for a second—you'll see a bubble with the name of the object you are pointing to (**Figure 5.3**).

- Another way to select an area of a chart is to select its name in the Chart Objects field on the toolbar (**Figure 5.5**).

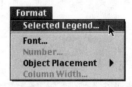

Figure 5.3 A selected object has selection handles.

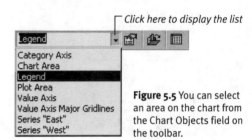

Figure 5.4 When the legend is selected, the Format menu offers the command Selected Legend.

Click here to display the list

| Legend |
| Category Axis |
| Chart Area |
| Legend |
| Plot Area |
| Value Axis |
| Value Axis Major Gridlines |
| Series "East" |
| Series "West" |

Figure 5.5 You can select an area on the chart from the Chart Objects field on the toolbar.

Figure 5.6 This legend uses the default border.

Figure 5.7 After formatting, the legend border has a shadow.

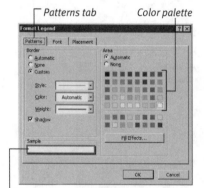

Patterns tab   *Color palette*

A preview of your current formatting selections

Figure 5.8 Use this dialog box to format the legend.

Figure 5.9 Click the Style field to display this list.

Figure 5.10 Click the Weight field to display this list.

Formatting the Legend

By default, the legend has a thin border around it (**Figure 5.6**). If you like, you can thicken the border, add a shadow, shade the background, or remove it altogether. In **Figure 5.7** the legend is formatted with a heavier line weight and a shadow.

To format the legend:

1. Select the legend and then choose Format > Selected Legend.

   or

   Double-click the legend.

2. Select the Patterns tab (**Figure 5.8**).

3. To choose a different border style (such as dashed lines), display the Style list (**Figure 5.9**) and choose one of the styles.

4. To choose a different line thickness, display the Weight list (**Figure 5.10**) and choose one of the weights.

5. To add a shadow, select the Shadow checkbox.

6. To shade the background of the legend, click one of the colors in the palette (**Figure 5.8**).

7. Click OK.

✔ Tips

- To enlarge the legend, drag the selection handles.

- To remove the legend border, go to the Patterns tab of the Format Legend dialog box and choose None under Border.

   To format the legend text, see Formatting Chart Text later in this chapter.

   To reposition or remove the legend, see the next page.

Repositioning the Legend

You can place the legend in a variety of standard positions on the chart (**Figure 5.11**).

To reposition the legend:

1. Select the legend, and choose Format > Selected Legend.

   or

   Double-click the legend.

2. Select the Placement tab (**Figure 5.12**).

3. Choose one of the placement positions.

4. Click OK.

✔ Tips

- Another way to reposition the legend is to drag it to the desired location (**Figure 5.13**).

- To remove a legend, select it and press Delete.

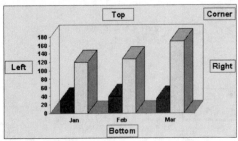

Figure 5.11 Graph offers five standard positions for the legend.

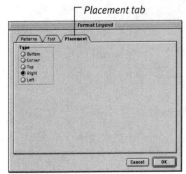

Figure 5.12 Choose a legend position in the Placement tab.

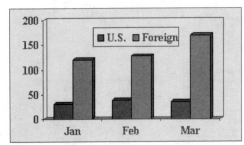

Figure 5.13 The legend was positioned inside the plot area by dragging it manually.

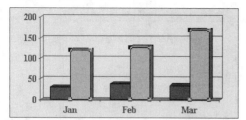

Figure 5.14 The second data series is selected in this column chart.

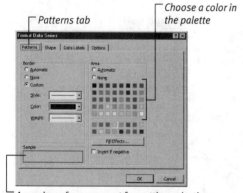

⌐ Patterns tab

⌐ Choose a color in the palette

⌐ A preview of your current formatting selections

Figure 5.15 Use this tab to assign patterns and colors to bar, column, area, and surface charts.

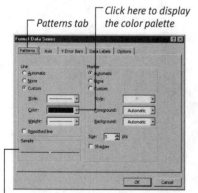

⌐ Click here to display the color palette

⌐ Patterns tab

⌐ A preview of your current formatting selections

Figure 5.16 The Patterns tab for line charts offers options specific to this chart type.

Changing the Color of a Data Series

You can assign new colors to each of the data series in a chart to help viewers differentiate the series.

To change the color of a data series:

1. Click one of the data series (there should be selection handles on each point in the series as shown in **Figure 5.14**) and choose Format > Selected Data Series.

   or

   Double-click any point in the series.

2. Select the Patterns tab (**Figures 5.15** and **5.16**).

   Note that the Format Data Series dialog box has different options depending upon the chart type.

3. Choose a color in the palette.

4. Click OK.

CHANGING THE COLOR OF A DATA SERIES

Filling a Data Series with Textures or Patterns

You can assign textures to chart elements to help define data. **Figure 5.17** shows an area chart with a texture assigned to one of its data series.

To fill a data series with textures or patterns:

1. Click one of the data series (there should be selection handles on each point in the series) and choose Format > Selected Data Series.

   or

   Double-click the series.

2. Select the Patterns tab.

3. Click Fill Effects.

4. Select the Gradient tab and choose a shading style.

   or

   Select the Texture tab and click a texture (**Figure 5.18**).

   or

   Select the Pattern tab and click a pattern (**Figure 5.19**).

5. Click OK.

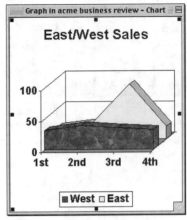

Figure 5.17 The West data series has a marble texture.

Texture tab

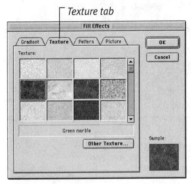

Figure 5.18 You can choose from a variety of textures.

Pattern tab

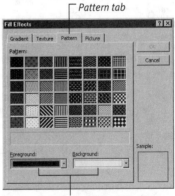

Choose the colors of the pattern here

Figure 5.19 Use the Pattern tab to choose from among dozens of patterns.

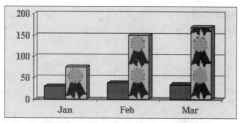

Figure 5.20 The second data series is filled with a ribbon graphic.

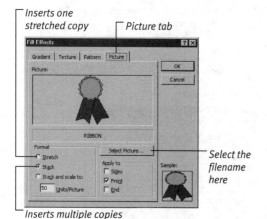

Inserts one stretched copy   *Picture tab*

Select the filename here

Inserts multiple copies

Figure 5.21 Use the Picture tab in the Fill Effects dialog box to fill a data series with a graphics file.

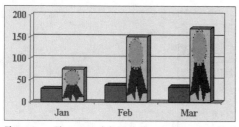

Figure 5.22 The second data series contains stretched graphics.

Filling a Data Series with a Graphics File

You can include graphics in a chart to provide information or extra interest. **Figure 5.20** shows a column chart that has one of its data series filled with a graphics file.

To fill a data series with a graphics file:

1. Click the data series you want to fill (there should be selection handles on each point in the series) and choose Format > Selected Data Series.

   or

   Double-click the series.

2. Select the Patterns tab.

3. Click Fill Effects.

4. Select the Picture tab (**Figure 5.21**).

5. Click Select Picture.

6. Navigate to the drive and folder containing the graphics file.

   The Microsoft Office folder contains a Clipart folder with dozens of graphics files.

7. Choose the filename and click OK.

8. To insert a single copy of the graphic (as in **Figure 5.22**), choose Stretch.

   or

   To have multiple copies of the graphic sit on top of each other (as in **Figure 5.20**), choose Stack.

9. For 3-D charts, select the Front checkbox to place the graphic on the front face of the area, and unselect the Sides and End checkboxes.

10. Click OK twice to return to the chart.

Formatting Data Markers

Data markers are symbols, such as circles or squares, that appear at data points on line, XY, and radar charts. The markers also appear in the legend to help you identify each data series (**Figure 5.23**).

To format data markers:

1. Click one of the data series (there should be selection handles at each data point) and choose Format > Selected Data Series.

   or

   Double-click the series.

2. Select the Patterns tab (**Figure 5.24**).

3. In the Marker section, display the Style list and choose a marker style (**Figure 5.25**).

4. If desired, increase the marker size.

5. Click OK.

✔ Tip

■ In the Marker section, choose None if you don't want any markers on the line. Make sure, though, that each line is a different color so you have some way of differentiating the series.

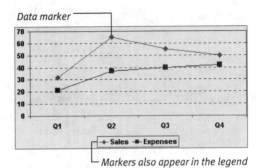

Data marker

Markers also appear in the legend

Figure 5.23 Data markers help you identify data series in this line chart.

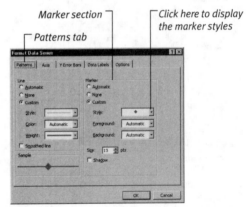

Marker section

Click here to display the marker styles

Patterns tab

Figure 5.24 Choose a marker style in the Patterns tab.

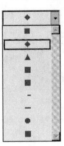

Figure 5.25 Click the Style field to display a list of marker styles.

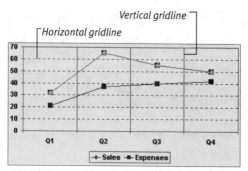

Figure 5.26 A line chart with horizontal and vertical gridlines.

Figure 5.27 The Graph toolbar offers buttons for turning gridlines on and off.

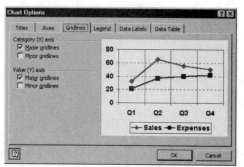

Figure 5.28 You can select gridlines from the Gridlines tab.

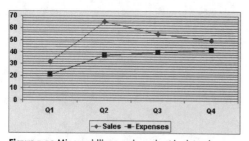

Figure 5.29 Minor gridlines make a chart look too busy.

Inserting/Removing Gridlines

Gridlines are the lines that extend from the tick marks on a chart's axes (**Figure 5.26**). They are useful for interpreting the actual values of the data points when you're not using data labels. Horizontal gridlines extend from the value axis, and vertical gridlines extend from the category axis.

The Graph toolbar contains buttons to quickly insert or remove gridlines (**Figure 5.27**). These buttons are toggles—they will insert or remove gridlines each time you click them.

To insert or remove gridlines:

1. To insert or remove vertical gridlines, click the Category Axis Gridlines button on the toolbar.

2. To insert or remove horizontal gridlines, click the Value Axis Gridlines button on the toolbar.

✔ Tip

■ Another way to turn gridlines on and off is by choosing Chart > Chart Options and selecting the Gridlines tab (**Figure 5.28**). In this tab, you can also insert *minor gridlines*—lines that extend from the minor tick marks (ticks between the scale increments). Minor gridlines are rarely used as they make the chart too busy (**Figure 5.29**).

Formatting Gridlines

You can change both the thickness and the style of the gridlines. **Figure 5.30** shows the dotted style .

To format a gridline:

1. Select one of the gridlines and choose Format > Selected Gridlines.

   or

   Double-click a gridline.

2. Select the Patterns tab (**Figure 5.31**).

3. To choose a different line style (such as dashed lines), display the Style list and choose one of the styles.

4. To choose a different color, click the Color field and choose a color.

5. To choose a different line thickness, display the Weight list and choose one of the weights.

6. Click OK.

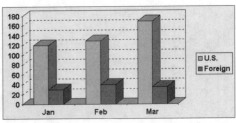

Figure 5.30 This chart uses gridlines with a dotted style.

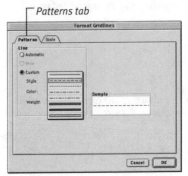

Figure 5.31 Choose a different format for the gridlines from the Patterns tab.

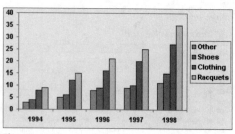

Figure 5.32 The x- and y-axes have outside tick marks.

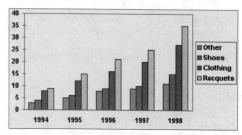

Figure 5.33 On this chart, the tick marks cross the y-axis; no marks appear on the x-axis.

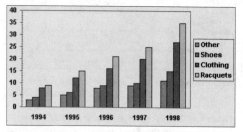

Figure 5.34 The y-axis has major tick marks on the outside and minor tick marks on the inside.

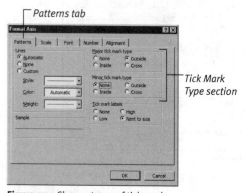

Figure 5.35 Choose types of tick marks from the Patterns tab.

Formatting Tick Marks

Tick marks are tiny lines next to the labels on an axis, similar to divisions on a ruler. You can place tick marks inside, outside, or crossing the axis (**Figures 5.32** and **5.33**). You can also choose to have *minor tick marks* between the major tick marks (**Figure 5.34**).

To format the tick marks:

1. Select the axis whose tick marks you want to format and choose Format > Selected Axis.

   or

   Double-click the axis.

2. Select the Patterns tab (**Figure 5.35**).

3. In the Major Tick Mark Type section, select the type of mark: None, Inside, Outside, or Cross.

4. Select the Minor Tick Mark Type: None, Inside, Outside, or Cross.

5. Click OK.

✔ Tip

■ The frequency of the tick marks depends on the major and minor units.

   See Scaling the Axis on the next page for information on specifying the major and minor units.

Scaling the Axis

On the *value axis* (such as the y-axis in **Figure 5.36**), Microsoft Graph lets you adjust the maximum value (the value at the top of the axis), minimum value (the value at the bottom), and major unit (increments between values). On the *category axis* (such as the x-axis in **Figure 5.36**), you can adjust the number of categories between labels and tick marks. **Figure 5.37** shows the line chart after adjusting the scales.

To scale the value or category axis:

1. Select the axis to be scaled and choose Format > Selected Axis.

   or

   Double-click the axis.

2. Select the Scale tab (**Figure 5.38**).

3. For the value axis, enter new values for the Minimum, Maximum, Major Unit, and/or Minor Unit. (The checkmark disappears in the Auto column when you change a value from its default.)

   or

   For the category axis, enter new values for Number Of Categories Between Tick-Mark Labels and/or Number Of Categories Between Tick Marks.

4. Click OK.

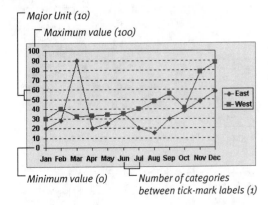

Figure 5.36 This chart uses the default y-axis and x-axis scales.

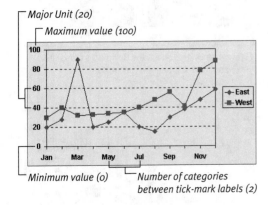

Figure 5.37 On this chart, the number of categories on the x-axis and the major unit on the y-axis were changed.

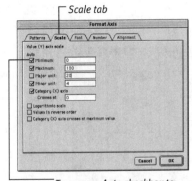

Turn on an Auto checkbox to return to the default scale value

Figure 5.38 Change the scale of the value (Y) axis in the Scale tab.

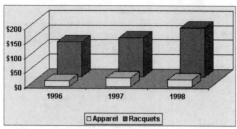

Figure 5.39 The numbers on the value axis have been given a Currency format.

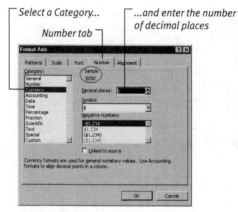

Select a Category... *...and enter the number of decimal places*

Number tab

Figure 5.40 Format axis numbers in the Number tab.

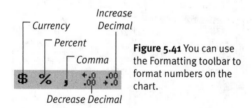

Increase Decimal

Currency

Percent

Comma

Decrease Decimal

Figure 5.41 You can use the Formatting toolbar to format numbers on the chart.

Formatting Axis Numbers

You can format axis values to indicate date, time, currency, and other specifics. **Figure 5.39** shows a value axis in which the numbers have been formatted to display dollar signs.

To format the axis numbers:

1. Select the axis whose numbers you want to format and then choose Format > Selected Axis.

   or

   Double-click the axis.

2. Select the Number tab (**Figure 5.40**).

3. From the Category list, choose the appropriate formatting category (such as Number, Percentage, or Currency).

4. If desired, change the value in the Decimal Places field.

5. Click OK.

✔ Tips

- You can also apply currency, percent, and comma format using buttons on the Formatting toolbar (**Figure 5.41**).

- Look at the Sample (circled in **Figure 5.40**) to preview what the number will look like.

- Instead of formatting all the numbers to currency, you can insert an axis title that explains that the values are in dollars.

  See Inserting Titles in Chapter 4.

Formatting Chart Text

You can format the text in each chart area (legend, titles, and so forth) with a particular typeface, size, and style (**Figures 5.42** and **5.43**).

To format chart text:

1. Select the area whose text you want to format.

   or

   Within a selected text box, drag across the individual characters you want to format.

2. Choose Format > Font (**Figure 5.44**).

3. In the Font list, choose the desired typeface.

4. Select the desired Font Style (Regular, Italic, Bold, Bold Italic).

5. In the Size list, choose the desired point size.

6. Select a different color, if desired.

7. Click OK.

✔ Tip

■ To format all the chart text to the same font, select the entire chart area. An easy way to select the chart area is to choose it from the Chart Objects field on the toolbar.

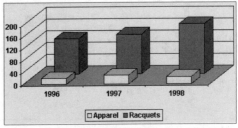

Figure 5.42 The text in this chart uses the default typeface (Arial) and size (18 points).

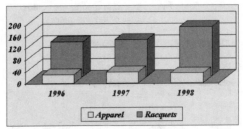

Figure 5.43 The text in this chart has been formatted to 22-point Bookman italic.

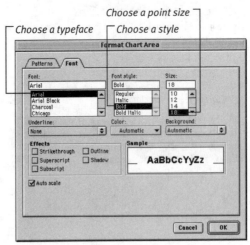

Figure 5.44 You can format chart text in the Font tab.

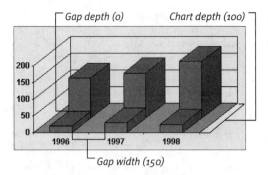

Figure 5.45 This 3-D column chart uses the default 3-D settings.

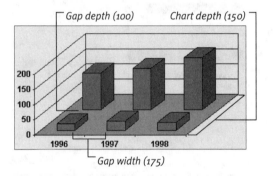

Figure 5.46 The same 3-D column chart has been altered.

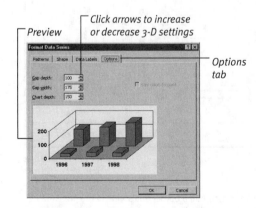

Figure 5.47 Adjust 3-D settings for a 3-D column chart in the Options tab.

Adjusting 3-D Effects

You can adjust the dimensionality of your 3-D charts—their gap depth, gap width, and chart depth. **Figure 5.45** shows a 3-D column chart with the default 3-D settings and **Figure 5.46** shows the same chart after formatting.

You can see in **Figures 5.45** and **5.46** that the *gap depth* is the vertical distance between each data point, the *gap width* is the horizontal distance between each data point, and the *chart depth* is the depth of the chart's base.

To adjust 3-D effects on a chart:

1. Select one of the data series. (It doesn't matter which one.)

2. Choose Format > Selected Data Series.

3. Select the Options tab (**Figure 5.47**).

4. Click the arrows to adjust each 3-D setting. Watch the preview in the dialog box to see how the new values affect the three-dimensionality of the chart.

5. Click OK.

✔ Tip

■ You can also adjust the 3-D view of a chart (that is, the viewer's perspective). By choosing the Chart > 3-D View command, you can adjust a chart's elevation, rotation, and perspective.

Formatting the Plot Area

The *plot area* is the rectangle formed by the horizontal and vertical axes. **Figure 5.48** shows a chart with a formatted plot area.

To format the plot area:

1. Click the Chart Objects field on the toolbar and choose Plot Area (**Figure 5.49**).

2. Choose Format > Selected Plot Area. The Format Plot Area dialog box appears (**Figure 5.50**).

   or

   Double-click the border of the plot area.

3. To place a border around the plot area, select Automatic in the Border section.

4. To shade the plot area, choose a color from the palette.

5. Click OK.

✔ Tips

- In the Format Plot Area dialog box, you can also adjust the line style, weight, and color of the border.

- Use the Fill Effects button in the Format Plot Area dialog box (**Figure 5.50**) to select a texture or gradient for the plot area.

  See Filling a Data Series with Textures or Patterns earlier in this chapter.

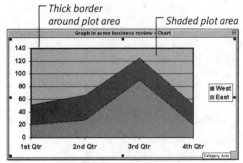

Thick border around plot area ⌐ Shaded plot area

Figure 5.48 This area chart includes a formatted plot area.

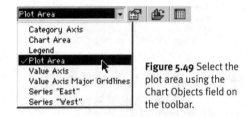

Figure 5.49 Select the plot area using the Chart Objects field on the toolbar.

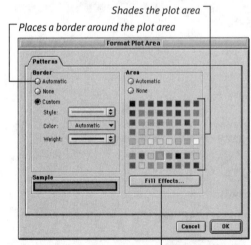

Shades the plot area ⌐
⌐ Places a border around the plot area

Click here to choose a gradient or texture

Figure 5.50 Add a border and shade to the plot area in the Format Plot Area dialog box.

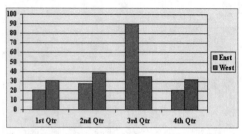

Figure 5.51 A column chart before applying a custom chart type.

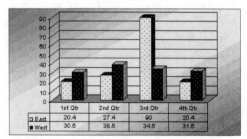

Figure 5.52 The same chart after applying a custom chart type.

Choosing a Custom Chart Type

With Microsoft Graph's built-in custom chart types, you can create a professional-looking chart that is preformatted with a coordinated set of options. **Figures 5.51** and **5.52** show a chart before and after applying a custom chart type.

To choose a custom chart type:

1. Choose Chart > Chart Type.

2. Select the Custom Types tab (**Figure 5.53**).

3. Make sure the Built-In option is selected.

4. Click a chart type in the list; look at the sample, and read its description.

5. When you have found a built-in custom chart type you like, click OK.

   See the next page for information on creating your own custom formats.

First select Built-in...

...then choose a chart type

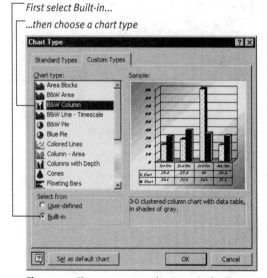

Figure 5.53 Choose a custom chart type in the Custom Types tab.

Defining a Custom Chart Type

Suppose you want to format a series of charts with the same settings. You can create your own chart type and then apply it to any chart; this is called *user-defined* chart type.

To define a custom chart type:

1. Format a chart with the exact settings you want to save. This chart should be the active chart.

2. Choose Chart > Chart Type.

3. Select the Custom Types tab.

4. Select the User-Defined option (**Figure 5.54**).

5. Click Add.

    The Add Custom Chart Type dialog box appears (**Figure 5.55**).

6. In the Name field, type a name for the format (up to 31 characters).

7. In the Description field, describe the format in more detail.

8. Click OK twice to return to the chart.

First select User-Defined...

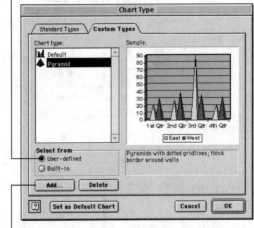

...then click here to add a custom chart type

Figure 5.54 Once you select the User-Defined option, you can add and delete your own custom chart types.

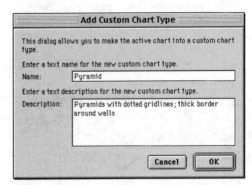

Figure 5.55 Enter the name and description for the custom chart type.

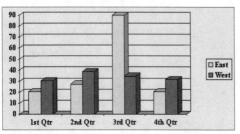

Figure 5.56 A chart before applying a user-defined chart type.

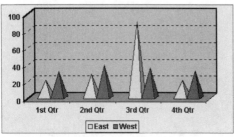

Figure 5.57 The same chart after applying a user-defined chart type.

Applying a User-Defined Chart Type

After you create a user-defined style, you can apply it to existing charts. **Figures 5.56** and **5.57** show a chart before and after applying a user-defined chart type.

To apply a user-defined chart type:

1. Display the chart you want to format.
2. Choose Chart > Chart Type.
3. Select the Custom Types tab.
4. Select the User-Defined option.
5. In the Chart Type list, click the name you want to use (**Figure 5.58**).
6. Click OK.

First select User-Defined...

...then choose a chart type

Preview of selected chart type

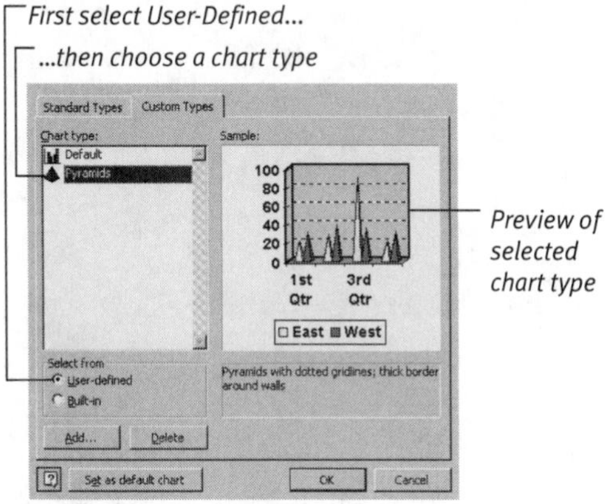

Figure 5.58 Apply a user-defined chart type in the Custom Types tab.

CREATING PIE CHARTS

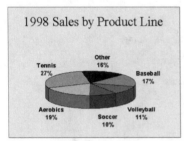

Figure 6.1 Use a 3-D pie chart to clearly show relative values.

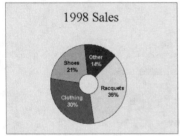

Figure 6.2 Doughnut charts show the breakdown of a total at a certain point in time.

A pie chart shows the relative proportions of several items. By looking at the relative size of the pie slices and their accompanying percentage figures, you can clearly see the relationship between the items (**Figure 6.1**).

Unlike column and line charts, which typically show different values over time, pie charts show values at a particular point in time (such as 1999 sales). Pie charts are one of the simplest types of charts to create because they have only one data series.

Microsoft Graph offers a number of ways to enhance your pie charts. For instance, you can explode a slice, assign new colors or patterns to the slices, and rotate the pie.

A chart type similar to the pie is the doughnut (**Figure 6.2**). Like pie charts, doughnut charts show the breakdown of a total at a certain point in time.

Inserting a Pie Slide

Like all charts, pie charts use one of the chart AutoLayouts.

To insert a pie chart slide:

1. Click the New Slide button on the Standard toolbar. 🔲

2. In the New Slide dialog box, choose one of the chart layouts (**Figure 6.3**).

3. Click OK.

   The slide appears with title and chart (and possibly text) placeholders (**Figure 6.4**).

4. Click the title placeholder and type the title of your chart.

5. Double-click the chart placeholder to create your chart.

6. Choose Chart > Chart Type.

   The Chart Type dialog box appears (**Figure 6.5**).

7. Click the Pie chart type.

8. Click the desired sub-type.

9. Click OK.

You are now ready to fill in the datasheet.

See Entering Pie Data on the next page.

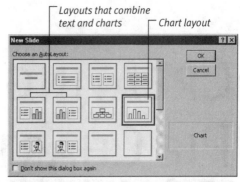

Layouts that combine text and charts — Chart layout

Figure 6.3 Choose a chart layout in the New Slide dialog box.

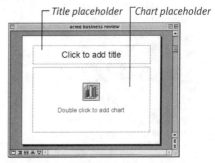

— Title placeholder — Chart placeholder

Figure 6.4 This slide uses the Chart layout.

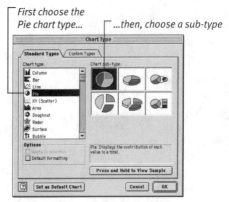

First choose the Pie chart type... ...then, choose a sub-type

Figure 6.5 Choose a chart type from the Chart Type dialog box's Standard Types tab.

INSERTING A PIE SLIDE

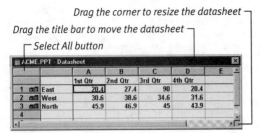

Drag the corner to resize the datasheet ⌐

Drag the title bar to move the datasheet ⌐

⌐ Select All button

Figure 6.6 Before typing in your data, delete the sample data in the datasheet.

⌐ This column can be left blank

Enter slice labels in this row ⌐

Enter slice values in this row ⌐

Figure 6.7 Enter pie data in the datasheet.

Figure 6.8 Another way to enter pie data is to type the labels and values into columns.

Entering Pie Data

You enter your chart data in the datasheet window (**Figure 6.6**). The datasheet contains sample data that you erase before entering your own data.

To enter pie chart data:

1. If you haven't already done so, double-click the chart placeholder to launch Microsoft Graph.

2. If the datasheet window isn't already displayed, click the View Datasheet button. ▤

3. To erase the sample data, click the Select All button (**Figure 6.6**) and press Delete (Windows) or Del (Mac OS).

4. Enter the chart data (**Figure 6.7**).

5. To view the chart, move or close the datasheet.

✔ Tips

■ Alternatively, you can enter slice labels in the first column and values in the second column of the datasheet (**Figure 6.8**). But you must use the Data > Series In Columns command to let Graph know that the data series are entered into columns instead of rows.

■ Be sure to use the Select All button when deleting the sample data. If you just delete a range of cells and your data consumes fewer columns than the sample data, Microsoft Graph will still insert a slice label for this data on the chart. To fix this problem, choose the Exclude Row/Col command on the Data menu. This command tells Graph not to chart the data in the selected row or column.

ENTERING PIE DATA

Showing Data Labels

When you first create a pie chart, it includes a legend but no data labels. **Figures 6.9** and **6.10** show some of the types of data (slice) labels you can add to a pie chart.

To place data labels on a pie chart:

1. Choose Chart > Chart Options.

2. Select the Data Labels tab.

3. Choose one of the options in the Data Labels dialog box (**Figure 6.11**).

4. Click OK.

✔ Tips

■ When you display only value or percent labels, you will need a legend to identify the slices (**Figure 6.9**).

■ If your pie chart has identifying labels next to its slices, you don't need a legend. You can remove the legend by selecting it and pressing Delete.

■ To reposition a data label, select it and drag it to the desired location.

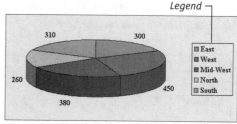

Legend

Figure 6.9 This chart shows values next to each slice.

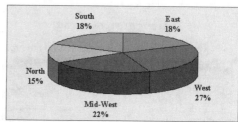

Figure 6.10 This chart shows labels and percentages next to each slice.

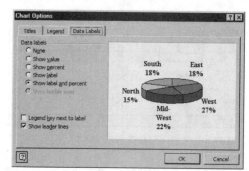

Figure 6.11 Choose the type of data labels you want to appear on your pie chart.

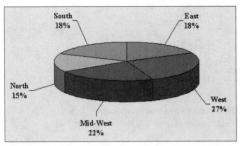

Figure 6.12 This pie chart shows leader lines between the labels and the slices.

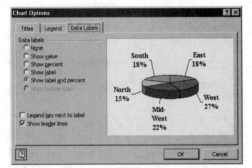

Figure 6.13 Go to the Data Labels tab in the Chart Options dialog box to select the leader line option.

Drag the border to move the label

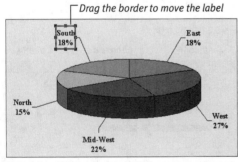

Figure 6.14 The South data label is currently selected.

Using Leader Lines

When a data label is moved away from the edge of the pie, you can use a leader line to point to its slice (**Figure 6.12**).

To use leader lines on a pie chart:

1. Choose Chart > Chart Options.

2. Select the Data Labels tab.

3. Make sure the Show Leader Lines checkbox is selected (**Figure 6.13**).

4. Click OK.

   If you have already moved your data labels away from the pie, your leader lines will automatically appear. If you haven't moved your data labels yet, continue on with step 5.

5. Click the data label you want to move; click until you see selection handles around the one label only (**Figure 6.14**).

6. Drag the border of the selected label to the desired position.

   A leader line will automatically appear.

7. Repeat steps 5 and 6 for each data label.

✔ Tips

- A leader line will not appear if the label is close to or inside the slice.

- Double-click a leader line to format its style, color, and weight.

Formatting Data Labels

You can format the numbers (percents or values) and the text in the slice data labels.

To format data labels:

1. Select the slice labels. (Make sure there are selection handles around all the labels as shown in **Figure 6.15**.)

2. Choose Format > Selected Data Labels.

3. If you want to format the numbers:
   - ◆ Select the Number tab (**Figure 6.16**).
   - ◆ From the Category list, choose the appropriate formatting category (such as Number, Currency, or Percentage).
   - ◆ If desired, change the value in the Decimal Places field.

4. If you want to format the text:
   - ◆ Select the Font tab (**Figure 6.17**).
   - ◆ In the Font list, choose the desired typeface.
   - ◆ Select the desired Font Style (Regular, Italic, Bold, Bold Italic).
   - ◆ In the Size list, choose the desired point size.
   - ◆ If you like, you can choose a different color.

5. Click OK.

✔ Tips

- ■ Look at the Sample (in **Figure 6.17**) to preview what the formatted text or number will look like.

- ■ One way to select all the slice labels is to choose Series 1 Data Labels in the Chart Objects field on the toolbar.

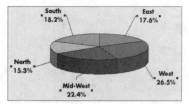

Figure 6.15 The selection handles show that the data labels are currently selected.

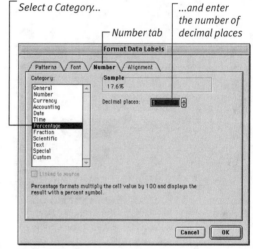

Figure 6.16 You can format numeric labels here.

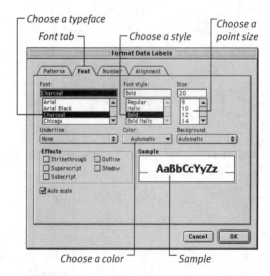

Figure 6.17 You can format text in data labels.

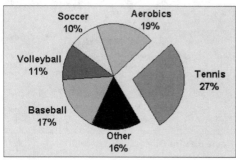

Figure 6.18 The Tennis slice is exploded from the pie to emphasize that it has the greatest portion of sales.

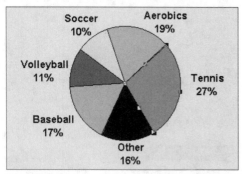

Figure 6.19 Selection handles indicate that the Tennis slice is selected.

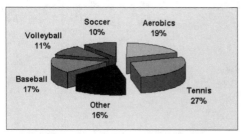

Figure 6.20 All slices are exploded in this pie chart.

Exploding a Slice

To emphasize one of the pie slices, you can *explode* it as shown in **Figure 6.18**.

To explode a pie slice:

1. Click the pie to select it.

2. Click the slice you want to explode. You'll see selection handles around it (**Figure 6.19**).

3. Place the mouse pointer inside the slice, and drag away from the pie center until the slice is the desired distance from the rest of the pie.

✔ Tips

- The more space you have between the pie chart and the exploded piece, the greater emphasis or importance you are placing on the piece.

- To unexplode a slice, select it and drag it back toward the pie center.

- To explode all the slices (**Figure 6.20**), select the entire pie and drag any slice—all slices will explode.

- If you want the exploded slice to be in a particular position (for instance, at the 5:00 position on the pie), rotate the pie until the slice is in the desired place.

  See Rotating a Pie later in this chapter.

Coloring the Slices

You can assign new colors to any of the slices in a pie chart.

To color the pie slices:

1. Click the pie to select it.

2. Click the slice you want to color. You should see selection handles around it (**Figure 6.21**).

3. Choose Format > Selected Data Point.

   or

   Double-click the slice.

4. Select the Patterns tab (**Figure 6.22**).

5. Choose a color in the palette.

6. Click OK.

7. Repeat steps 2 through 6 for each slice.

✔ Tip

■ You can also use the Fill Color button on the toolbar to apply a color to a selected pie slice.

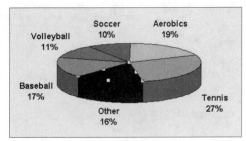

Figure 6.21 The Other slice is selected.

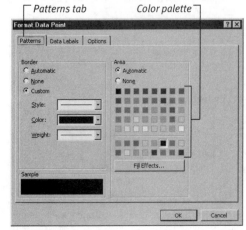

Figure 6.22 To change the color of a slice, choose a color in the palette.

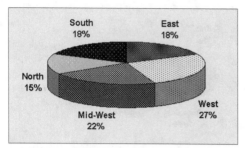

Figure 6.23 Each slice has a different pattern, which helps to differentiate the slices.

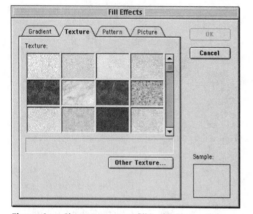

Figure 6.24 Choose a texture fill in the Texture tab.

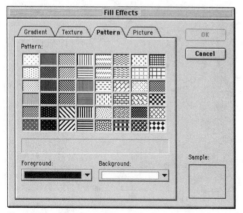

Figure 6.25 Choose a pattern fill in the Pattern tab.

Filling Slices with a Pattern

Slices can also be filled with distinguishing patterns and textures (**Figure 6.23**).

To fill a slice with a pattern:

1. Click the pie to select it.

2. Click the slice you want to fill. You should see selection handles around it.

3. Choose Format > Selected Data Series.
   or
   Double-click the slice.

4. Select the Patterns tab.

5. Click Fill Effects.

6. Select the Gradient tab and choose a shading style.
   or
   Select the Texture tab and click a texture (**Figure 6.24**).
   or
   Select the Pattern tab and click a pattern (**Figure 6.25**).

7. Click OK twice to return to the chart.

Rotating a Pie

To control the positioning of the slices, you can rotate the pie (**Figures 6.26** and **6.27**).

To rotate a pie:

1. Select the pie.

2. Choose Format > Selected Data Series.

3. Select the Options tab (**Figure 6.28**).

4. In the Angle Of First Slice field, click the up arrow to rotate the pie clockwise in 10-degree increments, or click the down arrow to rotate the pie counterclockwise.

5. Click OK.

✔ Tips

- The angle is measured from the 12:00 position on the pie.

- Watch the preview box (**Figure 6.28**) as you click the arrows in the Angle Of First Slice field—the pie rotates with each click.

- Though data labels will rotate with the slices, you still may need to reposition some of them after rotating.

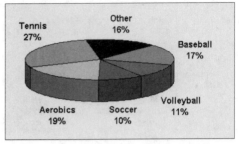

Figure 6.26 Before rotating the pie, the angle=45.

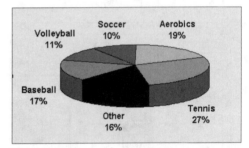

Figure 6.27 After rotating the pie, the angle=225.

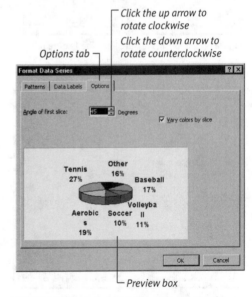

Figure 6.28 To rotate a pie, change the angle of the first slice.

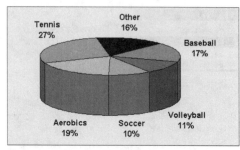

Figure 6.29 This pie chart has a height of 200%.

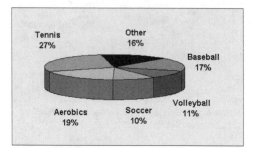

Figure 6.30 This pie chart has an elevation of 10 (the minimum).

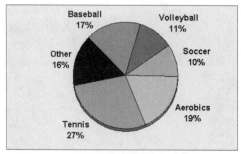

Figure 6.31 This pie chart has an elevation of 80 (the maximum).

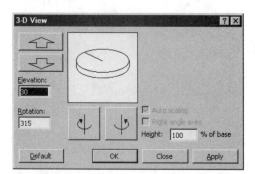

Figure 6.32 Change the elevation and height of a 3-D pie chart in the 3-D View dialog box.

Formatting 3-D Effects

For 3-D pies, you can control the height of the pie (**Figure 6.29**) and the angle from which you're viewing it (its elevation as shown in **Figures 6.30** and **6.31**).

To format a pie's 3-D effects:

1. Choose Chart > 3-D View.

   The 3-D View dialog box appears (**Figure 6.32**).

2. Click the large up or down arrows to increase or decrease the Elevation angle.

3. Enter a percentage in the Height field.

   The Height value is a percentage of the default height (100%). For instance, 50% is half the default height and 200% is twice the default height.

4. Click Apply to see the result of your changes without closing the dialog box.

5. Repeat steps 2 through 4 until you are satisfied with the results.

6. Click OK.

✔ Tips

- With a low elevation value, the pie looks as if you are standing next to the pie and looking at it from the side. With a high value, it looks as if you are in an airplane and viewing the pie from above.

- To return to the default settings, click Default in the 3-D View dialog box.

- Because you may need to rotate your pie after adjusting the elevation and height, the 3-D View dialog box has a Rotation field.

Resizing and Repositioning a Pie

After you format and modify a pie chart, you may notice that it seems too small or that it is no longer centered in the chart. You can solve these types of problems by manipulating the plot area.

To resize and reposition a pie:

1. Choose Plot Area in the Chart Objects field on the toolbar (**Figure 6.33**).

2. To resize the pie, drag any corner selection handle (**Figure 6.34**).

3. To reposition the pie, drag from any border line of the selected plot area.

✔ Tip

■ When resizing or moving a pie, the data labels move with their respective slices. However, you still may need to manually reposition some of them.

Figure 6.33 Select the plot area in the Chart Objects field on the toolbar.

Drag any border line to reposition the pie   *Drag any corner handle to resize the pie*

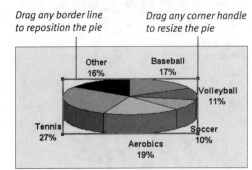

Figure 6.34 The selected plot area is surrounded by selection handles.

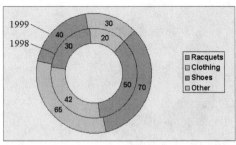

Figure 6.35 A doughnut chart can show two data series.

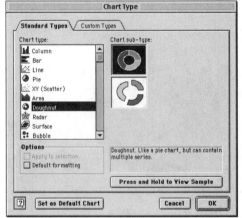

Figure 6.36 Choose the doughnut chart type from the Standard Types tab.

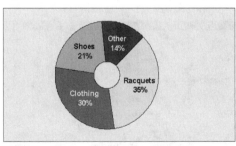

Figure 6.37 You can add labels on the inside of the doughnut pieces.

Creating a Doughnut

A doughnut chart is more than just a two-dimensional pie chart with a hole in the center: Unlike a pie, it can display more than one data series (**Figure 6.35**).

To create a doughnut chart:

1. Insert a chart slide and fill in the data sheet with each data series in a different row.

   See Inserting a Pie Slide and Entering Pie Data earlier in this chapter.

2. Choose Chart > Chart Type.

   The Chart Type dialog box appears (**Figure 6.36**).

3. Click the Doughnut chart type.

4. Click OK.

✔ Tips

- To label the doughnut pieces (**Figure 6.37**), use the Chart > Chart Options command and select the Data Labels tab. Notice that the labels are inside the pieces.

- Because the legend identifies the doughnut pieces, not the data series, you need to identify the data series yourself. In **Figure 6.35**, this was accomplished by returning to PowerPoint and typing the labels *1998* and *1999* with the Text Box tool and drawing the pointers with the Line tool. (These tools are located on the Drawing toolbar.) ▣ ◥

   See Creating a Text Box in Chapter 3 and Drawing Lines in Chapter 10.

CREATING A DOUGHNUT

Resizing the Doughnut Hole

If there isn't enough room inside the dough-nut pieces for the data labels (**Figure 6.38**), you can reduce the doughnut hole size. **Figure 6.39** shows the same chart after the doughnut hole size was reduced.

To resize the doughnut hole:

1. Click the doughnut to select it.

2. Choose Format > Selected Data Series.

3. Select the Options tab (**Figure 6.40**).

4. Click the up or down arrows in the Doughnut Hole Size field to increase or decrease the size of the hole.

5. Click OK.

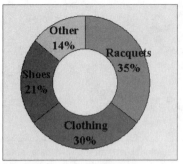

Figure 6.38 With the default doughnut hole size, the Racquets label doesn't fit.

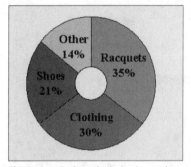

Figure 6.39 Reduce the hole size so that the labels fit inside the pieces.

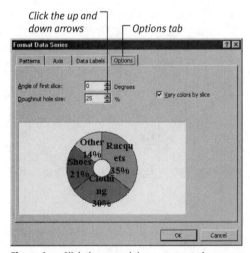

Figure 6.40 Click the up and down arrows to increase or decrease the hole size.

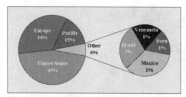

Figure 6.41 The smaller pie is a breakdown of the other slice in the larger pie.

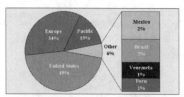

Figure 6.42 The bar shows a breakdown of the other slice.

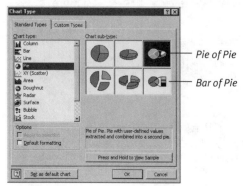

Pie of Pie

Bar of Pie

Figure 6.43 Choose one of the linked pie chart types.

Creating Linked Pies

The chart shown in **Figure 6.41** contains a second pie that is linked to the first pie—the pie on the right provides a detailed break-down of a single slice in the main pie. PowerPoint calls this type of chart Pie of Pie. A similar chart type, Bar of Pie (**Figure 6.42**), shows the second pie in a columnar style.

To create linked pies:

1. Create a new slide with the Chart layout.

2. Click the title placeholder and type the title of your chart.

3. Double-click the chart placeholder to create your chart.

4. Choose Chart > Chart Type.
   The Chart Type dialog box appears (**Figure 6.43**).

5. Click the Pie chart type.

6. Click the Pie of Pie or Bar of Pie sub-type.

7. Click OK.

Entering Data for Linked Pies

Entering data for a Pie of Pie or Bar of Pie chart is not exactly intuitive. The values for both pies are entered into a single column on the datasheet (**Figure 6.44**).

PowerPoint offers a variety of ways to designate how to split the series into two pies. In this example, we've specified that the last four values in the series are for the second plot (**Figure 6.45**).

To enter data for linked pies:

1. If the datasheet window isn't open, click the View Datasheet button.

2. To erase the sample data, click the Select All button and press Delete (Windows) or Del (Mac OS).

3. Enter the slice labels in the first column; do not enter a label for "Other."

4. Enter the slice values in the second column.

5. Click the By Column button on the toolbar.

   This button indicates the data are entered into columns, not rows.

6. Select either pie.

7. Choose Format > Selected Data Series.

8. Select the Options tab (**Figure 6.45**).

9. To designate how to split the series into two pies:

   ◆ Choose one of the options in the Split Series By field (Position, Value, Percent Value, or Custom).

   ◆ Enter a value in the next field.

10. Click OK.

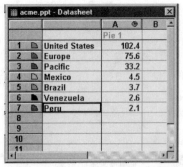

Figure 6.44 Enter the data for both pies as shown; be sure to enter the values in descending order.

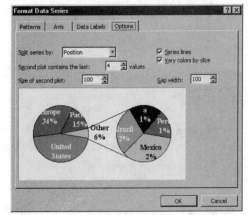

Figure 6.45 The four last values in the datasheet are assigned to the second plot.

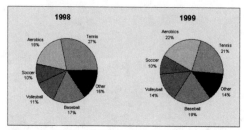

Figure 6.46 You can display two pie charts on a slide (created with the Chart & Text layout) to compare information.

Creating Two Pies on a Slide

If you want to compare two pie charts on the same slide (**Figure 6.46**) but one of the pies is not a sub-set of the other, don't use the Pie of Pie chart type. Instead, use the Chart & Text layout.

The procedure for creating this type of slide is described in Creating Two Charts on a Slide in Chapter 4.

✔ Tip

■ Because the pies are smaller when you have two to a slide, you may have to reduce the size of the data labels. (This was done in **Figure 6.46**.)

BUILDING ORGANIZATION CHARTS

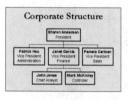

Figure 7.1
This organization chart illustrates a corporation's structure.

Peter is Sharon's assistant   *Sharon is manager of Peter, Patrick, Janet, and Pamela*

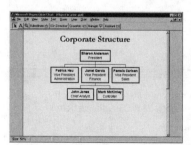

Patrick, Janet, and Pamela are co-workers and are subordinates to Sharon

Figure 7.2 An org chart uses several types of boxes.

The most common use for an organization chart (or *org chart*) is to illustrate a corporation's structure (**Figure 7.1**). It identifies the names and titles of the key people in a company or division. You can also use org charts to create a simple flowchart, an outline of tasks in a project, a family tree, or even a diagram of your hard disk's directory structure.

Organization charts can include managers, subordinates, co-workers, or assistants (**Figure 7.2**). A *manager* is someone who has other people—*subordinates*—reporting to him/her. *Co-workers* are subordinates who have the same manager. An *assistant* provides administrative assistance to a manager.

Org charts are created in a separate program called Microsoft Organization Chart (**Figure 7.3**). You launch Organization Chart by double-clicking the org chart placeholder or an embedded org chart.

Figure 7.3 Use Microsoft Organization Chart to create your org charts. (The Windows version is shown here; the Mac OS version is shown on the next page.)

Inserting an Org Chart Slide

PowerPoint offers an AutoLayout specific to organization charts.

To insert an organization chart slide:

1. Click the New Slide button on the toolbar. 🖻

2. In the New Slide dialog box, choose the Organization Chart layout (**Figure 7.4**).

3. Click OK.

   The slide appears with title and org chart placeholders (**Figure 7.5**).

4. Click the title placeholder and type the title of your org chart.

5. Double-click the org chart placeholder to create your organization chart.

   This action launches Microsoft Organization Chart in its own window (**Figure 7.6**).

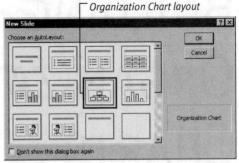

Figure 7.4 Choose the Organization Chart layout.

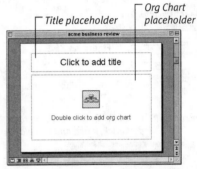

Figure 7.5 This slide uses the Organization Chart layout.

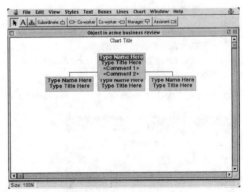

Figure 7.6 A new chart appears in Microsoft Organization Chart. (Mac OS is shown here.)

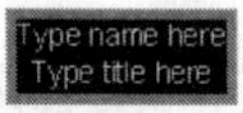

Figure 7.7 A box before any text is entered.

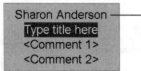

Type the name and press Tab

Figure 7.8 After you enter the name, type the title in this area.

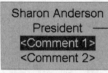

Type the title and press Tab

Figure 7.9 After you enter the title, enter comments in the Comment 1 area.

Entering Text into Boxes

You can have up to four lines of text in a box: name, title, and two comment lines.

To enter text into the boxes:

1. Click the box into which you want to enter text (**Figure 7.7**).

2. Type the name and press Tab (**Figure 7.8**). The next line is highlighted.

3. Type the title and press Tab (**Figure 7.9**). The next line is highlighted.

4. If needed, type a comment and press Tab.

5. Type an additional comment line, if desired.

6. When you're finished, click another box or click elsewhere in the window.

   See the next page for information on inserting additional boxes on the org chart.

✔ Tips

- Instead of pressing Tab, you can press Enter or Return to go to the next line in the box.

- To edit the text in a box, click the box to select it; click again in the text to see the text cursor.

- If you prefer using the keyboard, you can move between boxes by holding down Ctrl (Windows) or Option (Mac OS) as you press the arrow keys. Then press Enter or Return to edit the text.

- Boxes automatically resize to fit the text you type inside. To make a box smaller, choose a smaller point size for the text.

  See Formatting Box Text later in this chapter.

Inserting a Box

Since the default org chart has only four boxes, it's likely that you'll want to insert additional boxes.

To insert a box:

1. Click the appropriate box tool (**Figure 7.10**) for the type of box you want to insert.

2. Click the existing box to which the new box should be attached (**Figure 7.11**).

   Figure 7.12 shows a newly-inserted subordinate box.

✔ Tips

- Note that there are two Add Co-worker tools. The first tool inserts a box to the left of the selected box, and the second tool inserts one to the right.

- To delete a box, select it and press Delete.

- If you accidentally insert a box in the wrong location, choose Edit > Undo.

- **Table 7.1** shows the keyboard shortcuts for inserting boxes into an org chart.

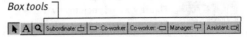

Box tools

Figure 7.10 Select a box tool on the toolbar.

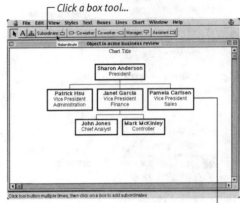

Click a box tool...

...then click an existing box to attach a new box

Figure 7.11 Insert a subordinate box.

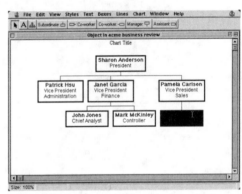

Figure 7.12 Pamela Carlsen's box now has a new subordinate box attached.

Table 7.1

Keyboard Shortcuts for Inserting Boxes	
FUNCTION KEY	DESCRIPTION
F2	Creates of subordinate for the selected box
F3	Creates a co-worker to the left of the selected box
F4	Creates a co-worker to the right of the selected box
F5	Creates a manager for the selected box
F6	Creates an assistant for the selected box

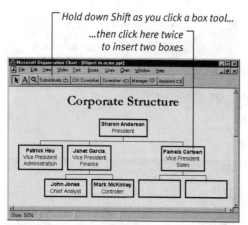

Figure 7.13 Insert multiple boxes with the Shift+click technique.

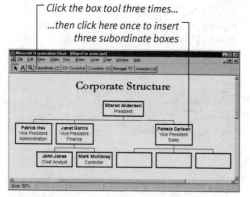

Figure 7.14 Insert multiple boxes with the multiple-click technique.

Inserting Multiple Boxes

Using the following technique, you can easily insert multiple boxes of the same type.

To insert multiple boxes:

1. Hold down Shift as you click the appropriate box tool, such as the Subordinate or Co-worker tool.

2. Click the existing box to which you want to attach the new box (**Figure 7.13**).

3. Repeat step 2 for each new box you want to insert.

4. Press Esc to deactivate the box tool.

✔ Tip

- Another way to insert multiple boxes is to click the box tool multiple times. For example, if you click the Subordinate tool three times and then click a box on your chart, three subordinate boxes will be inserted below the box you clicked (**Figure 7.14**).

Returning to PowerPoint

When you are finished editing your org chart, you'll want to exit from Microsoft Organization Chart and return to PowerPoint.

To return to PowerPoint (Windows):

1. Select one of the following commands:

   ◆ Choose File > Close And Return To *xxx.ppt* where *xxx.ppt* is the name of your PowerPoint presentation (**Figure 7.15**).

   or

   ◆ Choose File > Exit And Return To *xxx.ppt*.

   or

   ◆ Click the close button on the Microsoft Organization Chart window (**Figure 7.16**).

2. When asked if you want to update the object, select Yes.

To return to PowerPoint (Mac OS):

1. Select one of the following commands:

   ◆ Choose File > Close And Return To *xxx* where *xxx* is the name of your PowerPoint presentation (**Figure 7.17**).

   or

   ◆ Choose File > Quit And Return To *xxx*.

   or

   ◆ Click the close box on the object window (**Figure 7.18**).

2. When asked if you want to update the object, select Yes.

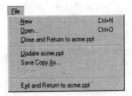

Figure 7.15 The File menu in Microsoft Organization Chart (Windows) has two options for returning to PowerPoint.

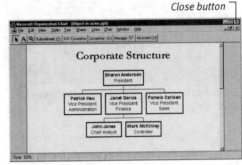

Figure 7.16 Click the close button to exit from Microsoft Organization Chart (Windows).

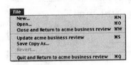

Figure 7.17 The File menu in Microsoft Organization Chart (Mac OS).

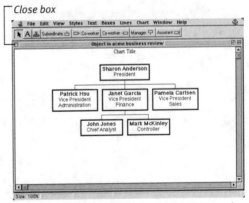

Figure 7.18 Click the close box to exit from Microsoft Organization Chart (Mac OS).

Embedded org chart

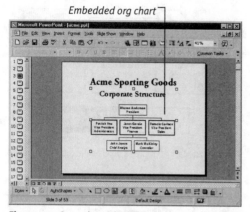

Figure 7.19 Open the embedded org chart by double-clicking it.

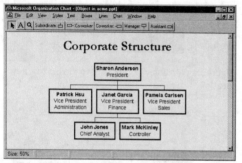

Figure 7.20 The chart after it is opened in Microsoft Organization Chart (Windows).

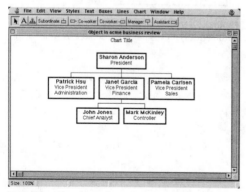

Figure 7.21 The chart after it is opened in Microsoft Organization Chart (Mac OS).

Editing an Existing Org Chart

To edit a previously-created org chart, you need to reopen it in Microsoft Organization Chart.

To edit an existing org chart:

1. In Slide or Normal view, double-click the embedded org chart (**Figure 7.19**).

   Figure 7.20 shows the org chart as it appears in the Windows version of Microsoft Organization Chart, and **Figure 7.21** shows the chart in Mac OS.

2. Make any desired changes to the chart (insert and/or rearrange the boxes, format the lines and boxes, and so forth).

3. When you're finished, exit from Microsoft Organization Chart.

   See Returning to PowerPoint on the previous page.

Rearranging Boxes

You can easily restructure an organization chart by dragging the boxes (**Figures 7.22** and **7.23**).

To rearrange boxes:

1. Press Esc or click the background to make sure nothing is selected.

2. Point to the box to be moved and drag it over its new manager or co-worker.

3. Release the mouse button.

✔ Tips

- As you drag one box over another, the pointer displays an icon to indicate the new positioning of the box:

  ▷ Box will be inserted as a co-worker to the right

  ◁ Box will be inserted as a co-worker to the left

  ⊔ Box will be inserted as a subordinate

- To move an entire branch, drag the manager's box; subordinates automatically move when you move a manager (**Figure 7.24**).

- Another way to move a box is by cutting and pasting. Select the box and choose Edit > Cut. Then, select the box of the new manager and choose Edit > Paste Boxes.

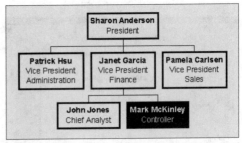

Figure 7.22 Mark McKinley's box is selected to be moved.

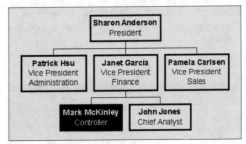

Figure 7.23 McKinley's box has been moved to a new location.

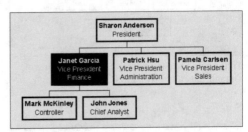

Figure 7.24 Moving Janet Garcia to the left automatically moves her subordinates as well.

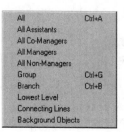

Figure 7.25 Choose
Edit > Select to display
this menu.

Figure 7.26 Choose Edit > Select
Levels to display this dialog box.

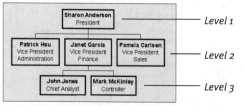

Figure 7.27 This organization chart uses
three levels.

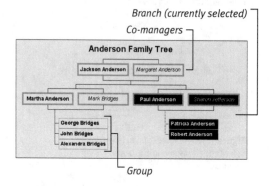

Figure 7.28 Elements of an organization chart.

Selecting Boxes

To format the boxes in an org chart, you
must first select them.

To select boxes:

Use any of the following techniques:

♦ Hold down Shift as you click each box.

♦ Click and drag a marquee around the
boxes.

♦ Choose Edit > Select and choose the item
you wish to select (**Figure 7.25**). *See
terms below.*

♦ Choose Edit > Select Levels and enter a
range of levels to select
(**Figures 7.26** and **7.27**).

When selecting boxes (**Figure 7.28**), it's
helpful to be familiar with the following terms:

Group All boxes with the same manager
(or the same parent in a family tree).

Branch All the boxes that report to the
currently-selected manager, all the way to
the bottom of the chart.

Co-Managers Those who share responsi-
bility for the same group of subordinates,
such as each set of spouses in **Figure 7.28**.
(The co-manager relationship is created via
styles. *See Choosing a Style on the next page.*)

✔ Tips

■ To select all the boxes on the chart,
press Ctrl+A (Windows) or Command+A
(Mac OS).

■ Before choosing Group or Branch from
the Select menu, click one of the boxes of
the group or branch.

Choosing a Style

You can apply a variety of styles to the different levels or groups of boxes on your organization charts.

To choose a style:

1. Select the boxes (such as a level or a group) that will be formatted with the new style (**Figure 7.29**).

   See Selecting Boxes on the previous page.

2. Click Styles on the menu bar.

3. Choose the desired style (**Table 7.2**).

   The org charts in **Figures 7.30**, **7.31**, and **7.32** are examples of some of the styles.

✔ Tip

■ The styles with vertical orientation are typically used on the lowest level of an organization chart.

Table 7.2

Org Chart Styles

BUTTON	DESCRIPTION
🔲🔲🔲	*Standard horizontal orientation*
🔳	*Vertical orientation with boxes*
🔳🔳	*Aligns boxes into columns*
🔳🔳 🔳🔳	*Aligns boxes into two sets of columns*
▯	*Vertical orientation without boxes*
▯	*Combines selected boxes into one box*
🔲🔲🔲	*Selected boxes become assistants*
🔲🔲🔲	*Selected boxes become co-managers*

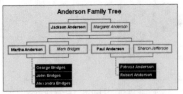

Figure 7.29 The lowest level (level 3) of this organization chart is selected.

Each married couple was formatted with the Co-Manager style

Figure 7.30 The lowest level is vertically oriented; each name is in a box.

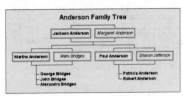

Figure 7.31 The lowest level is vertically oriented; the names are not boxed.

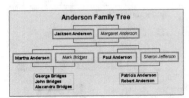

Figure 7.32 The lowest level is vertically oriented; all names in a group are in one box.

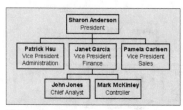

Figure 7.33 All the names are in bold.

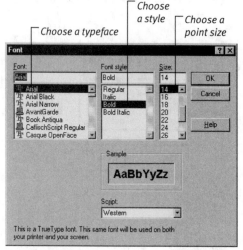

Figure 7.34 Format box text in the Font dialog box (Windows).

Choose a style

Choose a typeface

Choose a point size

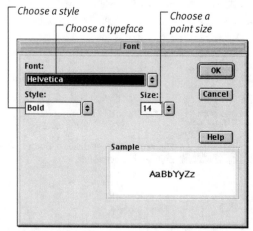

Figure 7.35 Format box text in the Font dialog box (Mac OS).

Formatting Box Text

You can format all or any part of the text inside the boxes (**Figure 7.33**).

To format box text:

1. To format a selection of text, click inside the box and then drag across the characters you want to select.

   or

   To format all the text in one or more boxes, select the boxes.

   See Selecting Boxes earlier in this chapter.

2. Choose Text > Font.

   The Font dialog box appears (**Figures 7.34 and 7.35**).

3. In the Font list, choose the desired typeface.

4. Select the desired Font Style (Regular, Italic, Bold, or Bold Italic).

5. In the Size list, choose the desired point size.

6. Click OK.

✔ Tips

- New boxes that you insert will automatically inherit the formatting of the currently-selected box. For example, if a manager has a bolded name, all subordinate boxes that you insert will have bolded names.

- You can also change the alignment of text within the boxes. On the Text menu, choose Left, Right, or Center. (Center is the default.)

- You can also change the text color. On the Text menu, choose Color.

Formatting the Boxes

You can choose a different border style (**Figure 7.36**), add a shadow (**Figure 7.37**), or change the color inside your boxes.

To format the boxes:

1. Select the boxes you want to format.

   See Selecting Boxes earlier in this chapter.

2. Click Boxes on the menu bar.

3. Choose any of the following formatting commands on the Boxes menu:

   ◆ Choose Color to change the background color of the boxes.

   ◆ Choose Shadow to add a shadow effect (**Figure 7.38**).

   ◆ Choose Border Style to change the line style of the borders (**Figure 7.39**).

   ◆ Choose Border Color to change the color of the borders.

   ◆ Choose Border Line Style to change the style of the borders.

✔ Tip

■ To format all the boxes, select them first with Ctrl+A (Windows) or Command+A (Mac OS).

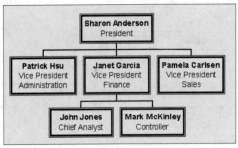

Figure 7.36 The boxes have a double-line border.

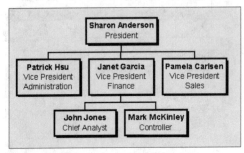

Figure 7.37 The boxes have shadows.

Figure 7.38 Choose Boxes > Shadow and select a style.

Figure 7.39 Choose Boxes > Border Style and select a style.

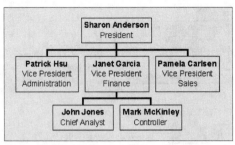

Figure 7.40 The connecting lines were formatted with a heavy line weight.

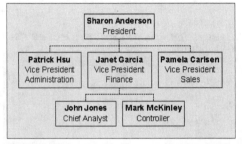

Figure 7.41 The connecting lines were formatted with a dotted line style.

Figure 7.42 Choose Lines > Thickness and select a line weight.

Figure 7.43 Choose Lines > Style and select a line style.

Formatting the Lines

The lines that connect the boxes to each other can also be formatted. You can adjust their thickness (**Figure 7.40**), style (**Figure 7.41**), or color.

To format the lines in the chart:

1. To format all connecting lines, choose Edit > Select > Connecting Lines.

   or

   To format a single line, click the line.

2. Click Lines on the menu bar.

3. Choose any of the following formatting commands on the Lines menu:

   ♦ Choose Thickness to change the weight of the lines (**Figure 7.42**).

   ♦ Choose Style to select a different line style (**Figure 7.43**).

   ♦ Choose Color to change the color of the lines.

✔ Tips

■ To select several lines, hold down Shift as you click each one.

■ It's difficult to see lines when they are selected—the lines are dotted when they are selected.

Zooming In and Out

The View menu (**Figure 7.44**) offers ways to zoom in (get up closer) or zoom out (step back) to change your view of the screen. (It does not affect the printed size of the chart.) You can also change your view using the Zoom button (**Figure 7.45**).

Figures 7.46 and **7.47** show examples of some of the zoom levels.

Table 7.3 defines the items on the View menu.

To zoom in or out:

1. Click the Zoom button (**Figure 7.45**).

2. Click the area of the chart you want to look at.

✔ Tip

■ The Zoom button zooms in to Actual Size and zooms out to Size to Window.

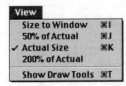

Figure 7.44 Use the View menu to change your view of the organization chart.

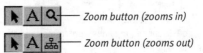

— Zoom button (zooms in)

— Zoom button (zooms out)

Figure 7.45 The icon for the Zoom button looks different depending upon the current view.

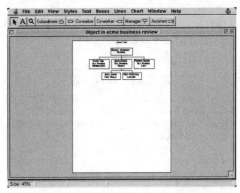

Figure 7.46 The Size to Window command gives you an overall feel for the chart (though you may not be able to actually read the text).

Table 7.3

View menu items	
MENU ITEM	DESCRIPTION
Size to Window	Zoom out to fit the entire page within the current window (readjusts as you change window size)
50% of Actual	Display the chart at half its printed size (the default view)
Actual Size	Zoom in to display the chart at the same size as printed
200% of Actual	Zoom way in to see the chart at twice its printed size

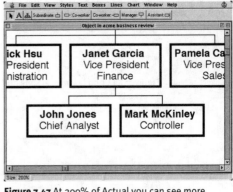

Figure 7.47 At 200% of Actual you can see more detail.

CREATING TABLES (WINDOWS)

Medical Plans		
	Indemnity Plan	**HMO**
Services Available	Any doctor	HMO facility
Premium	$100 / month	None
Deductible	$500 / month	None
Co-insurance	80% / 20%	$7 visit

Figure 8.1 This table has three columns.

What is the Smart Health Program?	A health care plan designed to maximize your benefits by utilizing a network of participating physicians and hospitals.
Is my physician a provider in the network?	Check with your physician or get a copy of the Smart Health Program Directory of Physicians. To order a copy, call 800-555-2323.
What about claim forms?	The participating provider is responsible for submitting forms for you.

Figure 8.2 This table has side-by-side paragraphs.

The best way to present columns of data is in a Table slide. **Figures 8.1** and **8.2** show examples of tables you can create in PowerPoint.

Think of a table as a mini-spreadsheet, similar to the ones you may have created in Microsoft Excel or Lotus 1-2-3. Unlike in previous versions of the program, you create tables directly in PowerPoint, not in Microsoft Word.

Inserting a Table Slide

PowerPoint offers one AutoLayout for tables (**Figure 8.3**).

To insert a table slide:

1. Click the New Slide button on the toolbar.

2. In the New Slide dialog box, choose the Table layout (**Figure 8.3**).

3. Click OK. The slide appears with title and table placeholders.

4. Click the title placeholder and type the title of your table.

5. Double-click the table placeholder to create your table.

   You are asked to specify the number of columns and rows (**Figure 8.4**).

6. Specify the Number of Columns and press Tab.

7. Specify the Number of Rows and click OK.

   An empty table appears on the slide (**Figure 8.5**).

✔ Tip

■ When you initially create a table, all the columns and rows are the same size. However, the column widths and row heights can be adjusted at any time.

   See Adjusting Column Widths and Adjusting Row Heights later in this chapter.

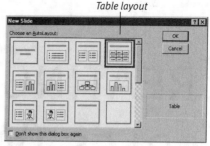

Table layout

Figure 8.3 To create a table slide, first choose the Table layout.

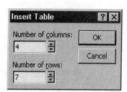

Figure 8.4 Specify the number of columns and rows in your table.

Tables and Borders toolbar

Click this button to display the Tables and Borders toolbar

Click the close button to close the toolbar

Figure 8.5 A new table with 4 columns and 7 rows.

What is the Smart Health Program?	A health care plan designed to maximize your benefits by utilizing a network of participating physicians and hospitals.
Is my physician a provider in the network?	Check with your physician or get a copy of the Smart Health Program Directory of Physicians. To order a copy, call 800-555-2323.
What about claim forms?	The participating provider is responsible for submitting forms for you.

Figure 8.6 Text automatically wraps within each cell, and the row heights automatically adjust.

Entering Text into a Table

A table is made up of rows and columns; the intersection of a row and column is called a *cell*.

To type text into a table:

1. Click a cell and start typing.

   As you reach the right edge of the cell, text will wrap automatically to the next line in the cell (**Figure 8.6**).

2. Press Tab to move the cursor to the next cell to the right.

   or

   Press the down arrow key to move down to the next cell.

3. After entering text in the last cell in the row, press Tab; this moves the cursor to the first cell in the next row.

✔ Tips

- If you enter more text than fits in the original size cell, the entire row becomes taller to accommodate all the extra characters.

- Pressing Enter in a cell drops the cursor down to the next line in the same cell. It does *not* move the cursor to a different cell.

- Pressing Tab from the last cell in a table inserts a new row and places the cursor in the first cell.

- If text wraps in a cell but you want it to fit on a single line, you can either decrease the type size or adjust the column width.

  See Formatting Table Text and Adjusting Column Widths later in this chapter.

Selecting Cells

Before you can format cells in your table, you need to select them.

To select parts of a table:

Use any of the following techniques:

◆ Click Table on the Tables and Borders toolbar and choose Select Table, Select Column, or Select Row.

◆ You can select the next cell or the previous cell by pressing Tab or Shift+Tab.

◆ With the mouse, you can select a range of cells by dragging across them (**Figure 8.7**).

◆ You can select an entire column by clicking directly above the column (**Figure 8.8**). The mouse pointer becomes a down arrow when it is positioned properly for selecting the column.

✔ Tips

■ Before dragging across cells, make sure the Draw Table or Eraser tools aren't selected. If the pointer appears as a pencil or an eraser, press Esc to cancel the tool.

■ The keyboard shortcut for selecting the entire table is Ctrl+5 (on the numeric keypad). For this shortcut to work, Num Lock *must not* be turned on.

Click and drag across cells to select a range

	1998	1999	Change
Jones	35,600	60,980	25,380
Smith	12,950	23,700	10,750
Black	24,500	27,100	2,600
Johnson	90,000	125,000	35,000
Goldman	54,200	25,400	-28,800
Totals	217,250	262,180	44,930

Figure 8.7 A range of cells is currently selected.

Click here to select a column

	1998	1999	Change
Jones	35,600	60,980	25,380
Smith	12,950	23,700	10,750
Black	24,500	27,100	2,600
Johnson	90,000	125,000	35,000
Goldman	54,200	25,400	-28,800
Totals	217,250	262,180	44,930

Figure 8.8 Click above the first cell in a column to select the entire column.

Column border ⌐

	1998	1999	Change
Jones, Bob	35,600	60,980	25,380
Smith, Mary	12,950	23,700	10,750
Black, John	24,500	27,100	2,600
Johnson, Joe	90,000	125,000	35,000
Goldman, A.J.	54,200	25,400	-28,800
Totals	217,250	262,180	44,930

Figure 8.9 Dragging the column border is one way to adjust the column width.

⌐Double-click here

	1998	1999	Change
Jones, Bob	35,600	60,980	25,380
Smith, Mary	12,950	23,700	10,750
Black, John	24,500	27,100	2,600
Johnson, Joe	90,000	125,000	35,000
Goldman, A.J.	54,200	25,400	-28,800
Totals	217,250	262,180	44,930

Figure 8.10 To quickly set the width of the first column, double-click the column border.

Adjusting Column Widths

Although a new table starts out with columns of equal width, it's easy to make the columns wider or narrower. You can either manually adjust the width of a column or have PowerPoint do it for you automatically.

To adjust the width of a column:

1. Press Esc to make sure no cells are selected. (Otherwise, the width will change for only the selected cells.)

2. Place the pointer on the right border line of the column (**Figure 8.9**).

   or

   If your table doesn't have vertical borders, place the pointer between the columns, where the border would be.

3. When the pointer becomes two arrows pointing left and right, do one of the following:

   ◆ Drag to the left to narrow the column, or drag to the right to widen it.

   or

   ◆ Double-click the column border to automatically find the best fit according to the widest entry (**Figure 8.10**).

Adjusting Row Heights

Although you can increase row heights in order to add extra space between rows, you can't make the row height shorter than its tallest entry.

To adjust the height of a row:

1. Place the pointer on the border line beneath the row (**Figure 8.11**).

   or

   If your table doesn't have horizontal borders, place the pointer between the rows, where the border would be.

2. When the pointer becomes two arrows pointing up and down, drag up to decrease the row height or drag down to increase the height.

✔ Tip

■ If you are unable to decrease the height of an empty row, it's because PowerPoint won't let you make the row shorter than its formatted point size. (This feature prevents characters from being truncated.) When this happens, select the row and choose a smaller font size (**Figure 8.12**).

Drag the row border to adjust the row height...   *...or if there isn't a border, drag to where the border would be*

	Indemnity Plan	HMO
Services Available	Any doctor	HMO facility
Premium	$100 / month	None
Deductible	$500 / month	None
Co-insurance	80% / 20%	$7 visit

Figure 8.11 To adjust the row height, drag the row border.

Select the row and choose a smaller font size

	1998	1999	Change
Jones, Bob	35,600	60,980	25,380
Smith, Mary	12,950	23,700	10,750
Black, John	24,500	27,100	2,600
Johnson, Joe	90,000	125,000	35,000
Goldman, A.J.	54,200	25,400	-28,800
Totals	217,250	262,180	44,930

Figure 8.12 Dragging the row border will not shorten a blank row until you decrease the font size.

The cursor is sitting after "Jones"

	1998	1999	Change
Jones	35,600	60,980	25,380
Smith	12,950	23,700	10,750
Black	24,500	27,100	2,600
Johnson	90,000	125,000	35,000
Goldman	54,200	25,400	-28,800
Totals	217,250	262,180	44,930

Figure 8.13 You can choose to insert a row either above or below the cursor.

Inserted row

	1998	1999	Change
Jones	35,600	60,980	25,380
Smith	12,950	23,700	10,750
Black	24,500	27,100	2,600
Johnson	90,000	125,000	35,000
Goldman	54,200	25,400	-28,800
Totals	217,250	262,180	44,930

Figure 8.14 Use the Table > Insert Rows Above command to insert this row.

Figure 8.15 Click the Table button on the Tables and Borders toolbar to display the menu. (You may need to wait a few seconds for the Insert Rows option to appear.)

Inserting Rows and Columns

If you underestimated the number of rows or columns in your table when initially creating it, you can insert them later. **Figures 8.13** and **8.14** show a table before and after inserting a row.

To insert a row:

1. Click the text cursor in the table where you'd like to insert the new row.

2. Click Table on the Tables and Borders toolbar.
   The Table menu appears (**Figure 8.15**).

3. Choose Insert Rows Above or Insert Rows Below.

To insert a column:

1. Click the text cursor in the table where you'd like to insert the new column.

2. Click Table on the Tables and Borders toolbar.
   The Table menu appears (**Figure 8.15**).

3. Choose Insert Columns to the Left or Insert Columns to the Right.

✔ Tips

- To insert multiple rows (or columns) in the same location, first select the number of rows (columns) you wish to insert. For instance, to insert two rows, select two rows and choose Insert Rows Above (or Insert Rows Below) on the Table menu.

- To insert a new row after the last row, position the cursor in the last cell in the table, and press Tab.

- You can also insert rows and columns with the Draw Table tool.

  See Drawing Table Borders later in this chapter.

Deleting Rows and Columns

When you delete rows and columns, you not only remove the contents of the cells, you remove the cells as well (**Figures 8.16** and **8.17**).

To delete rows or columns:

1. Select the rows or columns to be deleted (**Figure 8.16**).

   See Selecting Cells earlier in this chapter.

2. Click Table on the Tables and Borders toolbar.

   The Table menu appears (**Figure 8.18**).

3. Choose Delete Rows or Delete Columns.

✔ Tips

- If the Tables and Borders toolbar isn't displayed, choose View > Toolbars > Tables and Borders.

- If you accidentally delete columns or rows, immediately choose the Edit > Undo command.

- To erase the contents of selected cells, just press Delete. (The empty cells remain.)

	1998	1999	Change
Jones	35,600	60,980	25,380
Smith	12,950	23,700	10,750
Black	24,500	27,100	2,600
Johnson	90,000	125,000	35,000
Goldman	54,200	25,400	-28,800
Totals	217,250	262,180	44,930

Figure 8.16 A row is selected for deleting.

	1998	1999	Change
Jones	35,600	60,980	25,380
Smith	12,950	23,700	10,750
Johnson	90,000	125,000	35,000
Goldman	54,200	25,400	-28,800
Totals	217,250	262,180	44,930

Figure 8.17 The row with Black's data has been deleted and removed from the table.

Figure 8.18 Click the Table button on the Tables and Borders toolbar to display the menu. (You may need to wait a few seconds for the Delete options to appear.)

	Indemnity Plan	HMO
Services Available	Any doctor	HMO facility
Premium	$100 / month	None
Deductible	$500 / month	None
Co-insurance	80% / 20%	$7 visit

Figure 8.19 This text is 28-point Times New Roman.

	Indemnity Plan	**HMO**
Services Available	Any doctor	HMO facility
Premium	$100 / month	None
Deductible	$500 / month	None
Co-insurance	80% / 20%	$7 visit

Figure 8.20 After formatting, this text is 22-point Arial with bolded column headings.

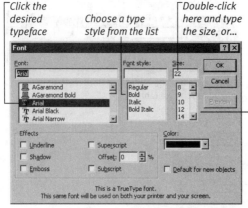

Click the desired typeface *Choose a type style from the list* *Double-click here and type the size, or...*

...choose a size on the list

Figure 8.21 Choose a font for table text in the Font dialog box.

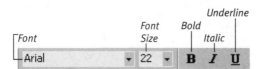

Font *Font Size* *Bold* *Italic* *Underline*

Figure 8.22 You can also format table text using the Formatting toolbar.

Formatting Table Text

You can apply many kinds of formats to the text in the table, including typeface, size, and style (**Figures 8.19** and **8.20**).

To format table text:

1. Select the cells whose text you want to format; or within a cell, drag across the individual characters you want to format.

   See Selecting Cells earlier in this chapter.

2. Choose Format > Font (**Figure 8.21**).

3. In the Font list, choose the desired typeface.

4. Select the desired Font Style (Regular, Italic, Bold, or Bold Italic).

5. In the Size list, choose the desired point size.

6. If you like, you can add an underline, or other effect, to the selection.

7. Click OK.

✔ Tip

■ Instead of displaying the Font dialog box, you can use the Font, Font Size, Bold, Italic, and Underline buttons on the Formatting toolbar (**Figure 8.22**).

Adding Borders

By default, borders appear around the outside and inside of new tables (**Figure 8.23**). These default borders are solid lines with a 1-point line weight. You can remove any of these borders or apply different line styles or weights to existing borders (**Figure 8.24**).

To add new or format existing borders:

1. Select the cells where you'd like to add or change borders.

   See Selecting Cells earlier in this chapter.

2. On the Tables and Borders toolbar (**Figure 8.25**), click the arrow next to the Border Style button and choose a line style (**Figure 8.26**).

3. Click the arrow next to the Border Width button and then choose a line weight (**Figure 8.27**).

4. To apply the borders to the selected area, click the arrow next to the Apply Borders button and then choose a border type (**Figure 8.28**).

   See **Table 8.1** for a description of the border buttons.

To remove borders:

1. Select the cells whose borders you want to remove.

2. On the Tables and Borders toolbar (**Figure 8.25**), click the arrow next to the Border Style button and choose No Border (**Figure 8.26**).

3. To remove the borders from the selected area, click the arrow next to the Apply Borders button and choose which border to remove (**Figure 8.28**).

	Indemnity Plan	HMO
Services Available	Any doctor	HMO facility
Premium	$100 / month	None
Deductible	$500 / month	None
Co-insurance	80% / 20%	$7 visit

Figure 8.23 This table has 1-point borders around all the cells.

	Indemnity Plan	HMO
Services Available	Any doctor	HMO facility
Premium	$100 / month	None
Deductible	$500 / month	None
Co-insurance	80% / 20%	$7 visit

Figure 8.24 This table has 3-point inside vertical borders and a bottom border under the column headings. (The other borders were removed.)

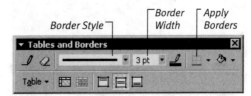

Figure 8.25 Use the Tables and Borders toolbar to apply borders to a table.

Figure 8.26 Choose a border style from the list.

Figure 8.27 Choose a border width from the list.

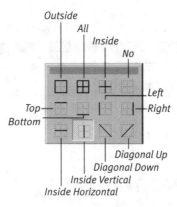

Figure 8.28 Click the Apply Borders button to choose a border type.

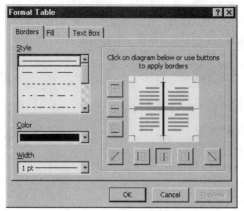

Figure 8.29 Use the Format > Colors and Lines command to display this dialog box.

✔ Tips

- If the Tables and Borders toolbar isn't displayed, choose View > Toolbars > Tables and Borders.

- To remove all borders from the table, select the table and choose the No Border style on the Apply Borders button.

- Another way to specify borders is with the Format > Colors and Lines command (**Figure 8.29**). However, the Tables and Borders toolbar is more intuitive to use than this dialog box.

- Click the Border Color button on the Tables and Borders toolbar to select a different color for the borders. ▟

Table 8.1

Apply Border Buttons

BORDER BUTTON	DESCRIPTION
Outside Borders	Outline around the selected area
All Borders	Lines around and inside the selected area
Inside Borders	Horizontal and vertical lines inside the selected area
No Border	Removes lines from the selected area
Top Border	Horizontal line on the top of the selected area
Bottom Border	Horizontal line on the bottom edge of the selected area
Left Border	Vertical line on the left side of the selected area
Right Border	Vertical line on the right side of the selected area
Inside Horizontal Border	Horizontal lines between cells in the selected area
Inside Vertical Border	Vertical lines between cells in the selected area
Diagonal Down Border	Diagonal lines that extend from the upper-left to the lower-right corner of each cell in the selected area
Diagonal Up Border	Diagonal lines that extend from the lower-left to the upper-right corner of each cell in the selected area

ADDING BORDERS

Drawing Table Borders

With the Draw Table and Eraser tools (**Figure 8.30**), you can change the structure of your table by simply drawing on it. These tools allow you to "draw" new rows and columns, or merge cells by "erasing" their borders. It gives you a lot of flexibility in the layout of your table as shown in **Figure 8.31**.

To draw a new table border:

1. On the Tables and Borders toolbar (**Figure 8.30**), click the arrow next to the Border Style button and choose a line style.

2. Click the arrow next to the Border Width button and choose a line weight.

3. Click the Draw Table button.
   The pointer is now shaped like a pencil.

4. Drag the pencil-shaped pointer where you want to draw a line (such as between two rows or columns).

5. Repeat step 4 to draw additional lines.

6. Press Esc when you're finished drawing.

To erase a border:

1. Click the Eraser button (**Figure 8.30**).

2. Drag across a border until it is selected.

3. Release the mouse button.
   The selected border is removed and the adjoining cells are merged into one.

4. Press Esc when you're finished erasing.

✔ Tips

- If the Tables and Borders toolbar isn't displayed, choose View > Toolbars > Tables and Borders.

- You can't draw new rows or columns outside of existing table boundaries. Instead, position the cursor and choose the Insert Rows or Insert Columns command.

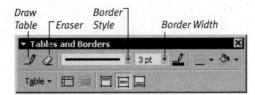

Draw Table   *Eraser*   *Border Style*   *Border Width*

Figure 8.30 The Draw Table tool creates new rows and columns in your table; the Eraser tool removes the borders between cells.

Model Number	Options			Mfg. Cost	Retail Price*
	A	B	C		
490	✓			5,348	6,348
500		✓		5,470	6,470
510			✓	5,600	6,600
520	✓	✓		5,850	6,850
530		✓	✓	5,960	6,960
540	✓	✓	✓	6,100	7,100
* Retail price includes a $1000 markup					

Figure 8.31 With the Draw Table tool, you can easily create complex tables that have columns within columns and rows within rows.

Model Number	Options			Mfg. Cost	Retail Price*
	A	B	C		
490	✓			5,348	6,348
500		✓		5,470	6,470
510			✓	5,600	6,600
520	✓	✓		5,850	6,850
530		✓	✓	5,960	6,960
540	✓	✓	✓	6,100	7,100
* Retail price includes a $1000 markup					

Figure 8.32 The top row in this table has a dark gray shade.

Fill Color

Figure 8.33 Use the Fill Color button to apply shades or colors to selected cells in a table.

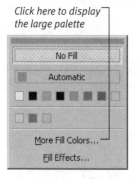

Click here to display the large palette

No Fill

Automatic

More Fill Colors...

Fill Effects...

Figure 8.34 The small color palette appears when you click the arrow next to the Fill Color button.

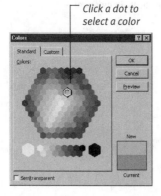

Click a dot to select a color

Figure 8.35 Choose from hundreds of colors in the Standard or Custom tabs.

Shading Table Cells

To emphasize a range of cells, you can shade the cell background (**Figure 8.32**).

To add shading:

1. Select the cells that you'd like to shade.

   See Selecting Cells earlier in this chapter.

2. On the Tables and Borders toolbar (**Figure 8.33**), click the arrow next to the Fill Color button to display a color palette.

3. Choose a color from the palette (**Figure 8.34**).

   or

   Click More Fill Colors and choose a color from the Standard or Custom tab (**Figure 8.35**).

4. Click OK.

✔ Tips

■ If the Tables and Borders toolbar isn't displayed, choose View > Toolbars > Tables and Borders.

■ The Automatic fill color is determined by the slide color scheme.

   See Changing the Default Colors in Chapter 12.

SHADING TABLE CELLS

Aligning Text within a Cell

By default, table text is aligned at the top-left edge of each cell (**Figure 8.36**). Using PowerPoint's table and paragraph formatting commands, you can adjust the horizontal and vertical alignment of text within a cell (**Figure 8.37**).

To align cells horizontally:

1. Select the cells whose alignment you want to change.

   See Selecting Cells earlier in this chapter.

2. Click an alignment button on the Formatting toolbar (**Figure 8.38**) or use a keyboard shortcut (**Table 8.2**).

To align cells vertically:

1. Select the cells whose alignment you want to change.

2. Choose a vertical alignment button on the Tables and Borders toolbar (**Figure 8.39**).

✔ Tip

- If the Tables and Borders toolbar isn't displayed, choose View > Toolbars > Tables and Borders.

	Indemnity Plan	HMO
Services Available	Any doctor	HMO facility
Premium	$100 / month	None
Deductible	$500 / month	None
Co-insurance	80% / 20%	$7 visit

Figure 8.36 The text in this table has the default alignment.

	Indemnity Plan	HMO
Services Available	Any doctor	HMO facility
Premium	$100 / month	None
Deductible	$500 / month	None
Co-insurance	80% / 20%	$7 visit

Figure 8.37 By changing horizontal and vertical alignment in the cells, you can improve the appearance of this table.

Center
Align Left *Align Right*

Figure 8.38 Use the Formatting toolbar to control the horizontal alignment of text.

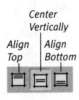

Center Vertically
Align Top *Align Bottom*

Figure 8.39 Use the Tables and Borders toolbar to control the vertical alignment of text.

Table 8.2

Keyboard Shortcuts for Aligning Cells

TYPE OF ALIGNMENT	SHORTCUT
Align left	Ctrl+L
Center	Ctrl+E
Align right	Ctrl+R
Justify	Ctrl+J

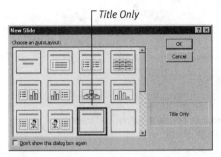

Title Only

Figure 8.40 The Title Only layout is a good choice when you are planning on inserting a Word table.

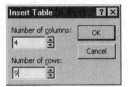

Figure 8.41 Specify the number of columns and rows in your table.

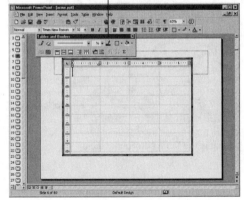

To see this toolbar, choose View > Toolbars > Tables and Borders

Figure 8.42 When you're creating a table in Word, a thick border surrounds the object and rulers appear on the top and left side.

Inserting a Word Table

An alternative to creating a table using PowerPoint's table features is to embed a Word table object onto a slide. Creating a table in this way allows you to take advantage of several advanced table features offered in Word—such as autoformatting and performing calculations.

To insert a Word table:

1. Insert a Title Only slide (**Figure 8.40**).

2. Choose Insert > Picture > Microsoft Word Table.

   You are asked to specify the number of columns and rows (**Figure 8.41**).

3. Specify the Number of Columns and press Tab.

4. Specify the Number of Rows and click OK.

   An empty table appears on the slide (**Figure 8.42**). Though the title bar still says PowerPoint, you are now in Microsoft Word.

5. Type data into the Word table just as you would in PowerPoint.

6. When you are finished with the table, click outside the table anywhere on the slide.

   The thick outside table border and rulers disappear. You are now back in PowerPoint.

✔ Tip

■ To return to the Word table from PowerPoint, double-click the table. (The thick outside table border and rulers reappear.)

   See also AutoFormatting a Word Table and Entering Formulas.

INSERTING A WORD TABLE

AutoFormatting a Word Table

With Word's Table AutoFormat feature, you can add borders, shading, and other formatting attributes by choosing one of several dozen predesigned formats. **Figures 8.43** and **8.44** show a table before and after choosing an AutoFormat. Not only is this feature a big time-saver, but it also assures you of professional-looking results.

Note: You can apply an AutoFormat to an embedded Word table only—not a table created in PowerPoint.

See Inserting a Word Table on the previous page.

To AutoFormat a Word table:

1. If you aren't currently editing the table in Word, double-click the embedded table.

2. Choose Table > Table AutoFormat.

3. Click different formats in the Formats list, and look at the Preview box to see what each one looks like (**Figure 8.45**).

4. Unselect the formatting options you don't want to apply: Borders, Shading, Font, Color, and/or AutoFit.

5. Select whether you want to apply special formatting to the Heading Rows, First Column, Last Row, and/or Last Column.

6. Click OK.

✔ Tips

■ The AutoFit option automatically adjusts the column widths and size of the table. You may want to unselect this option if you've already adjusted the column widths to your liking.

■ If you don't like an AutoFormat after you have applied it, choose Edit > Undo.

	1998	1999	Change
Jones	35,600	60,980	25,380
Smith	12,950	23,700	10,750
Black	24,500	27,100	2,600
Johnson	90,000	125,000	35,000
Goldman	54,200	25,400	-28,800
Totals	217,250	262,180	44,930

Figure 8.43 This table has not yet been formatted.

	1998	1999	Change
Jones	35,600	60,980	25,380
Smith	12,950	23,700	10,750
Black	24,500	27,100	2,600
Johnson	90,000	125,000	35,000
Goldman	54,200	25,400	-28,800
Totals	217,250	262,180	44,930

Figure 8.44 This table has been formatted with the List 4 AutoFormat.

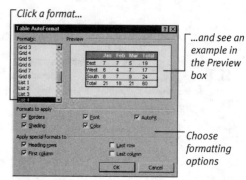

Click a format...

...and see an example in the Preview box

Choose formatting options

Figure 8.45 Select a predesigned format in the Table AutoFormat dialog box.

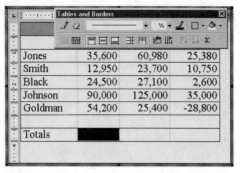

Figure 8.46 Click where you want the sum to appear.

Click the AutoSum
button...

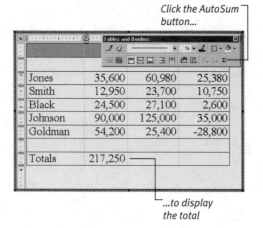

...to display
the total

Figure 8.47 After you click the AutoSum button, the result of the calculation appears in the cell.

Click here to see a list
of available functions

Figure 8.48 To average a row, enter a formula in the Formula dialog box.

Entering Formulas

Just as in a spreadsheet program, Word tables can make some simple calculations, such as totaling and averaging. Summing a column of numbers or row of numbers is particularly easy with the AutoSum button.

Note: You can perform calculations in an embedded Word table only—not a table created in PowerPoint.

See Inserting a Word Table earlier in this chapter.

To sum a column or row:

1. If you aren't currently editing the table in Word, double-click the embedded table.

2. Click the cell at the end of the row or bottom of the column that you want to sum (**Figure 8.46**).

3. If the Tables and Borders toolbar isn't displayed, choose View > Toolbars > Tables and Borders.

4. Click the AutoSum button on the Tables and Borders toolbar. Σ

   The result is shown in **Figure 8.47**.

To enter a formula:

1. If you aren't currently editing the table in Word, double-click the embedded table.

2. Click the cell where you want the calculation to appear.

3. Choose Table > Formula.

4. Enter the formula in the Formula box (**Figure 8.48**). For example, type = *AVERAGE (left)* to average a row of numbers or = *AVERAGE (above)* to average a column.

5. Click OK.

   The result appears in the cell.

CREATING TABLES (MAC OS)

Medical Plans

	Indemnity Plan	HMO
Services Available	Any doctor	HMO facility
Premium	$100 / month	None
Deductible	$500 / year	None
Co-insurance	80% / 20%	$7 visit

Figure 9.1 A table slide presents data.

The best way to present columns of data is in a Table slide. **Figure 9.1** shows an example of a table you can create in PowerPoint.

Think of a table as a mini-spreadsheet, similar to the ones you may have created in Microsoft Excel or Lotus 1-2-3. You can even build formulas in PowerPoint tables.

When you create tables in PowerPoint, you actually use the Microsoft Word program. When you're creating or editing a table, you'll notice the Word application icon in the upper right corner of your screen (**Figure 9.2**).

Word application icon

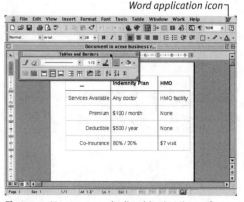

Figure 9.2 You create and edit tables in Microsoft Word.

Inserting a Table Slide

PowerPoint offers one AutoLayout for tables (**Figure 9.3**).

To insert a table slide:

1. Click the New Slide button on the toolbar.

2. In the New Slide dialog box, choose the Table layout (**Figure 9.3**).

3. Click OK. The slide appears with title and table placeholders.

4. Click the title placeholder and type the title of your table.

5. Double-click the table placeholder to create your table.

   You are asked to specify the number of columns and rows (**Figure 9.4**).

6. Specify the Number of Columns (maximum of 30) and press Tab.

7. Specify the Number of Rows and click OK.

   A table appears in Word (**Figure 9.5**).

✔ Tips

- Although the maximum number of rows you can specify in the Insert Word Table dialog box is seven, you can insert more rows later.

  See Inserting Rows and Columns later in this chapter.

- When you initially create a table, all the columns and rows are the same size. However, the column widths and row heights can be adjusted at any time.

  See Adjusting Column Widths and Adjusting Row Heights later in this chapter.

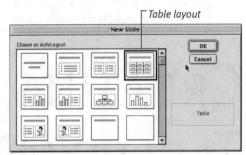

Figure 9.3 To create a table slide, first choose the Table layout.

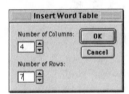

Figure 9.4 Specify the number of columns and rows in your table.

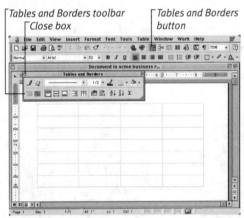

Figure 9.5 After you specify the number of columns and rows, an empty table appears in Word.

Vertical
ruler   Cell   Gridline   Horizontal
ruler

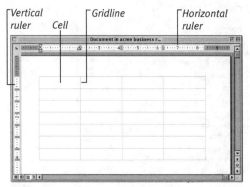

Figure 9.6 A table is a grid of cells.

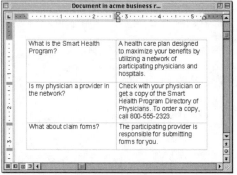

Figure 9.7 Text automatically wraps within each cell, and the row heights adjust automatically.

Entering Text into a Table

A table is made up of rows and columns; the intersection of a row and column is called a *cell* (**Figure 9.6**).

To type text into a table:

1. Click a cell and start typing.

   As you reach the right edge of the cell, text will wrap automatically to the next line in the cell (**Figure 9.7**).

2. Press Tab to move the cursor to the next cell to the right.

   or

   Press the down arrow key to move down to the next cell.

3. After entering text in the last cell in the row, press Tab; this moves the cursor to the first cell in the next row.

✔ Tips

- Use the Zoom field on the toolbar to zoom out and see more of the table at once.

- If you don't see gridlines between cells in your table, choose Table > Gridlines.

- Pressing Return in a cell drops the cursor to the next line in the same cell. It does *not* move the cursor to a different cell.

- Pressing Tab from the last cell in a table inserts a new row and places the cursor in the first cell.

- If text wraps in a cell but you want it to fit on a single line, you can either decrease the type size or adjust the column width.

  See Formatting Table Text and Adjusting Column Widths later in this chapter.

Returning to PowerPoint

When you are finished with your table, you need to exit Microsoft Word and return to PowerPoint.

To return to PowerPoint:

Select one of the following commands:

◆ Choose File > Close and Return To *xxx* where *xxx* is the name of your PowerPoint presentation (**Figure 9.8**).

   or

◆ Choose File > Quit to exit Microsoft Word.

✔ Tips

■ The File > Quit command closes Microsoft Word while the File > Close and Return command leaves it open.

■ Use the File > Close and Return command if you know that you'll be editing the table in the same work session or if you'll be creating other tables. (Tables will open faster when Word is already open.)

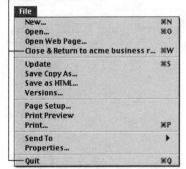

Choose either of these options to return to PowerPoint

Figure 9.8 Use Word's File menu when you're finished with your table.

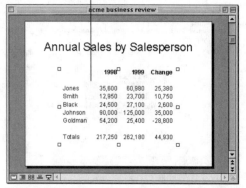

Figure 9.9 To edit an existing table, you double-click it.

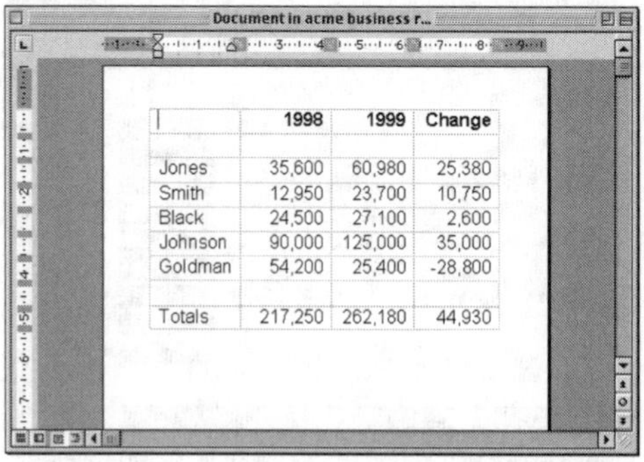

Figure 9.10 After you double-click an embedded table, it opens in Word.

Editing an Existing Table

To edit a previously-created table, you need to reopen it in Microsoft Word.

To edit an existing table:

1. In Slide view, double-click the table (**Figure 9.9**).

   The table opens up in Microsoft Word (**Figure 9.10**).

2. Make any desired changes to the table—edit text, add borders, change the font, adjust column widths, and so forth.

   Note: the rest of this chapter explains how to make these types of changes.

3. When you're finished, return to PowerPoint.

   See Returning to PowerPoint on the previous page.

✔ Tip

■ You can adjust the size of the table place-holder by dragging its selection handles when you're in PowerPoint.

Selecting Cells

Before you can format cells in your table, you need to select them.

To select parts of a table:

Use any of the following techniques:

- The Table menu offers ways to select the current row, column, or the entire table.

- You can select the next or previous cell by pressing Tab or Shift+Tab.

- You can select a range of cells by dragging across them with the mouse (**Figure 9.11**).

- You can select an entire column by clicking directly above the column (**Figure 9.12**). The mouse pointer becomes a down arrow when it is positioned properly for selecting the column.

- To select an entire row (**Figure 9.13**), click the beginning of the row—to the left of the cell contents. The mouse pointer points up and to the right when it is positioned properly for selecting the row.

✔ Tips

- A keyboard shortcut for selecting the entire table is Option+Num Lock.

- A shortcut for selecting a column is to hold down Option as you click a cell.

Click and drag across cells to select a range

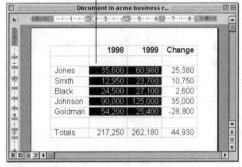

Figure 9.11 A range of cells is currently selected.

Click here to select a column

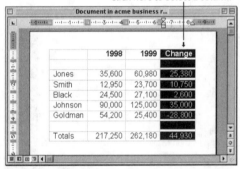

Figure 9.12 Click above the first cell in a column to select the entire column.

Click here to select a row

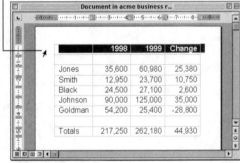

Figure 9.13 Click to the left of the first cell in a row to select the entire row.

Column markers

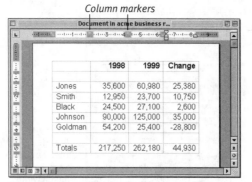

Figure 9.14 The column markers in the ruler display where columns appear.

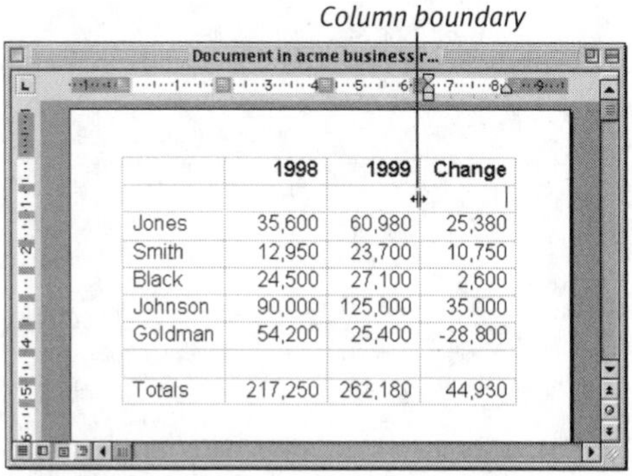

Column boundary

Figure 9.15 You can drag the column boundary to adjust column width.

Figure 9.16 The horizontal ruler displays column width measurements.

Adjusting Column Widths

Although a new table starts out with columns of equal width, it's easy to make the columns wider or narrower.

To adjust the width of a column manually:

1. Click anywhere in the table to make sure no cells are selected. (Otherwise, the width will change for only the selected cells.)

2. To change the width of a column without changing the width of any other columns, drag the column marker in the ruler to the right or left (**Figure 9.14**).

   or

   To change the width of a column without changing the overall width of the table, drag the column boundary to the right or left (**Figure 9.15**).

✔ Tips

- If the rulers are hidden, choose View > Ruler.

- You can display column width measurements on the horizontal ruler by holding down Option as you drag the column marker or boundary (**Figure 9.16**).

ADJUSTING COLUMN WIDTHS

Setting Column Widths Automatically

The AutoFit feature automatically sets an appropriate width for a column, based on the longest entry in the column.

To set the column width automatically:

1. Click anywhere in the column whose width you want to set.

   or

   To change all column widths, select the entire table.

2. Choose Table > Cell Height and Width.

3. Select the Column tab.

4. Click the AutoFit button (**Figure 9.17**).

5. Click OK.

✔ Tips

- Double-click a column marker in the ruler to bring up the Cell Height and Width dialog box.

- To AutoFit with the mouse, select the column and double-click the right column boundary.

- If the text in one column is right-aligned and the text in the next column is left-aligned, the text will be too close together. You can fix this problem by adding extra space between columns (**Figure 9.17**).

Adds extra padding between all columns

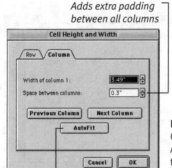

Sets an appropriate width for the column

Figure 9.17
Click the AutoFit button to set the column width.

Drag here to adjust the row height

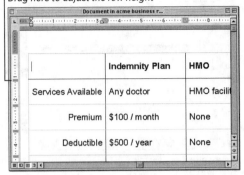

Figure 9.18 To adjust the row height visually, drag the row markers in the ruler.

Click Exactly for the Height...

Row tab   *...then enter a new value here*

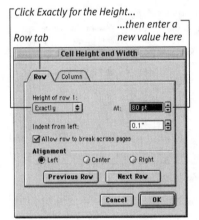

Figure 9.19 To adjust the row height precisely, use the Cell Height and Width dialog box.

Select the row and choose a smaller font size

	1998	1999	Change
Jones	35,600	60,980	25,380
Smith	12,950	23,700	10,750
Black	24,500	27,100	2,600
Johnson	90,000	125,000	35,000
Goldman	54,200	25,400	-28,800
Totals	217,250	262,180	44,930

Figure 9.20 Dragging the row markers will not shorten a blank row until you decrease the font size.

Adjusting Row Heights

PowerPoint offers two ways to adjust the row height: You can drag the row marker in the vertical ruler (**Figure 9.18**) to visually adjust the height, or you can use the Cell Height and Width dialog box (**Figure 9.19**) to enter a precise value.

To adjust the height of a row visually:

1. If the horizontal ruler is displayed but the vertical ruler isn't, choose View > Page Layout.

   or

   If neither the vertical nor horizontal ruler is displayed, choose View > Ruler.

2. Drag the row marker up to decrease the row height or drag down to increase the height (**Figure 9.18**).

To adjust the height of a row precisely:

1. Select the row(s) whose height you want to adjust.

2. Choose Table > Cell Height and Width.

3. Select the Row tab (**Figure 9.19**).

4. For the Height, choose Exactly.

5. In the At box, specify the number of points for the row height.

6. Click OK.

✔ Tip

- If you are unable to decrease the height of an empty row, it's because PowerPoint won't let you make the row shorter than its formatted point size. (This feature prevents characters from being truncated.) When this happens, select the row and choose a smaller font size (**Figure 9.20**).

Inserting Rows and Columns

If you underestimated the number of rows or columns in your table when you created it, you can insert them later. **Figures 9.21** and **9.22** show a table before and after inserting a row.

To insert a row:

1. Click the text cursor anywhere in the row. (The new row will insert *above* the cursor.)

2. Choose Table > Insert Rows.

To insert a column:

1. Select an entire column. (The new column will insert to the *left* of the selected column).

   See Selecting Cells earlier in this chapter.

2. Choose Table > Insert Columns.

✔ Tips

- You can also insert rows (or columns) using the Insert Rows (or Insert Columns) button on Word's Standard toolbar (**Figures 9.23** and **9.24**).

- To insert multiple rows (or columns) in the same location, first select the number of rows (columns) you wish to insert. For instance, to insert two rows, select two rows and choose Table > Insert Rows.

- To insert a new row after the last row, position the cursor in the last cell in the table and press Tab.

- Another way to insert rows and columns is with the Draw Table tool. ✐

   See Drawing Table Borders later in this chapter.

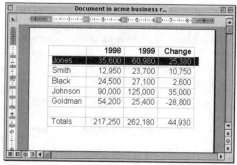

Figure 9.21 The new row will be inserted above the selected row.

Inserted row

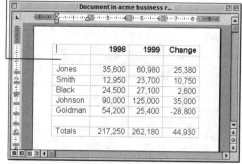

Figure 9.22 Use the Table > Insert Rows command to insert a row.

Insert Rows

Figure 9.23 You can also insert rows with the Insert Rows button on the Standard toolbar.

Insert Columns

Figure 9.24 If a column is selected, the Insert Columns button displays.

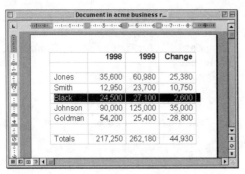

Figure 9.25 A row is selected for deleting.

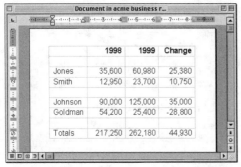

Figure 9.26 The row with Black's data has been deleted and removed from the table.

Deleting Rows and Columns

When you delete rows and columns, you not only remove the contents of the cells, you remove the cells as well, as shown in **Figures 9.25** and **9.26**.

To delete rows or columns:

1. Select the rows or columns to be deleted (**Figure 9.25**).

   See Selecting Cells earlier in this chapter.

2. Choose Table > Delete Rows or Table > Delete Columns.

✔ Tips

- If you accidentally delete rows or columns, immediately choose the Edit > Undo command.

- To erase the contents of selected cells, just press Del. (The empty cells remain, as shown in **Figure 9.27**.)

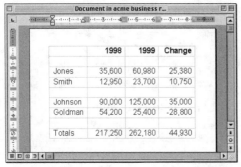

Figure 9.27 The row that had contained Black's data has been erased by pressing Del; the row is now empty.

143

Formatting Table Text

You can apply many kinds of formats to the text in the table, including font, size, and style (**Figures 9.28** and **9.29**).

To format table text:

1. Select the cells whose text you want to format; or within a cell, drag across the individual characters you want to format. *See Selecting Cells earlier in this chapter.*

2. Choose Format > Font.
   The Font dialog box appears (**Figure 9.30**).

3. In the Font list, choose a typeface.

4. Select a Font Style (Regular, Italic, Bold, or Bold Italic).

5. In the Size list, choose a point size.

6. If you like, you can add an underline or another effect to the selection.

7. Click OK.

✔ Tips

- Instead of displaying the Font dialog box, you can use the Font, Font Size, Bold, Italic, and Underline buttons on the Formatting toolbar (**Figure 9.31**).

- You can also select a typeface from the Font menu.

	Indemnity Plan	HMO
Services Available	Any doctor	HMO facility
Premium	$100 / month	None
Deductible	$500 / year	None
Co-insurance	80% / 20%	$ 7 visit

Figure 9.28 The default text is 32-point Arial.

	Indemnity Plan	HMO
Services Available	Any doctor	HMO facility
Premium	$100 / month	None
Deductible	$500 / year	None
Co-insurance	80% / 20%	$ 7 visit

Figure 9.29 After formatting, this text is 20-point Arial Black.

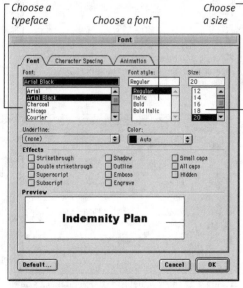

Figure 9.30 Choose a font for table text in the Font tab of the Font dialog box.

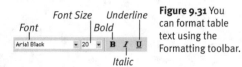

Figure 9.31 You can format table text using the Formatting toolbar.

	1998	1999	Change
Jones	35,600	60,980	25,380
Smith	12,950	23,700	10,750
Black	24,500	27,100	2,600
Johnson	90,000	125,000	35,000
Goldman	54,200	25,400	-28,800
Totals	217,250	262,180	44,930

Figure 9.32 The gridlines between cells do not print.

	1998	1999	Change
Jones	35,600	60,980	25,380
Smith	12,950	23,700	10,750
Black	24,500	27,100	2,600
Johnson	90,000	125,000	35,000
Goldman	54,200	25,400	-28,800
Totals	217,250	262,180	44,930

Figure 9.33 This table has inside (single line style) and outside (double line) borders.

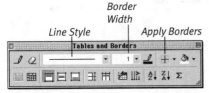

Figure 9.34 Use the Tables and Borders toolbar to apply borders to a table.

Adding and Removing Borders

The gridlines between cells (**Figure 9.32**) in a table do not print—they appear on-screen to help you distinguish cells. To print boundaries between cells, you can add borders (**Figure 9.33**).

To add new or format existing borders:

1. Select the cells in which you'd like to add or change borders.
   See Selecting Cells earlier in this chapter.

2. If the Tables and Borders toolbar isn't displayed (**Figure 9.34**), choose View > Toolbars > Tables and Borders.

3. Click the arrow next to the Line Style button and choose a style (**Figure 9.35**).

4. Click the arrow next to the Border Width button and choose a line weight (**Figure 9.36**)

5. To apply the borders to the selected area, click the Apply Borders button and choose a border type (**Figure 9.37**).
   See **Table 9.1** for a description of the border buttons.

Table 9.1

Apply Border Buttons

BORDER BUTTON	DESCRIPTION	BORDER BUTTON	DESCRIPTION
Outside Border	Outline around the selected area	All Borders	Lines around and inside the the selected area
Top Border	Horizontal line on the top of the selected area		
Bottom Border	Horizontal line on the bottom edge of the selected area	Inside Border	Horizontal and vertical lines inside the selected area
Left Border	Vertical line on the left side of the selected area	Inside Horizontal Border	Horizontal lines between cells in the selected area
Right Border	Vertical line on the right side of the selected area	Inside Vertical Border	Vertical lines between cells in the selected area
		No Border	Removes lines from the selected area

ADDING AND REMOVING BORDERS

To remove borders:

1. Select the cells whose borders you want to remove.

2. On the Tables and Borders toolbar (**Figure 9.34**), click the arrow next to the Line Style button and choose No Border (**Figure 9.35**).

3. To remove the borders from the selected area, click the arrow next to the Apply Borders button and choose which border to remove (**Figure 9.37**).

4. When you're finished with the Tables and Borders toolbar, click its close box.

✔ Tips

- Another way to specify borders is with the Format > Borders and Shading command (**Figure 9.38**). However, the Tables and Borders toolbar is more intuitive than the Borders and Shading dialog box.

- You can display the Tables and Borders toolbar by clicking the Tables and Borders button on the Standard toolbar.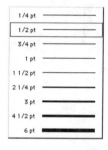

- Use the AutoFormat feature to automatically apply professional looking borders to a table.

  See AutoFormatting a Table later in this chapter.

Figure 9.35 These are just a few of the line styles that are available.

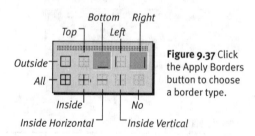

Figure 9.36 Choose a border width from the list.

Figure 9.37 Click the Apply Borders button to choose a border type.

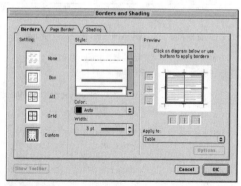

Figure 9.38 Use the Format > Borders and Shading command to display this dialog box.

ADDING AND REMOVING BORDERS

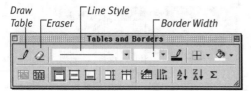

Figure 9.39 The Draw Table tool creates new rows and columns in your table; the Eraser tool removes the borders between cells.

| Model | Options | | | Mfg. | Retail |
Number	A	B	C	Cost	Price*
490	✓			5,348	6,348
500		✓		5,470	6,470
510			✓	5,600	6,600
520	✓	✓		5,850	6,850
530		✓	✓	5,960	6,960
540	✓	✓	✓	6,100	7,100
*Retail price includes a $1,000 markup.					

Figure 9.40 With the Draw Table tool, you can easily create complex tables that have columns within columns and rows within rows.

Drawing Table Borders

With the Draw Table and Eraser tools (**Figure 9.39**), you can change the structure of your table by simply drawing on it. These tools allow you to "draw" new rows and columns or merge cells by "erasing" their borders. It gives you a lot of flexibility in the layout of your table, as shown in **Figure 9.40**.

To draw a new table border:

1. If the Tables and Borders toolbar isn't displayed (**Figure 9.39**), choose View > Toolbars > Tables and Borders.

2. Click the arrow next to the Line Style button and choose a line style.

3. Click the arrow next to the Border Width button and choose a line weight.

4. Click the Draw Table button.
   The pointer is now shaped like a pencil.

5. Drag the pencil-shaped pointer where you want to draw a line (such as between two rows or columns).

6. Repeat step 5 to draw additional lines.

7. Press Esc when you're finished drawing.

To erase a border:

1. Click the Eraser button (**Figure 9.39**)

2. Drag across a border until it is selected.

3. Release the mouse button.
   The selected border is removed and the adjoining cells are merged into one.

4. Press Esc when you're finished erasing.

✔ Tip

■ Using the Draw Table tool, you can also trace along the gridlines to create borders. (But don't use the Eraser tool to remove these borders because this tool will merge cells together.)

Shading Table Cells

To emphasize a range of cells, you can shade the cell background (**Figure 9.41**).

To add shading:

1. Select the cells that you'd like to shade.
   See Selecting Cells earlier in this chapter.

2. If the Tables and Borders toolbar isn't displayed (**Figure 9.42**), choose View > Toolbars > Tables and Borders.

3. Click the arrow next to the Shading Color button to display a palette of gray shades and colors (**Figure 9.43**).

4. Point to a gray shade.
   The bubble indicates the percentage (such as Gray-25%).

5. Click the desired gray shade.

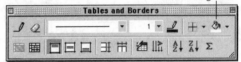

	1998	1999	Change
Jones	35,600	60,980	25,380
Smith	12,950	23,700	10,750
Black	24,500	27,100	2,600
Johnson	90,000	125,000	35,000
Goldman	54,200	25,400	-28,800
Totals	217,250	262,180	44,930

Figure 9.41 The top row in this table has a 20% gray shade

Shading Color

Figure 9.42 Use the Shading Color button to apply shades or colors to selected cells in a table.

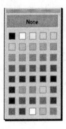

Figure 9.43 This palette of gray shades and colors appears when you click the arrow next to the Shading Color button.

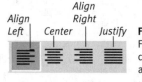

Figure 9.44
The text in this table has the default alignment.

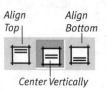

Figure 9.45
By changing alignment and indents, you can improve the appearance of this table.

Align Left | *Center* | *Align Right* | *Justify*

Figure 9.46 Use the Formatting toolbar to control the horizontal alignment of text.

Align Top | *Align Bottom*

Center Vertically

Figure 9.47 Use the Tables and Borders toolbar to control the vertical alignment of text.

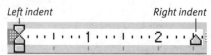

Left indent | *Right indent*

Figure 9.48 Drag the indent markers to position text horizontally in a cell.

Aligning Text within a Cell

By default, table text is aligned at the top-left edge of each cell (**Figure 9.44**). Using Word's table and paragraph formatting commands, you can adjust the horizontal and vertical alignment of text within a cell (**Figure 9.45**).

To control the horizontal alignment:

1. Select the cells whose alignment you want to change.

   See Selecting Cells earlier in this chapter.

2. Choose an alignment button on the Formatting toolbar (**Figure 9.46**).

To control the vertical alignment:

1. Select the cells whose alignment you want to change.

2. Choose a vertical alignment button on the Tables and Borders toolbar (**Figure 9.47**).

✔ Tip

■ To add an indent to the left or right of the text, drag the indent markers on the ruler (**Figure 9.48**).

AutoFormatting a Table

With Word's AutoFormat feature, you can add borders, shading, and other formatting attributes by choosing one of several dozen predesigned formats. **Figures 9.49** and **9.50** show a table before and after choosing an AutoFormat. Not only is this feature a big time-saver, but it also helps to assure you of professional-looking results.

To automatically format a table:

1. Choose Table > Table AutoFormat.

    or

    Click the Table AutoFormat button on the Tables and Borders toolbar. 📖

2. Click different formats in the Formats list, and look at the Preview box to see how each one looks (**Figure 9.51**).

3. Unselect the formatting options you don't want to apply: Borders, Shading, Font, Color, and/or AutoFit.

4. Select the areas to which you want to apply special formatting: Heading Rows, First Column, Last Row, and/or Last Column.

5. Click OK.

✔ Tips

- The AutoFit option automatically adjusts the column widths and size of the table. You may want to unselect this option if you've already adjusted the column widths to your liking.

- As you preview a format, enable and disable the various options under Apply Special Formats To while looking at the Preview box. This box lets you see how the table will look with these options.

- If you don't like an AutoFormat after you have applied it, choose Edit > Undo.

	1998	1999	Change
Jones	35,600	60,980	25,380
Smith	12,950	23,700	10,750
Black	24,500	27,100	2,600
Johnson	90,000	125,000	35,000
Goldman	54,200	25,400	-28,800
Totals	217,250	262,180	44,930

Figure 9.49 This table has not yet been formatted.

	1998	1999	Change
Jones	35,600	60,980	25,380
Smith	12,950	23,700	10,750
Black	24,500	27,100	2,600
Johnson	90,000	125,000	35,000
Goldman	54,200	25,400	-28,800
Totals	217,250	262,180	44,930

Figure 9.50 This table has been formatted with the List 4 AutoFormat.

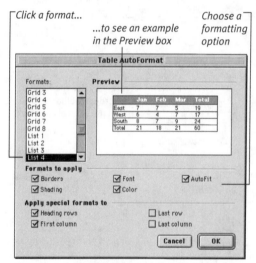

Figure 9.51 Select a predesigned format in the Table AutoFormat dialog box.

Figure 9.52 Click where you want the sum to appear.

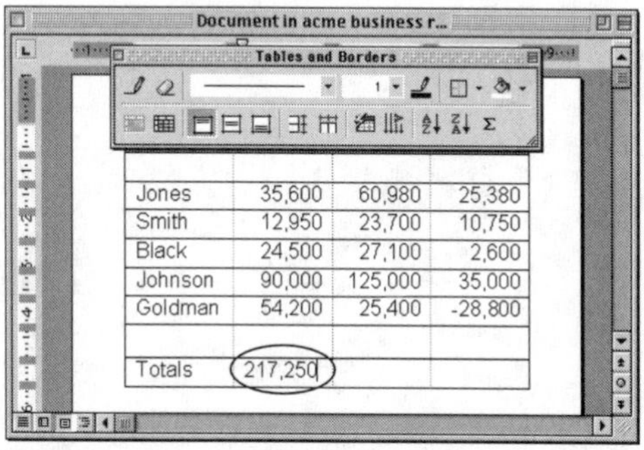

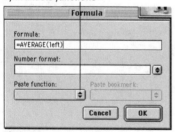

Figure 9.53 After you click the AutoSum button, the result of the calculation appears in the cell.

Click here to see a list of available functions

Figure 9.54 To average a row, enter a formula in the Formula dialog box.

Entering Formulas

Just as in a spreadsheet program, Word can make some simple calculations, such as totaling and averaging. Summing a column of numbers or a row of numbers is particularly easy with the AutoSum button.

To sum a column or row:

1. Click the cell at the end of the row or at the bottom of the column that you want to sum (**Figure 9.52**).

2. Click the AutoSum button on the Tables and Borders toolbar. Σ

    The result is shown in **Figure 9.53**.

To enter a formula:

1. Click the cell where you want the calculation to appear.

2. Choose Table > Formula.

3. Enter the formula in the Formula box (**Figure 9.54**). For example, you would type *=AVERAGE(left)* to average a row of numbers or *=AVERAGE(above)* to average a column.

4. Click OK.

    The result appears in the cell.

✔ Tip

- You can also enter formulas that perform calculations on individual cells, such as *=B3-C3*. (You have to figure out the cell coordinates yourself since the rows and columns aren't labeled.)

ENTERING FORMULAS

ADDING
GRAPHICAL OBJECTS

┌─ *Drawing toolbar*

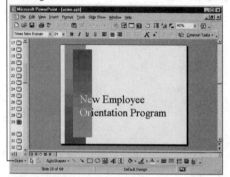

Figure 10.1 The Drawing toolbar appears near the bottom of the PowerPoint window.

Figure 10.2 The AutoShapes menu lists categories of shapes you can add to your slides.

Figure 10.3 Use the Clip Gallery to insert images on your slide.

Graphical elements contribute variety and interest to your slides. One way to add graphical objects is to use the Drawing toolbar (**Figure 10.1**) which offers tools for drawing lines, rectangles, circles, and so forth. And with the AutoShapes menu (**Figure 10.2**) you can easily insert predefined objects such as arrows, stars, hearts, and triangles.

The second way to add graphical objects is by inserting *clip art* images that come with PowerPoint (**Figure 10.3**).

Finally, you can import other graphics files—for example, an image created in CorelDRAW or Macromedia Freehand.

Drawing Lines

Figure 10.4 illustrates how lines can become a graphical element on a slide.

To draw a line:

1. On the Drawing toolbar, click the Line tool.

2. Place the crosshair pointer where you want to begin the line.

3. Hold down the mouse button as you drag in the direction you want the line to follow.

4. Release the mouse button when the line is the desired length.

✔ Tips

■ To make sure a line is perfectly straight (horizontally or vertically), hold down the Shift key as you draw the line.

■ To draw several lines, double-click the Line tool. When you are finished drawing lines, press Esc.

■ To change the length or angle of the line, click the line to select it (**Figure 10.5**) and drag a selection handle. To change the length without changing the angle, hold down Shift as you drag a handle.

■ To reposition the line, select it and drag it into position. (Make sure you don't drag a selection handle or you will change the length of the line.)

To change the line color, style, or thickness, see Formatting Lines on the opposite page.

These two lines were drawn with the Line tool

Figure 10.4 Use the Line tool to create lines on your slide.

Selection handles

Figure 10.5 When a line is selected, selection handles appear at each end.

DRAWING LINES

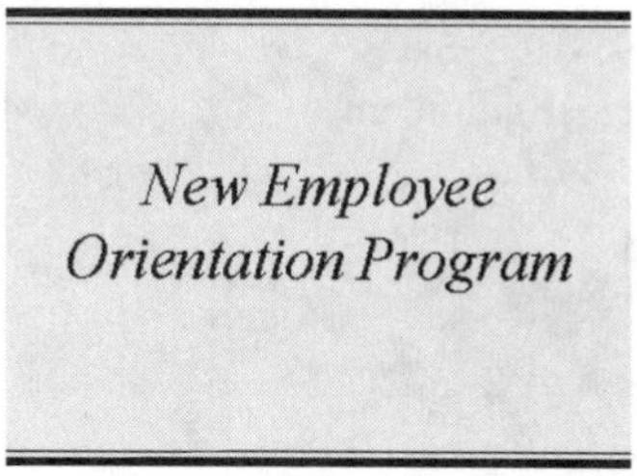

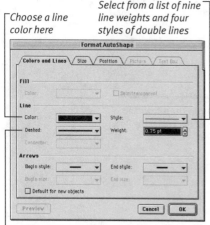

New Employee
Orientation Program

Figure 10.6
This slide has both thick and thin lines drawn on it.

Select from a list of nine line weights and four styles of double lines

Choose a line color here

Select a dashed line style

Figure 10.7 Format your lines in the Colors and Lines tab of the Format AutoShape dialog box.

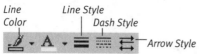

Line Color

Line Style

Dash Style

Arrow Style

Figure 10.8 Use tools on the Drawing toolbar to format lines.

Formatting Lines

You can format lines and object borders in a variety of ways. For instance, you can change the line thickness (**Figure 10.6**), choose a double-line style, or create a dashed line.

To format lines:

1. Select the line or shape to be formatted and choose Format > Colors and Lines.

   or

   Double-click the line or shape.

   The Colors and Lines tab of the Format AutoShape dialog box appears (**Figure 10.7**).

2. In the Line section of the dialog box, choose a color in the Color field.

3. In the Style field, click the style and weight of line that you want.

4. If desired, click one of the sample lines on the Dashed list.

5. Click OK.

✔ Tips

- The Style field offers a variety of styles and weights. If the list doesn't include the precise line thickness you need, make the line thicker or thinner in the Weight field.

- To select more than one line, hold down Shift as you click each one.

- You can also format lines with the Line Color, Line Style, and Dash Style tools on the Drawing toolbar (**Figure 10.8**).

- To turn a line into an arrow, use the Arrow Style tool (**Figure 10.8**).

  See Formatting Arrows later in this chapter.

Drawing Arrows

Arrows are helpful for pointing out important areas on a slide (**Figure 10.9**).

To draw an arrow:

1. On the Drawing toolbar, click the Arrow tool.

2. Place the crosshair pointer where you want to begin the arrow. (This point will be the beginning of the line—it will not have an arrowhead.)

3. Hold down the mouse button as you drag in the direction you want the arrow to point.

4. Release the mouse button when the line is the desired length.

   The arrowhead appears at the end of the line (**Figure 10.10**).

✔ Tips

- To make sure the line is perfectly straight (horizontally or vertically), hold down the Shift key as you draw the line.

- To draw several arrows, double-click the Arrow tool. When you're finished drawing arrows, press Esc.

- After drawing an arrow, you can change the arrowhead's shape, size, and position. *See Formatting Arrows on the facing page.*

- Another way to create an arrow is by drawing a connector line.

  See Adding Connector Lines later in this chapter.

Figure 10.9 The arrow was created with the Arrow tool.

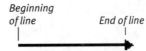

Figure 10.10 The arrowhead appears at the end of the line.

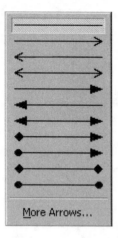

More Arrows...

Figure 10.11 Choose an arrow style from this list.

Choose an arrowhead shape for the beginning of the line... ...or for the end of the line

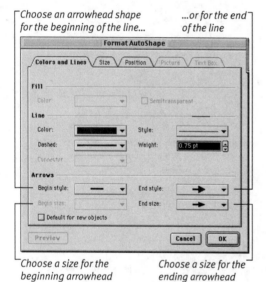

Choose a size for the beginning arrowhead

Choose a size for the ending arrowhead

Figure 10.12 When you click More Arrows on the arrow style list, this dialog box appears.

Formatting Arrows

PowerPoint offers a variety of ways to format arrows. For example, you can choose different arrowhead shapes and sizes for the beginning and/or end of the line.

To format an arrow:

1. Select the arrow to be formatted.

2. Click the Arrow Style button on the Drawing toolbar.

3. Click the arrow with the thickness, direction, or style you prefer (**Figure 10.11**).

   or

   Click More Arrows to open the Colors and Lines tab of the Format AutoShape dialog box (**Figure 10.12**).

✔ Tips

- To select more than one arrow, hold down Shift as you click each one.

- You can also open the Format AutoShape dialog box (**Figure 10.12**) by double-clicking the arrow.

  To change the line weight or color, see Formatting Lines earlier in this chapter.

- To convert an arrow to a line, use the Arrow Style tool and choose the first style in the list (the line without arrowheads).

Adding Connector Lines

PowerPoint offers a special type of line or arrow called a *connector line* that extends between two objects (**Figure 10.13**). The advantage of using a connector line rather than a regular line or arrow is that when you move or resize one of the connected objects, the line moves with the object and automatically adjusts (**Figure 10.14**).

To add a connector line:

1. On the Drawing toolbar, click AutoShapes to display the menu.

2. Choose Connectors.

3. Choose the desired style of connector line (**Figure 10.15**).

4. Point to the first object that you want to connect.

   Possible connection sites appear as blue squares on the object (**Figure 10.16**).

5. Click the blue square that you want to use as the connection point on the first object.

6. Point to the second object you want to connect.

   Again, blue squares indicate possible connection sites.

7. Click the blue square that you want to use as the connection point on the second object.

✔ Tips

- The red squares at the ends of a connector line indicate the line is locked onto an object. A green square indicates that the connector is unlocked—this happens after you move the line away from a connection site.

- You can connect to a different point by dragging the red square to another blue square on the object.

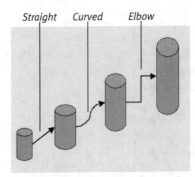

Figure 10.13 The three different types of connector lines.

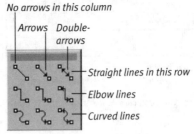

Figure 10.14 When you move an object, the connector lines automatically move with it.

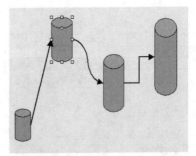

Figure 10.15 Choose the type of connector line you want.

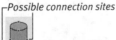

Figure 10.16 When you point to an object, blue squares appear on the object.

ADDING CONNECTOR LINES

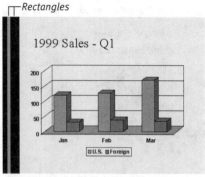

Rectangles

1999 Sales - Q1

Figure 10.17 The Rectangle tool created the black and gray boxes that border the left edge of this slide.

Begin dragging at one corner of the box...

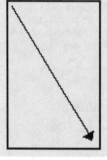

Figure 10.18 Click and drag with the Rectangle tool to draw a rectangle.

...then drag to the opposite corner until the box is the desired size

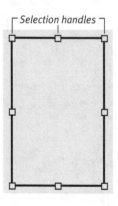

Selection handles

Figure 10.19 When a rectangle is selected, selection handles appear around the border.

Drawing Rectangles and Squares

Using the Rectangle tool, you can create rectangles and squares. **Figure 10.17** shows an example of how a rectangle can be used on a slide.

To draw a rectangle:

1. On the Drawing toolbar, click the Rectangle tool. ▢

2. Place the crosshair pointer where you want to begin the rectangle.

3. Hold down the mouse button as you drag towards the opposite corner of the box (**Figure 10.18**).

4. Release the mouse button when the box is the desired size.

✔ Tips

■ To create a perfect square, hold down Shift as you draw the rectangle.

■ To create several rectangles, double-click the Rectangle tool. When you are finished drawing rectangles, press Esc.

■ To change the size or shape of a rectangle, click on it and drag a selection handle (**Figure 10.19**).

■ To reposition a rectangle, just drag it into position. (Make sure you don't drag a selection handle or you will change the rectangle's size or shape.)

■ To type centered text inside a selected rectangle, just start typing. The text is actually part of the rectangle.

■ To change the border or fill color, use the Format > Color and Lines command.

DRAWING RECTANGLES AND SQUARES

Drawing Ovals

Using the Oval tool, you can create ovals and circles. **Figure 10.20** shows an example of how an oval can be used to annotate a slide.

To draw an oval:

1. On the Drawing toolbar, click the Oval tool. ⬭

2. Place the crosshair pointer where you want to begin the oval.

3. Hold down the mouse button as you drag in a diagonal direction (**Figure 10.21**).

4. Release the mouse button when the oval is the desired size.

✔ Tips

- To create a perfect circle, hold down Shift as you draw the oval.

- To create several ovals, double-click the Oval tool. When you are finished drawing ovals, press Esc.

- To change the size and position of an oval, see the tips for Drawing Rectangles on the previous page.

- To change the oval's border or fill color, use the Format > Colors and Lines command.

- To type centered text inside a selected oval, just start typing. The text is actually part of the oval. This technique was used in **Figure 10.20**. (The text does not wrap, however—you must press Enter or Return after each line.)

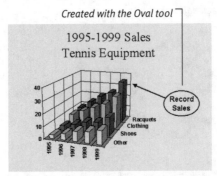

Created with the Oval tool

Figure 10.20 An oval encloses a chart annotation.

Begin dragging at one edge of the oval...

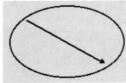

Figure 10.21 Click and drag with the Oval tool to draw an oval.

...then drag diagonally until the oval is the desired size

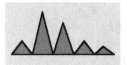

Figure 10.22 This geometric mountain range was created with the Freeform tool.

Figure 10.23 Hmmm...your author is obviously not artistically inclined and should stay clear of freehand drawing!

To create a closed shape, finish by clicking at the starting point

To create an open shape, finish by double-clicking at the ending point

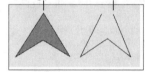

Figure 10.24 You can create closed or open shapes.

Freeform

Scribble

Figure 10.25 To select one of the special line tools, click the AutoShapes button and then choose Lines.

Creating Polygons and Freehand Drawings

The Freeform tool lets you create your own shapes, such as the one in **Figure 10.22**. Or, if you are artistically inclined, you can use the Scribble tool to create freehand drawings (**Figure 10.23**). Your shapes and drawings can be open or closed (**Figure 10.24**).

To create linked line segments:

1. On the Drawing toolbar, click AutoShapes and choose Lines.

2. Click the Freeform tool (**Figure 10.25**).

3. Click at each point of the shape you want to draw—PowerPoint draws a line segment between each point.

4. To finish the drawing, double-click (to create an open shape) or single-click the first point (to create a closed shape).

To create a freehand drawing:

1. On the Drawing toolbar, click AutoShapes and choose Lines.

2. Click the Scribble tool (**Figure 10.25**).

3. Place the pencil pointer at the starting point of the drawing.

4. Drag the mouse to draw with the pencil.

5. To finish the drawing, release the mouse button.

✔ Tips

■ Closed shapes are automatically filled with the default color; open shapes are not. Use the Fill Color tool on the Drawing toolbar to add, remove, or change the fill of a selected object.

■ To edit a drawing, click the Draw button on the Drawing toolbar and choose Edit Points. Drag any of the points that appear.

Using AutoShapes

PowerPoint comes with a set of built-in *AutoShapes* that you can add to any slide. The chart in **Figure 10.26** has been enhanced with a couple of these shapes. **Figure 10.27** shows the set of Basic Shapes.

To create an AutoShape:

1. On the Drawing toolbar, click the AutoShapes button to display the menu (**Figure 10.28**).

2. Choose the shape category (such as Basic Shapes).

3. Click the desired shape.

4. Place the crosshair pointer where you want to begin the object.

5. Hold down the mouse button as you drag diagonally to create the object, and release when the object is the desired size.

   or

   Click on the slide to create an object of the default size.

✔ Tips

■ To type centered text inside a selected AutoShape, just start typing. The text is actually part of the AutoShape object. This technique was used to type "Record Sales" in **Figure 10.26**. (The text does not wrap, however—you must press Enter or Return after each line.)

■ To replace an existing AutoShape with another, select the shape, click the Draw button on the Drawing toolbar, choose Change AutoShape, and choose the desired shape. The new shape will have the same size, text (if any), and line and fill attributes as the shape it replaces.

■ To create a shape whose height is equal to its width, hold down Shift as you draw the object.

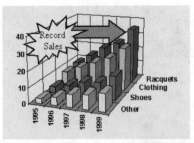

Figure 10.26 This chart was annotated with two AutoShapes (the "explosion" and the large arrow).

Figure 10.27 The basic set of AutoShapes contains special tools for creating crosses, cylinders, cubes, triangles, hearts, and so forth.

Figure 10.28 After clicking the AutoShapes button, this menu is displayed.

┌Adjustment handle

Figure 10.29 When you select an AutoShape, a diamond-shaped adjustment handle appears.

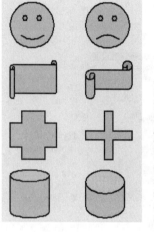

Figure 10.30 The first column shows several AutoShapes after they were inserted; the second column shows these same shapes after they were adjusted.

Customizing AutoShapes

You can customize many of the AutoShapes by dragging the diamond-shaped adjustment handle (**Figure 10.29**). **Figure 10.30** shows examples of the types of changes you can make to an AutoShape.

To customize an AutoShape:

1. Select the object.

2. Look for the yellow diamond inside or near the selected object (**Figure 10.29**). This diamond is an adjustment handle.

3. Drag the diamond in the direction you want to change the AutoShape.

✔ Tip

■ While not all AutoShapes have a diamond adjustment handle, some have more than one.

Filling an Object with Color

You can add, change, or remove the fill color for the rectangles, circles, freeform objects, and AutoShapes you create in PowerPoint.

To add or change a fill color:

1. Select the object you want to fill and click the arrow next to the Fill Color tool on the Drawing toolbar.

   The small color palette appears (**Figure 10.31**).

2. Choose a color from the palette.

   or

   Click More Fill Colors and choose a color from the Standard or Custom tab (**Figure 10.32**).

3. Click OK.

✔ Tips

- To remove the fill from a selected object, click the arrow next to the Fill Color tool and choose No Fill.

- To reapply the last fill color you used, select the object and click the Fill Color tool itself (not the arrow next it).

- You can also modify the fill color by double-clicking the object.

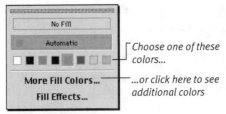

Choose one of these colors...

...or click here to see additional colors

Figure 10.31 This list appears when you choose the Fill Color tool.

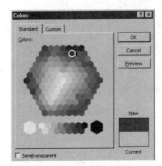

Figure 10.32 Hundreds of colors are available on the Standard and Custom tabs.

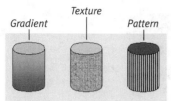

Figure 10.33 You can fill your shapes with any of several types of fills.

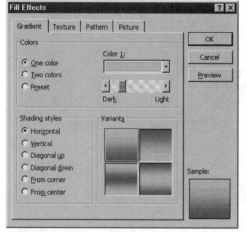

Figure 10.34 On the Gradient tab, you can fill an object with graduating shades of color.

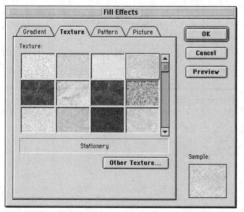

Figure 10.35 On the Texture tab, you can select from a variety of textures, such as granite, canvas, and sand.

Filling an Object with a Pattern

You can fill an object with a gradient, texture, or pattern. **Figure 10.33** shows examples of these types of fills.

To fill an object with a gradient, texture, or pattern:

1. Select the object you want to fill and click the arrow next to the Fill Color tool on the Drawing toolbar.

2. Click Fill Effects.

3. Select the Gradient tab and choose a shading style (**Figure 10.34**).

    or

    Select the Texture tab and click a texture (**Figure 10.35**).

    or

    Select the Pattern tab and click a pattern.

4. Click OK.

    For information on creating gradients, refer to Creating a Gradient Background in Chapter 12.

✔ Tip

■ To remove the border around an object, click the arrow next to the Line Color button and choose No Line.

Filling an Object with a Graphics File

Figure 10.36 shows an object that is filled with a graphics file.

Figure 10.36 The heart shape is filled with a graphic.

To fill an object with a graphics file:

1. Select the object you want to fill and click the arrow next to the Fill Color tool on the Drawing toolbar.

2. Click Fill Effects.

3. Select the Picture tab.

4. Click Select Picture to open the Select Picture dialog box (**Figures 10.37** and **10.38**).

5. Navigate to the drive and folder containing the graphics file.

6. Choose the filename and click OK.

7. Click OK when you're finished.

✔ Tip

■ If you aren't sure where your graphics files are, choose Tools > Find (Windows) or click Find File (Mac OS) in the Select Picture dialog box (**Figures 10.37** and **10.38**).

To locate graphics files, click here and choose Find

Figure 10.37 Select the name of the graphics file in the Select Picture dialog box (Windows).

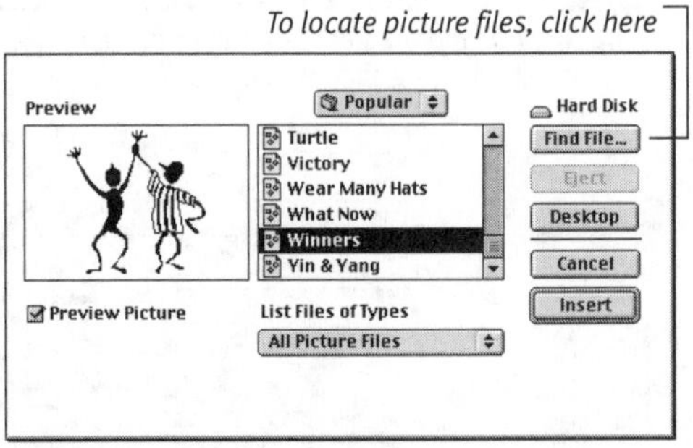

To locate picture files, click here

Figure 10.38 Select the name of the graphics file (Mac OS).

Figure 10.39 This rectangle has a shadow.

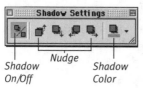

No Shadow

Shadow Settings...

Figure 10.40 This list of shadow styles displays after you click the Shadow button on the Drawing toolbar.

Shadow Settings

Shadow On/Off   *Nudge*   *Shadow Color*

Figure 10.41 Use the Shadow Settings toolbar to format a shadow.

Adding a Shadow

A shadow can add a feeling of depth to an object. **Figure 10.39** shows a rectangle with a shadow.

To add a shadow:

1. Select the object you want to shadow.

2. On the Drawing toolbar, click the Shadow button. ▣

3. Choose a shadow style (**Figure 10.40**).

To adjust the color and offset of a shadow:

1. Select the shadowed object.

2. Click the Shadow button on the Drawing toolbar and choose Shadow Settings. The Shadow Settings toolbar appears (**Figure 10.41**).

3. To adjust the shadow position, click the appropriate Nudge button(s) on the Shadow Settings toolbar.

4. To adjust the shadow color, click the arrow next to the Shadow Color button.

5. Choose a color from the palette.

   or

   Click More Shadow Colors and choose a color from the Standard or Custom tab.

6. When you are finished using the Shadow Settings toolbar, click its close button.

✔ Tips

■ A semi-transparent shadow allows you to see what's behind it.

■ To remove a shadow from a selected object, click the Shadow button on the Drawing toolbar and choose No Shadow.

ADDING A SHADOW

Adding 3-D Effects

You can add a 3-D effect to objects (such as rectangles or ovals) you have drawn in PowerPoint. After adding a 3-D effect, you can tilt the effect or change its depth and direction (**Figure 10.42**).

To add a 3-D effect:

1. Select the object to which you want to add a 3-D effect.

2. On the Drawing toolbar, click the 3-D button.

3. Choose a 3-D style (**Figure 10.43**).

To adjust the settings of a 3-D object:

1. Select the 3-D object.

2. Click the 3-D button on the Drawing toolbar and choose 3-D Settings.

   The 3-D Settings toolbar appears (**Figure 10.44**).

3. To tilt the object, click the appropriate Tilt button(s) on the 3-D Settings toolbar.

4. To adjust the depth of the object, click the Depth button and choose an amount (**Figure 10.45**).

5. To select the perspective of the 3-D effect, click the Direction button and choose a direction (**Figure 10.46**).

6. To adjust the color of the 3-D portion of the object, click the arrow next to the 3-D Color button. You can either choose a color from the small color palette, or you can click More 3-D Colors and choose a color from the Standard or Custom tab.

7. When you are finished using the 3-D Settings toolbar, click its close button.

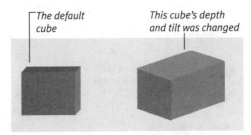

Figure 10.42 The cube on the left uses the default three-dimensional settings; the cube on the right has been formatted with different 3-D settings.

Figure 10.43 Select one of the 3-D styles from this list.

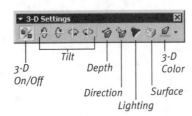

Figure 10.44 Use the 3-D Settings toolbar to format a three-dimensional object.

ADDING 3-D EFFECTS

Figure 10.45 Click the Depth button on the 3-D Settings toolbar to adjust the amount of the 3-D effect.

Figure 10.46 Click the Direction button on the 3-D Settings toolbar to adjust the viewer's perspective.

✔ Tips

■ To select the angle at which you want light to hit the object, click the Lighting button and choose the desired lighting angle.

■ To change the reflective tone of the object, click the Surface button and choose the desired surface type (such as Matte or Metal).

ADDING 3-D EFFECTS

Inserting Clip Art

PowerPoint comes with many *clip art* images that you can add to your slides. An easy way to insert these images is with the Microsoft Clip Gallery applet.

To insert a clip art image (Windows):

1. On the Drawing toolbar, click the Insert Clip Art button. 📷

   The Insert ClipArt window appears (**Figure 10.47**). This is the Microsoft Clip Gallery.

2. If necessary, select the Pictures tab.

3. Click a category (such as Conceptual or Animals).

4. To look through another category, click the Back button on the toolbar and choose a different one. ↩

5. Once you've found the image you like, drag it onto your slide (**Figure 10.48**).

✔ Tips

■ Although the window may not be visible, the Clip Gallery is a separate application and remains open after you drag an image onto your slide. To switch back to it (so that you can close it or insert another image), click the Insert ClipArt button on the Windows taskbar.

■ When adding a new slide, you can choose one of the two clip art AutoLayouts (**Figure 10.49**).

■ To maintain an image's original proportions as you resize it, select it and drag a *corner* selection handle. If you drag a *middle* handle the image will stretch out of proportion.

Figure 10.47 The Insert ClipArt window shows a variety of clip art (Windows).

Figure 10.48 Drag an image from the Clip Gallery onto your slide.

These two AutoLayouts have clip art placeholders

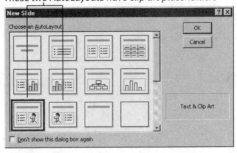

Figure 10.49 You may want to choose one of the AutoLayouts that have clip art placeholders.

Figure 10.50 Clicking the Insert Clip Art button starts Microsoft Clip Gallery (Mac OS).

Inserted clip art

New Employee Orientation Program

Figure 10.51 After inserting an image, you probably need to reposition and resize it.

To insert a clip art image (Mac OS):

1. On the Standard toolbar, click the Insert Clip Art button. 🖼

   The Microsoft Clip Gallery window appears (**Figure 10.50**).

2. If necessary, select the Clip Art tab.

3. Click a category (such as Animals or Industry).

4. If you find an image you like, click it and choose Insert (**Figure 10.51**).

   or

   If you don't see a picture you want, choose a different category.

✔ Tips

- When adding a new slide, you can choose one of the two clip art AutoLayouts (**Figure 10.49**).

- To maintain an image's original proportions as you resize it, select it and drag a *corner* selection handle. If you drag a *middle* handle the image will not maintain its original proportions.

- To move an image, select it and drag it into position. Make sure that you don't drag a selection handle, or you will resize the image.

Searching for Clip Art

An easy way to locate a particular clip art image is to have the Clip Gallery search for it. Each image has several keywords associated with it so you can search for images based upon one or more of these keywords.

To search for clip art (Windows):

1. On the Drawing toolbar, click the Insert Clip Art button. 🖼
   The Insert ClipArt window appears.

2. If necessary, select the Pictures tab.

3. In the Search for Clips field, type the keyword(s) you want to search for (**Figure 10.52**).

4. Press Enter.
   The Clip Gallery now displays pictures that match your specifications (**Figure 10.53**).

5. Click the Keep Looking button to see additional images.

6. If you find an image you like, drag it onto your slide.

✔ Tips

■ Click the Back button on the toolbar to view previously displayed images.

■ If you don't see a picture you want or if the Clip Gallery doesn't contain any matching images, try different keywords in the Search For Clips field.

■ After a search, click the All Categories button on the Clip Gallery toolbar to see all the categories again. 🖼

Enter keywords here

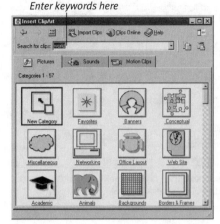

Figure 10.52 In this example, we will search for pictures with the keyword *world*.

Figure 10.53 The window now displays the images that have *world* as a keyword.

Click Find

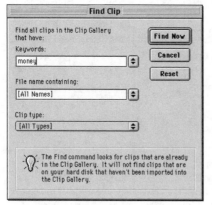

Figure 10.54 To search for clip art, click the Find button.

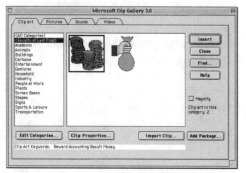

Figure 10.55 In this example, we are searching for pictures with *money* as a keyword.

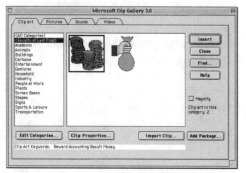

Figure 10.56 The window now displays the images that have *money* as a keyword.

To search for clip art (Mac OS):

1. On the Standard toolbar, click the Insert Clip Art button.

   The Microsoft Clip Gallery window appears (**Figure 10.54**).

2. If necessary, select the Clip Art tab.

3. Click Find.

   The Find Clip dialog box appears (**Figure 10.55**).

4. In the Keywords field, type the word(s) you want to search for.

   or

   Enter a filename or part of a filename in the File Name Containing field.

5. Click Find Now.

   The Clip Gallery now displays all pictures that match your specifications (**Figure 10.56**).

6. If you find an image you like, click it and choose Insert.

✔ Tip

- If you don't see a picture you want or if the Clip Gallery doesn't contain any matching images, try a different search word in the Keywords field.

Finding Clip Art on the Web (Windows Only)

If you can't find the appropriate image in the Microsoft Clip Gallery, you can search the online clip gallery on the Web—it contains thousands of images that you can download free of charge.

To find clip art on the Web:

1. On the Drawing toolbar, click the Insert Clip Art button.

2. In the Insert ClipArt window, click the Clips Online button (**Figure 10.57**).

3. Click OK.

   If you aren't currently connected to the Internet, you will be connected at this time. After a moment, the Clip Gallery Live Web site appears in your browser window.

4. Read the terms and click Accept.

5. In the Search Clips by Keyword field, type the word(s) that you want to search for (**Figure 10.58**).

6. Click Go.

   After a moment, the Clip Gallery Live window displays pictures that match your specifications (**Figure 10.59**).

7. Click More to view additional images.

8. If you find an image you want to download, click the download icon under the image.

✔ Tips

■ You can locate your downloaded images in Clip Gallery's Downloaded Clips category.

■ To download several images at once, click the checkbox under each image, click Selection Basket, and then click Download.

Click Clips Online

Figure 10.57 The Clips Online button is the gateway to the Clip Gallery Live Web site.

Enter keywords here...   ...and click Go

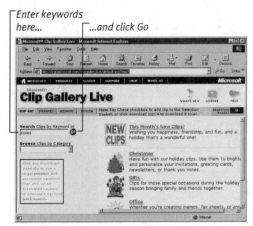

Figure 10.58 The Clip Gallery Live Web site appears in your browser window.

Displays additional images

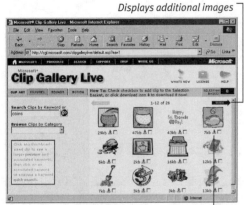

Figure 10.59 The window displays the results of the online search.   Download icon

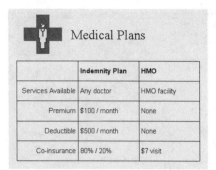

Figure 10.60 The doctor graphic is an imported Windows Metafile.

To locate picture files, click here ⌐

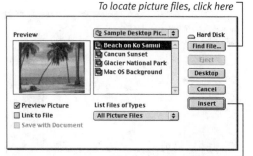

Click here to insert the image ⌐

Figure 10.61 Select the name of the graphics file (Mac OS).

To locate picture files, click here and choose Find

Click here to insert the image ⌐

Figure 10.62 Select the name of the graphics file in the Insert Picture dialog box (Windows).

Inserting Graphics Files

You may want your slides to include graphics files that you have created or purchased. **Figure 10.60** shows a graphic that has been imported to a PowerPoint slide.

To insert a graphics file:

1. Display the slide on which you want to insert the graphics file.

2. Choose Insert > Picture > From File.
   The Insert Picture dialog box appears (**Figures 10.61** and **10.62**).

3. Navigate to the drive and folder containing the graphics file.

4. Click the name of the graphics file.

5. Click Insert.

✔ Tips

■ If you aren't sure where your graphics files are, choose Tools > Find (Windows) or click Find File (Mac OS) in the Insert Picture dialog box.

■ To maintain an image's original proportions as you resize it, select it and drag a *corner* selection handle. If you drag a *middle* handle the image will not maintain its original proportions.

■ To move an image, select it and then drag it into position. Make sure that you don't drag a selection handle, or you will resize the image.

See Pasting Graphics on the next page for another way to insert graphics.

Pasting Graphics

If you have created a graphical image in another program (such as CorelDRAW), you may want to use the copy-and-paste routine to bring it into PowerPoint. One advantage to using this method is that the image becomes an *embedded object* (like org charts and pie charts) that you can easily modify.

To paste a graphic:

1. Select the graphic in the source application (**Figure 10.63**), and then choose Edit > Copy to copy it to the Clipboard.

2. Switch to PowerPoint and display the slide on which you want to insert the graphic.

3. Choose Edit > Paste.

   The graphic now appears on the current PowerPoint slide (**Figure 10.64**).

✔ Tip

- As with any embedded object, you can modify it by double-clicking the object. PowerPoint will then launch the application that created the image and display the graphic, ready for editing. When you exit the source application, the graphic is updated automatically in PowerPoint.

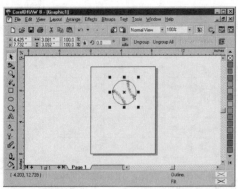

Figure 10.63 Copy the object in the source application.

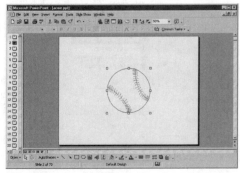

Figure 10.64 Paste the object onto a PowerPoint slide.

MANIPULATING GRAPHICAL OBJECTS

Figure 11.1 The star on the right was scaled to 50% of its original size.

Figure 11.2 The image on the right was cropped.

Figure 11.3 To center the cross inside the circle use PowerPoint's alignment commands.

PowerPoint offers a number of ways to manipulate the graphical objects you create with the drawing tools as well as the images imported from the Clip Gallery or other programs.

The figures on this page demonstrate some of the techniques you can use to manipulate graphical objects. You can scale (**Figure 11.1**), crop (**Figure 11.2**), align (**Figure 11.3**), flip, rotate, distribute, or recolor objects.

In this chapter, you will learn how to use PowerPoint's rulers, guides, and snap feature to place objects; copy graphical attributes; group a set of objects; and change the stacking order of objects.

Using Rulers and Guides

To help you precisely position graphical objects, you can use *rulers* and *guides* (**Figure 11.4**). For example, in **Figure 11.5**, the ruler helped us to position the squares exactly one inch apart and the horizontal guide enabled us to align the boxes along their baselines.

To display rulers:

◆ Choose View > Ruler.

The horizontal ruler appears above the slide; the vertical ruler appears to the left. Notice that the zero point is at the center of each ruler. This enables you to measure distances from the center of the slide.

To display the guides:

1. Choose View > Guides.

2. Drag the individual guides to place them at any position on the slide.

✔ Tips

■ Checkmarks next to Ruler and Guides on the View menu indicate the options are enabled (**Figure 11.6**).

■ The Ruler and Guides commands are toggles—choose them again to turn them off and the checkmark disappears.

■ You can turn the guides on and off by pressing Ctrl+G (Windows) or Command+G (Mac OS).

■ As you drag the guides, a measurement appears (**Figure 11.4**); this measurement represents the distance from the zero point. Thus, if you want to place objects exactly 1.25 inches down from the center of the slide, you can easily drag the horizontal guide to this position (with or without the ruler displayed).

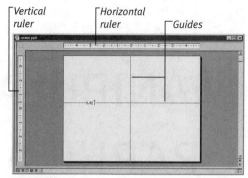

┌Vertical   ┌Horizontal
 ruler   ruler   ┌Guides

Figure 11.4 Rulers and guides are displayed.

Figure 11.5 Use rulers and guides to help position objects on your slides.

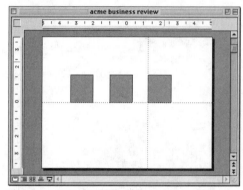

Figure 11.6 As the checkmarks indicate, the Ruler and Guides options are enabled.

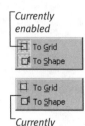

Currently enabled

Figure 11.7 A depressed icon indicates the option is enabled (Windows).

Currently disabled

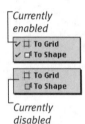

Currently enabled

Figure 11.8 A checkmark indicates the option is enabled (Mac OS).

Currently disabled

Using Grid Snap

Another tool that helps position objects is the *grid*, a series of invisible, horizontal and vertical lines, about 1/12 inch apart. Whenever you draw, size, or move an object, the object borders jump to the lines along the invisible grid, as though they were magnetized.

The grid is always there, although you can't actually see it; you can enable or disable the grid snap at any time.

To enable grid snap:

1. On the Drawing toolbar, click Draw to display the menu.

2. Choose Snap.

   To determine if grid snap is already enabled, check the icon next to To Grid (**Figures 11.7** and **11.8**). Grid snap is enabled if this icon is depressed (Windows) or if a checkmark appears next to it (Mac OS).

3. If grid snap is not enabled, click To Grid.

   or

   If grid snap is already enabled, press Esc until the menu is cleared.

✔ Tips

- To temporarily disable grid snap when positioning an object, hold down Alt (Windows) or Command (Mac OS) as you drag.

- You may want to disable grid snap if you're trying to position several objects and the grid snap is interfering.

- To disable grid snap, choose Draw > Snap > To Grid.

- The effect of snapping from one gridline to the next is more apparent in zoomed-in views.

   See Zooming In and Out later in this chapter.

Snapping to Shapes

PowerPoint offers a way to easily place shapes so their edges are touching—the *snap-to-shape* feature. This feature is useful when you want to attach a pointer line to the edge of an object or to stack objects directly on top of one another (**Figure 11.9**).

To enable snap to shape:

1. On the Drawing toolbar, click Draw to display the menu.

2. Choose Snap.

   To determine if snap to shape is already enabled, check the icon next to To Shape (**Figures 11.10** and **11.11**). Snap to shape is enabled if this icon is depressed (Windows) or if there is a checkmark next to it (Mac OS).

3. If snap to shape is not enabled, click To Shape.

   or

   If snap to shape is already enabled, press Esc until the menu is cleared.

✔ Tips

- To temporarily disable shape snap when positioning an object, hold down Alt (Windows) or Command (Mac OS) as you drag.

- To disable snap to shape, again choose Draw > Snap > To Shape.

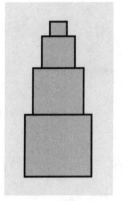

Figure 11.9 You can use the snap-to-shape feature to stack objects on top of one another.

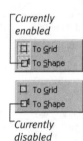

Figure 11.10 A dimmed icon indicates the option is enabled (Windows).

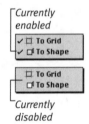

Figure 11.11 A checkmark indicates the option is enabled (Mac OS).

SNAPPING TO SHAPES

Zoom field

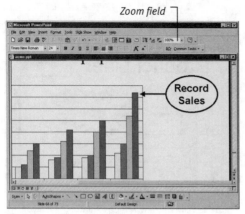

Figure 11.12 This slide is zoomed in to 100%.

*Click here
to display
a list*

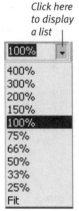

Figure 11.13 You can zoom in or out by selecting one of the percentages in the Zoom field.

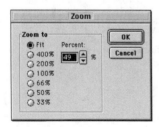

Figure 11.14 The Zoom dialog box is another way to zoom in or out.

Zooming In and Out

As you are drawing, sizing, and moving objects, you may want to zoom in to make sure they are positioned properly (**Figure 11.12**).

To zoom in and out:

◆ Click the arrow in the Zoom field to display a list of zoom percentages (**Figure 11.13**). Then click the desired number.

or

◆ Click the percentage in the Zoom field, type a number between 10 and 400, and press Enter or Return.

or

◆ Choose View > Zoom and choose the desired zoom percentage in the Zoom dialog box (**Figure 11.14**).

✔ Tips

■ Use the Fit zoom option to fit the whole slide in the window.

■ To zoom in on a particular area of the slide, click an object in this area before choosing a zoom percentage; the selected object will be centered in the window.

ZOOMING IN AND OUT

Displaying a Slide Miniature

When you are zoomed in while in Slide, Outline, or Normal view, it's helpful to display a *slide miniature* so you can see the complete slide as you are working on the detail (**Figure 11.15**).

To display the slide miniature (Windows):

1. Select one of the zoomed in views (such as 200%).

   Unless you manually closed the slide miniature in the past, a slide miniature of the current slide automatically appears (**Figure 11.16**).

2. If the slide miniature doesn't appear, choose View > Slide Miniature.

To display the slide miniature (Mac OS):

1. Choose View > Slide Miniature.

   A slide miniature of the current slide appears (**Figure 11.17**).

2. Hold down Control as you click the slide miniature, and then choose Black and White View or Color View from the shortcut menu.

✔ Tips

- If the slide miniature is blocking your work area, you can position it elsewhere in the PowerPoint window by dragging its title bar.

- To remove the slide miniature, click the close box on the slide miniature window.

- Switching to Black and White view is another way to automatically display the slide miniature (Windows only).

Slide miniature

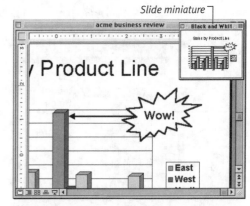

Figure 11.15 Displaying a slide miniature when you are zoomed in helps you see how your changes affect the entire slide.

Figure 11.16 The slide miniature appears when you zoom in (Windows).

Figure 11.17 Choose View > Slide Miniature to view the slide miniature (Mac OS).

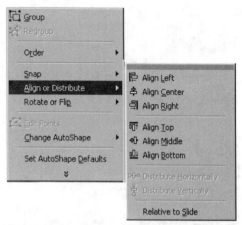

Figure 11.18 Use the options on the Align or Distribute menu to align several objects horizontally or vertically.

Figure 11.19 The star is centered horizontally and vertically inside the circle.

Figure 11.20 The lines are aligned on the left.

Aligning Objects

As explained on the preceding pages, you can use guides and rulers to help line up several objects. However, perhaps the easiest way to align objects is automatically with the Draw > Align or Distribute command (**Figure 11.18**). For example, you can center one object inside another (**Figure 11.19**) or align a group of objects on the left (**Figure 11.20**).

To align two or more objects:

1. Click to select the first object you want to align, and hold down Shift as you click additional objects to be aligned.

   or

   Drag around the objects to be selected.

2. On the Drawing toolbar, click Draw to display the menu.

3. Choose Align or Distribute.

4. To align the objects horizontally, choose Align Left, Align Center, or Align Right.

   or

   To align the objects vertically, choose Align Top, Align Middle, or Align Bottom.

✔ Tip

■ To center one object inside another, you need to issue two alignment commands: one to align the objects horizontally (Align Center) and the other to align vertically (Align Middle).

ALIGNING OBJECTS

Spacing Objects Equally

You can evenly space three or more objects, such as the rectangles in **Figure 11.21**, using PowerPoint's Distribute Horizontally command or Distribute Vertically command (**Figure 11.22**).

When you distribute objects, the top and bottom objects (or left and right objects in a horizontal distribution) remain stationary and the objects in between them are repositioned so that they are spaced evenly.

To space objects equally:

1. Click to select the first object you want to distribute, and hold down Shift as you click additional objects to be distributed.

   or

   Drag around the objects to be selected.

2. On the Drawing toolbar, click Draw to display the menu.

3. Choose Align or Distribute.

4. Choose Distribute Horizontally or Distribute Vertically.

✔ Tip

- By default, PowerPoint distributes objects relative to the first and last object in the group. If you want to evenly space objects across the slide, choose Draw > Align or Distribute > Relative to Slide before you choose the Distribute Horizontally or Distribute Vertically command.

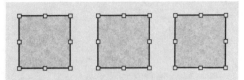

Figure 11.21 The three rectangles are evenly spaced.

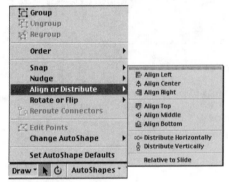

Figure 11.22 Use the Distribute Horizontally or Distribute Vertically commands to evenly space several objects.

Figure 11.23 All the objects in this design are selected.

Figure 11.24 After grouping the objects, one set of selection handles surrounds the design.

Grouping Objects

When you want to manipulate several objects as a single unit, you can *group* them. Once the objects are grouped, you can move, resize, scale, flip, and rotate the group as if it were a single object.

To group objects:

1. Click to select the first object you want in the group, and hold down Shift as you click additional objects to be grouped (**Figure 11.23**).

   or

   Drag around the objects.

2. On the Drawing toolbar, click Draw to display the menu.

3. Choose Group.

4. A single set of selection handles appears, and the group is now considered a single object (**Figure 11.24**).

✔ Tips

- You can also group objects by pressing Ctrl+Shift+G (Windows) or Command+Shift+G (Mac OS).

- To disassemble the group and modify the objects separately, choose the Draw > Ungroup command or press Ctrl+Shift+H (Windows) or Command+Shift+H (Mac OS).

- To re-create a disassembled group, you do not need to reselect the objects. Press Esc to unselect, and then choose Draw > Regroup.

- For more complex drawings, you can create groups within groups.

GROUPING OBJECTS

Copying Object Attributes

Use the Format Painter button to copy attributes from one object to another. You can copy all formatting characteristics, including color, pattern, shadow, and line thickness.

To copy object attributes:

1. Select the object whose formatting attributes you want to copy (**Figure 11.25**).

2. Click the Format Painter button on the Standard toolbar.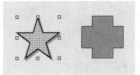

   The pointer changes to an arrow with a paintbrush.

3. Click the object you want to format (**Figure 11.26**).

✔ Tips

- If you don't see the Format Painter button on the Standard toolbar, click the More Buttons button to see other buttons (Windows only).

- To copy attributes to more than one object, select the object with the desired format to be copied and double-click the Format Painter button. Click as many objects as you want to format, and when done, press Esc.

- Format Painter can copy formatting attributes that were applied within PowerPoint only. Therefore, you cannot copy attributes of images imported or pasted from other applications.

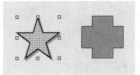

Figure 11.25 Select the object (the star, in this example) with the formatting attributes you want to copy.

The cross now has a thick border, a shadow, and a pattern fill

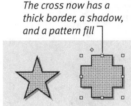

Figure 11.26 After selecting the Format Painter tool, click the cross to "paste" the star's attributes.

Picture tab

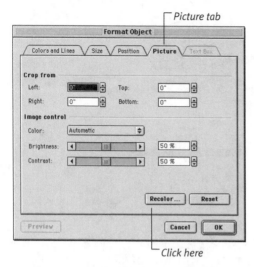

Click here

Figure 11.27 In the Picture tab, click Recolor.

Click here to choose a new color

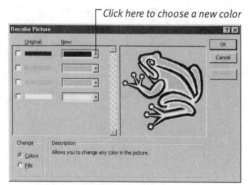

Figure 11.28 Look up the color you want to replace in the Original column and select the replacement color in the New column.

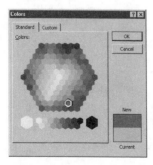

Figure 11.29 Select any color in the Standard or Custom tab.

Recoloring a Picture

Recoloring a picture involves replacing one color with another in a graphic or clip-art image you have inserted into PowerPoint. Note that you cannot recolor bitmap images or shapes created in PowerPoint.

To replace a color in a picture:

1. Select the picture to be recolored.

2. Choose Format > Picture (Windows) or Format > Object (Mac OS).

3. If necessary, select the Picture tab (**Figure 11.27**).

4. Click Recolor.

   The Recolor Picture dialog box appears (**Figure 11.28**).

5. Choose whether you want to change all Colors (fills and lines) or just the Fills.

6. In the Original column, locate the color you want to replace. This column lists all the original colors used in the picture.

7. Click the arrow in the adjacent New field to display the small palette.

8. Choose a color from the palette.

   or

   Click More Colors and choose a color from the Standard or Custom tab (**Figure 11.29**).

9. Repeat steps 6 through 8 for any other colors you want to change.

10. Click OK.

✔ Tip

■ If you want to return a changed color to the original color, select the appropriate checkbox in the Original column.

Scaling an Object

Scaling resizes the height and width of an object by a designated percentage. This feature is similar to the enlarge and reduce buttons on a copy machine.

Figure 11.30 shows an image that was copied and then scaled down. You can scale objects drawn in PowerPoint as well as pictures you have inserted.

To scale an object:

1. Select the object or group to be scaled.

2. To scale an inserted image, choose Format > Picture (Windows) or Format > Object (Mac OS).

   or

   To scale a shape drawn in PowerPoint, choose Format > AutoShape.

3. Select the Size tab (**Figure 11.31**).

4. In the Height field of the Scale section, specify a scaling percentage for the height. A number greater than 100 enlarges the object; a number less than 100 reduces it.

5. In the Width field of the Scale section, specify a scaling percentage for the width. To scale the object proportionally, the height and width percentages should be equal.

6. To see how the object looks with the new scale factors, click Preview.

7. If necessary, adjust the Height and Width values.

8. When you're satisfied with your scale values, click OK.

✔ Tip

■ To scale a bitmap image, use the Format > Picture command (Mac OS only).

Figure 11.30 To create the baby frog, copy the big frog and scale the copied image down to 40% of its original size.

Enter scaling percentages here

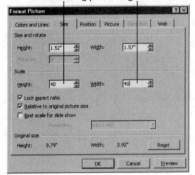

Figure 11.31 Enter scaling percentages in the Height and Width fields.

Figure 11.32 You must place the entire graphic when you insert a clip art image or graphics file.

Figure 11.33 After inserting a graphic, you can crop out the portions you don't want.

Crop

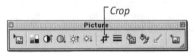

Figure 11.34 The Crop tool is on the Picture toolbar.

Drag this
handle down

Figure 11.35 After selecting the Crop tool, drag the indicated selection handle to crop the image as shown in Figure 11.33.

Cropping a Picture

Cropping is a term that refers to trimming away an unwanted section of a picture. For example, if a graphic displays a person's full body, you can crop it so that only the person's face appears. **Figures 11.32** and **11.33** show an example of cropping. Note that you can crop only the edges of the picture—you cannot crop out anything in the middle.

To crop a picture:

1. Select the picture to be cropped.

2. If the Picture toolbar doesn't appear (**Figure 11.34**), right-click the picture and choose Show Picture Toolbar on the shortcut menu (Windows).

    or

    Hold down Control as you click the picture and choose Show Picture Toolbar on the shortcut menu (Mac OS).

    The Picture toolbar appears.

2. Click the Crop button on the Picture toolbar.

3. Place the cropping pointer on a selection handle (**Figure 11.35**), and drag toward the middle of the picture until you have trimmed away the unwanted portion.

4. If necessary, drag other selection handles to crop other portions.

5. When you are finished cropping, click an empty area of the slide or press Esc.

✔ Tips

■ When you crop, you are temporarily hiding part of the picture. At any time, you can crop outwards to redisplay the hidden portion.

■ You may want to zoom in for more accuracy in cropping.

Changing the Stack Order

As you draw objects or place pictures on a slide, PowerPoint layers the new ones on top of the old ones. In **Figure 11.36**, you can see that the clouds and the airplane appear on different layers.

To change the order in which objects are stacked:

1. On the Drawing toolbar, click Draw to display the menu.

2. Choose Order (**Figure 11.37**).

3. Choose one of the following:

   ◆ Bring to Front to place an object at the top of the stack.

   ◆ Send to Back to place an object at the bottom of the stack.

   ◆ Bring Forward to bring an object one layer up in the stack.

   ◆ Send Backward to send an object one layer back in the stack.

✔ Tips

■ You can also change the stacking order by right-clicking (Windows) or Control-clicking (Mac OS) an object and making a selection from the Order menu.

■ Choosing the Send Backward command several times will ultimately produce the same results as choosing Send to Back once. Likewise, selecting Bring Forward several times is the equivalent of choosing Bring to Front.

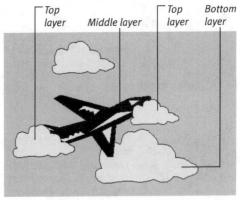

Figure 11.36 Overlapping objects are layered.

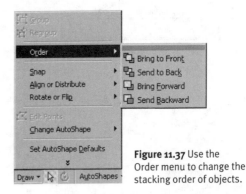

Figure 11.37 Use the Order menu to change the stacking order of objects.

Figure 11.38
The ribbon on
the right was
rotated.

Drag counterclockwise

Figure 11.39 To rotate the
ribbon as shown, drag a
handle in a counterclockwise
direction.

Rotating Objects

Figure 11.38 shows an example of an object
before and after it was rotated. You can rotate
any object drawn in PowerPoint. To rotate an
inserted graphic (such as a clip art image),
you must first ungroup it to convert it to a
Microsoft Office drawing, and then regroup it.

See Grouping Objects earlier in this chapter.

To rotate an object:

1. Select the object to be rotated.

2. On the Drawing toolbar, click the Free
   Rotate button. ↻

3. Place the tip of the rotate pointer on a
   green rotate handle (**Figure 11.39**).
   Drag in a clockwise or counterclockwise
   direction.

4. Release the mouse button when you have
   finished rotating.

5. If you want to rotate the object further,
   repeat steps 3 and 4.

6. Click off the object or press Esc to deactivate the Free Rotate tool.

✔ Tip

■ You can also rotate objects by clicking
  Draw on the Drawing toolbar and choosing Rotate or Flip. Choose Rotate Left to
  rotate an object 90 degrees counterclockwise or Rotate Right to rotate 90 degrees
  clockwise.

ROTATING OBJECTS

Flipping Objects

You can flip any object drawn in PowerPoint horizontally (**Figure 11.40**) or vertically (**Figure 11.41**). To flip an inserted graphic (such as a clip art image), you must first ungroup it to convert it to a Microsoft Office drawing, and then regroup it.

See Grouping Objects earlier in this chapter.

To flip an object:

1. Select the object to be flipped.

2. On the Drawing toolbar, click Draw to display the menu.

3. Choose Rotate or Flip (**Figure 11.42**).

4. Choose Flip Horizontal or Flip Vertical.

Figure 11.40 The balloon on the left is the original object; the balloon on the right was flipped horizontally.

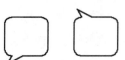

Figure 11.41 The balloon on the left is the original object; the balloon on the right was flipped vertically.

Figure 11.42 Use the Flip Horizontal or Flip Vertical command to flip the selected object.

MAKING GLOBAL CHANGES

```
                    Agenda
        1998 Annual Business Review
   • Introduction
   • Corporate Goals
   • 1998 Sales Performance
       – By Region
       – By Product Line
   • 1999 Budget
```

Figure 12.1 This bulleted list uses the default settings.

```
   Agenda
   1998 Annual Business Review

   ■ Introduction
   ■ Corporate Goals
   ■ 1998 Sales Performance
       ➤ By Region
       ➤ By Product Line
   ■ 1999 Budget
```

Figure 12.2 After modifying the Slide Master, all slides in the presentation are formatted exactly the same way.

Figure 12.3 Applying a template is a quick way to format an entire presentation.

This chapter shows you how to quickly format an entire presentation—without having to change each slide.

You make some global changes, such as replacing fonts and changing colors or backgrounds, with commands on the Format menu.

You can make other changes, such as formatting slide titles and adding logos or page numbers, by editing the *Slide Master*. The Slide Master contains default formatting as well as any background items you want repeated on each slide. **Figures 12.1** and **12.2** show a slide before and after modifying the Slide Master. While these figures show just one slide, bear in mind that *all* slides would be formatted similarly.

Perhaps the most dramatic global change you can make to your presentation is to apply a *template*. A template controls the color scheme, text formatting, and repeating graphical elements—and you apply it with a single command. **Figure 12.3** shows the same slide after applying a template.

Changing the Default Colors

Your presentation's color scheme includes color assignments for the slide background, slide titles, text and lines, shadows, object fills, and accents. Once you change the default colors, any new slides you create will automatically use the new color scheme.

To change the default colors:

1. Choose Format > Slide Color Scheme.

2. Select the Custom tab (**Figure 12.4**).

3. In the Scheme Colors area, click the color box associated with the element you want to change. For instance, click the color box next to Title Text to change the color of your titles.

4. Click Change Color.

   A color palette appears (**Figure 12.5**).

5. Click the color you want and then click OK.

6. Repeat steps 3 through 5 for each element you want to change.

7. Click Apply to All to apply the new colors to the entire presentation.

✔ Tips

- Use the Standard tab in the Color Scheme dialog box to select one of PowerPoint's built-in color schemes (**Figure 12.6**).

- When you change the Text and Lines color, it affects the color of bullet, chart, org chart, and table text. It also changes the color of object borders, lines inside charts (such as gridlines and legend borders), and connecting lines in org charts. The colors in embedded Word tables do not change, however.

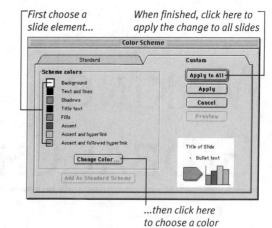

First choose a slide element... When finished, click here to apply the change to all slides

...then click here to choose a color

Figure 12.4 Use the Color Scheme dialog box to make global color changes in your presentation.

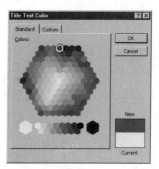

Figure 12.5 Choose a color in the Standard or Custom tab.

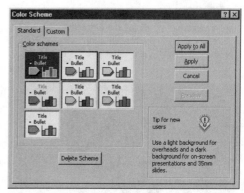

Figure 12.6 Select a color scheme in the Standard tab of the Color Scheme dialog box.

First assign new colors to slide elements...

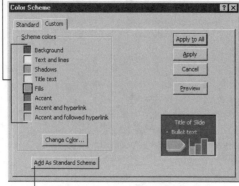

...then click here to create a scheme

Figure 12.7 You can also create your own color schemes.

Click the   Click the   Click here to
Standard tab   new scheme   apply the
                                      scheme

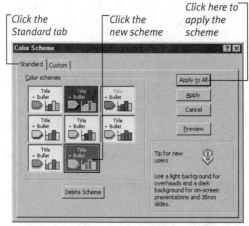

Figure 12.8 The new color scheme is now listed on the Standard tab.

Creating Color Schemes

In PowerPoint, you can create your own color schemes and apply them to individual slides or to the entire presentation.

To create a color scheme:

1. Choose Format > Slide Color Scheme.

2. Select the Custom tab.

3. Choose colors for the various slide elements.

   See Changing the Default Colors on the previous page.

4. When you're finished assigning colors, click Add As Standard Scheme (**Figure 12.7**).

5. Select the Standard tab.

   Your new color scheme is now listed on the Standard tab (**Figure 12.8**).

6. To apply the new scheme, select it and then click Apply to All (for all slides) or Apply (for one slide).

✔ Tip

■ If you're not happy with the colors after you apply a new color scheme, you can immediately choose Edit > Undo to restore your previous color scheme.

Creating a Gradient Background

A *gradient* is a gradual progression from one color to another. **Figure 12.9** shows a slide with a gradient background. Gradient fills have a primary color of your choosing and are blended with different amounts of black or white. Alternatively, you can blend any two colors, as explained on the next page.

To create a gradient background:

1. Choose Format > Background.

2. In the Background dialog box, click the arrow (**Figure 12.10**) and choose Fill Effects.

3. Select the Gradient tab.

4. Click One Color (**Figure 12.11**).

5. To choose the gradient's primary color, click the Color 1 field.

   The small color palette appears.

6. Choose a color from the palette.

   or

   Click More Colors and choose a color from the Standard or Custom tab.

7. Choose one of the Shading Styles (Horizontal, Vertical, etc.).

8. Click one of the Variants (these are variations of the style you selected in step 7).

9. To adjust the blended color, drag the scroll box in the Dark/Light slider.

10. Click OK.

11. Click Apply to All.

✔ Tip

■ As you darken the blended color, you are adding more black. As you lighten, you are adding more white.

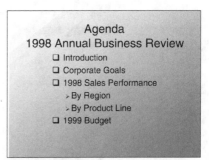

Figure 12.9 Gradients are an attractive (but not overly distracting) slide background.

Click here and choose Fill Effects

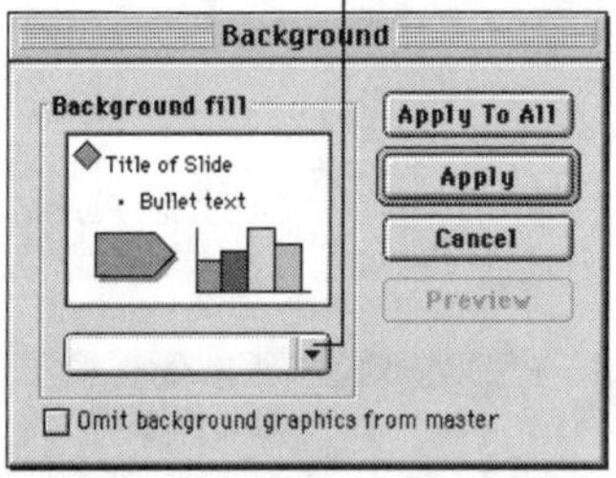

Figure 12.10 To choose a fill effect for the background, you must click the arrow next to the empty field.

Drag here to adjust the blended color

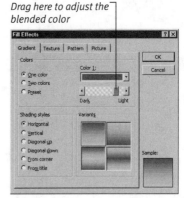

Figure 12.11 To create a gradient fill, you must choose a color, shading style, and a variant.

Click here and choose Fill Effects

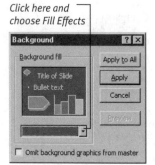

Figure 12.12 To choose a fill effect for the background, click the arrow next to the empty field.

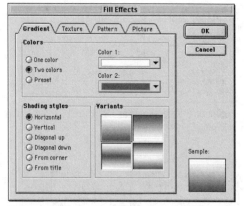

Figure 12.13 Choose Two Colors to create a blend with two different colors.

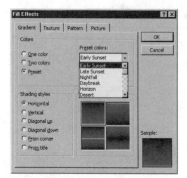

Figure 12.14 Be sure to look at the preset gradients—PowerPoint offers some unique multicolored blends.

Creating a Two-Color Gradient

In PowerPoint, you can blend two different colors to create vibrant backgrounds for your presentations.

To create a two-color gradient:

1. Choose Format > Background.

2. In the Background dialog box, click the arrow (**Figure 12.12**) and click Fill Effects.

3. Select the Gradient tab.

4. Click Two Colors (**Figure 12.13**).

5. To choose the gradient's first color, click the Color 1 field.

    The small color palette appears.

6. Choose a color from the palette.

    or

    Click More Colors and choose a color from the Standard or Custom tab.

7. To choose the shade's second color, click the Color 2 field and select a color.

8. Choose one of the Shading Styles (Horizontal, Vertical, etc.).

9. Click one of the Variants (these are variations of the style you selected in step 8).

10. Click OK.

11. Click Apply to All.

✔ Tip

■ You can also create a multicolor shade with the Preset option. Choose Preset instead of Two Colors, and then choose one of the samples from the Preset Colors list (**Figure 12.14**).

CREATING A TWO-COLOR GRADIENT

Replacing a Font

Suppose you want all your slide text to be in the Arial font instead of Times New Roman (**Figures 12.15** and **12.16**). You can accomplish this task easily with the Format > Replace Fonts command.

To globally replace one font with another:

1. Choose Format > Replace Fonts.

   The Replace Font dialog box appears (**Figure 12.17**).

2. In the Replace field, choose the font you want to replace in the presentation.

3. In the With field, choose the new font.

4. Click Replace.

5. Repeat steps 2 through 4 to replace other fonts.

6. When you're finished replacing fonts, click Close.

✔ Tips

- The Replace Fonts command does not substitute typefaces in charts, embedded Word tables, or org charts.

- To replace the font in only the slide titles or the bullet text, you need to edit the Slide Master.

  See Changing the Default Format for Text later in this chapter.

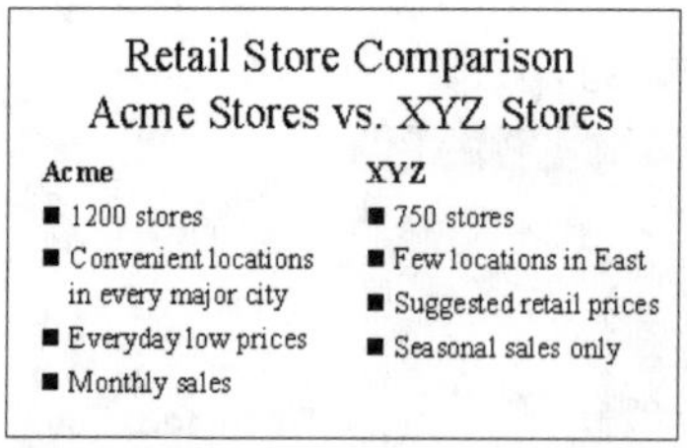

Figure 12.15 The current font for text on this slide (and all other slides) is Times New Roman.

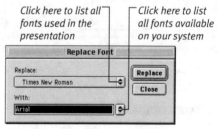

Figure 12.16 After replacing fonts, the text on all slides is in Arial.

Click here to list all fonts used in the presentation   *Click here to list all fonts available on your system*

Figure 12.17 Globally replace one font with another using the Format > Replace Fonts command.

REPLACING A FONT

Click this button to display a slide miniature

Object area placeholder

Master toolbar

Title area placeholder

Slide miniature

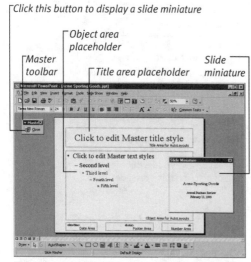

Figure 12.18 Edit the Slide Master to make global changes to your presentation.

Bullet shapes changed

Graphical objects added

Title formatted

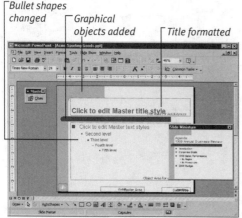

Figure 12.19 This figure shows some of the types of changes you can make on a Slide Master.

Figure 12.20 Click the Close button on the Master toolbar to close the Slide Master.

Editing the Slide Master

The Slide Master (**Figure 12.18**) contains the default formatting for your presentation as well as any background items you want to appear on each slide. Any changes you make on the Slide Master automatically affect all slides in your presentation. When you format the Master title and Master text, you are actually formatting all the titles and text in your presentation (except in embedded Word tables, charts, and org charts). **Figure 12.19** is an example of a formatted Slide Master.

To edit the Slide Master:

1. Choose View > Master > Slide Master. The Slide Master appears (**Figure 12.18**).

2. Make desired changes on the Master.

   See Changing the Default Format for Text, Adding Background Items, and Inserting Footers later in this chapter.

3. If you like, adjust the size and position of placeholders. (These placeholders are pointed out in **Figure 12.18**.)

4. Click the Close button on the Master toolbar (**Figure 12.20**).

   All slides now have the formatting and background items you added on the Master.

The following pages show some common ways to edit the Slide Master.

✔ Tips

- When you change an element on the Slide Master, only the elements with default formatting are affected. Elements with specific formats override those on the Slide Master.

- To quickly display the Slide Master, hold down Shift as you click the Slide View button. ▭

Inserting a Title Master

Frequently, you will want your title slides to be formatted differently from other slides in your presentation. For instance, your Slide Master may contain graphical elements that aren't appropriate for title slides (**Figure 12.21**). In PowerPoint, you can create a *Title Master* just for your title slides.

Note: A "title slide" is one that was created using the Title Slide layout in the Slide Layout dialog box.

To insert a Title Master:

1. Choose View > Master > Slide Master. The Slide Master appears.

2. Choose Insert > New Title Master. A new Title Master is inserted (**Figure 12.22**).

3. Make desired changes on the Master.

   See Changing the Default Format for Text and Adding Background Items on the following pages.

4. Click the Close button on the Master toolbar.

   All title slides will now have the formatting and background items you added to (or deleted from) the Title Master.

✔ Tips

■ To switch between the Title Master and the Slide Master, press Page Up and Page Down. (The status bar indicates which master is currently displayed.)

■ Once you have created a Title Master, you can edit it using the View > Master > Title Master command.

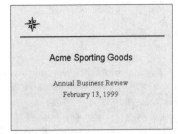

Figure 12.21 Since a star and a line were added to the Slide Master, they appear on every slide. But they look out of place on this title slide.

Figure 12.22 Insert a Title Master and delete the objects you don't want on your title slides (or add the ones you do want).

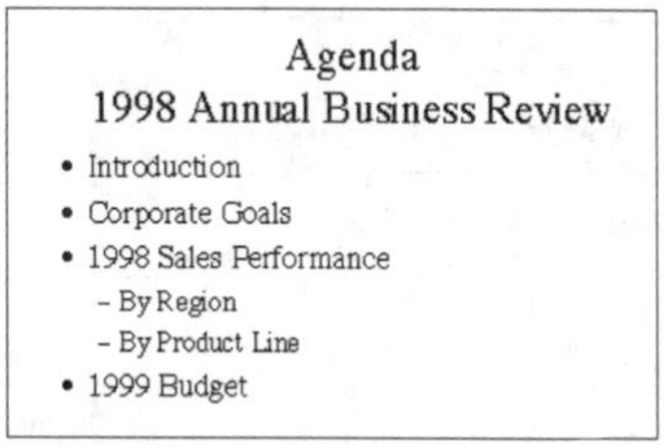

Agenda
1998 Annual Business Review

- Introduction
- Corporate Goals
- 1998 Sales Performance
  - By Region
  - By Product Line
- 1999 Budget

Figure 12.23 This slide uses the default Slide Master.

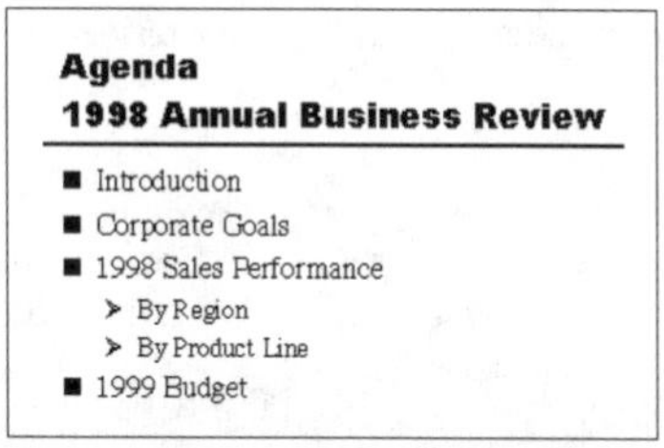

Agenda
1998 Annual Business Review

- Introduction
- Corporate Goals
- 1998 Sales Performance
  - By Region
  - By Product Line
- 1999 Budget

Figure 12.24 This slide illustrates what the text looks like after formatting the text on the Slide Master; all slides are formatted the same way.

Figure 12.25 Formatting the sample text on the Slide Master formats all the default text in the presentation.

Changing the Default Format for Text

Suppose you want all your slide titles to be in a larger type size and aligned on the left, all first-level bullets to be squares, and all bullet text to be anchored in the middle. By making these changes on the Slide Master, you need to format the text only once—all new and existing slides will conform to the modified format.

Figures 12.23 and **12.24** show a slide before and after editing the Slide Master. **Figure 12.25** shows the modified Slide Master.

To change the default format for text:

1. Choose View > Master > Slide Master.

2. To format slide titles, click the Master title and make desired changes.

3. To format first-level bullets in Bulleted List slides, click where it says *Click to edit Master text styles* and make desired changes.

   See Choosing Bullet Shapes, Adjusting Bullet Placement, and Formatting a Text Placeholder in Chapter 3.

4. To format other bullet levels, click the line (such as *Second level*) and make desired changes.

5. When you're finished, click the Close button on the Master toolbar.

✔ Tips

- When you format text on the Slide Master, only slide text with default formatting is affected. Text that has been directly formatted overrides the formatting on the Slide Master.

- To maintain consistent formatting throughout your presentation, try to use direct formatting as little as possible.

Adding Background Items

When background items are placed on the Slide Master, they are repeated on every slide in the presentation. Common background items are company names and logos, borders, rules, and graphics.

Figure 12.26 shows several examples of background items you may want repeated on every slide.

To add background items to all your slides:

1. Choose View > Master >Slide Master. The Slide Master appears.

2. Do any of the following to add background items:

   ◆ Use tools on the Drawing toolbar (**Figure 12.27**) to create graphical objects on the Master.

   See Chapter 10.

   ◆ Use the Text Box tool to insert text boxes on the Master.

   See Creating a Text Box in Chapter 3.

   ◆ Choose the Insert > Picture command or click the Insert Clip Art button to add graphics on the Master. 🖾

   See Inserting Clip Art and Inserting Graphics Files in Chapter 10.

3. When you're finished, click the Close button on the Master toolbar.

✔ Tips

■ To create the border shown in **Figure 12.26**, use the Rectangle tool to draw a box around the slide, and choose No Fill. Use the Line Style button to choose one of the double line styles.

■ If you've inserted a Title Master, you may choose to add background items to it also.

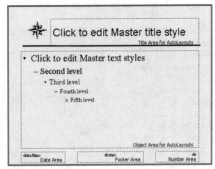

Figure 12.26 The star, line, and border are background items added on the Slide Master.

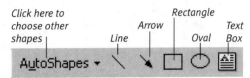

Figure 12.27 Use the tools on the Drawing toolbar to add shapes to the background of your slide.

Figure 12.28 This slide, and all other slides in the presentation, contain footers with the date, presentation title, and slide number.

Figure 12.29 The Date Area, Footer Area, and Number Area are placeholders on the Slide Master.

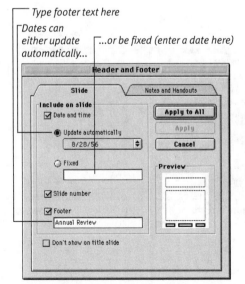

Figure 12.30 Use the Header and Footer dialog box to specify which elements to include in the footer.

Inserting Footers

With a single command, you can place a footer on each slide containing the date, customizable text (such as the presentation title), and/or the slide number (**Figure 12.28**). Footer text will be placed in the placeholders on the Slide Master (**Figure 12.29**).

To insert footers:

1. From any view, choose View > Header and Footer.

   The Header and Footer dialog box appears (**Figure 12.30**).

2. Select the checkboxes for the items you want: Date and Time, Slide Number, and/or Footer.

3. If you select Date and Time, click Update Automatically to use the current date or click Fixed to use a date that you type in.

4. If you select Footer, type your footer text in the empty text box (**Figure 12.30**).

5. To prevent the footer from appearing on title slides, select the checkbox for Don't Show on Title Slide.

6. Click Apply to All.

✔ Tips

- To format the footer text, format each footer placeholder on the Slide Master.

- To change the starting page number, choose File > Page Setup and specify a new number for Number Slides From.

Applying a Template

PowerPoint comes with built-in *templates* that include predesigned formats and color schemes. Applying a specific template to a presentation gives it a particular look that you can easily copy to other presentations. By applying a template, you can instantly change the format of the text, add background items to each slide, and adjust the colors used in the presentation. PowerPoint includes more than a dozen professionally designed templates.

Figure 12.31 shows a slide before applying a template; **Figure 12.32** shows the same slide after applying a template.

To apply a template to a presentation:

1. Choose Format > Apply Design Template (Windows) or Format > Apply Design (Mac OS).

2. If necessary, navigate to the Presentation Designs folder. (This folder is a subfolder of the Microsoft Office Templates folder.)

3. Click a template filename.

   A preview of this template is shown in the preview box (**Figure 12.33**).

4. Preview other templates, and when you find one you like, click Apply.

   The template's design is applied to all the slides in the presentation.

✔ Tips

- You can also choose a template as you are creating a new presentation.

  See Choosing a Template in Chapter 2.

- You can use any PowerPoint presentation file as a template. To select a presentation file when you're applying a template, choose All Files in the Files of Type field.

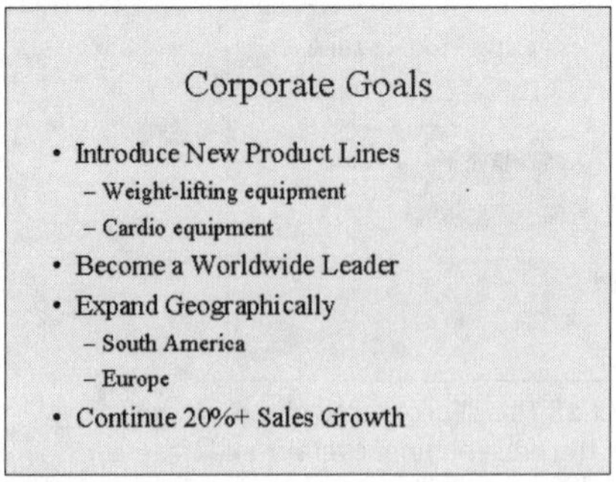

Figure 12.31 This is how the slide looks before applying a template.

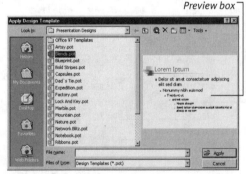

Figure 12.32 This is how the slide looks after applying a template.

Preview box

Figure 12.33 In the Apply Design Template dialog box, you can choose the template filename to apply.

WORKING IN
OUTLINE VIEW

Outline view displays each slide's title and main text, such as bulleted items, in classic outline form (**Figures 13.1** and **13.2**). Outline view is ideal for seeing the structure of your presentation, for reorganizing bulleted points, and for reordering slides. It also offers a quick way to type a series of bulleted lists. In this chapter, you will see how easy it is to type lists, insert new slides, and move slides around.

Normal view (Windows only) also displays an outline of your presentation (**Figure 13.3**). Note that everything in this chapter also applies to the outline pane in Normal view.

For more information on Normal view, see Using Normal View in Chapter 2.

Outline pane   Notes pane   Slide pane

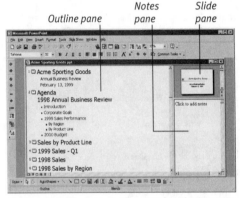

Figure 13.1 In Windows, Outline view has three panes; drag the pane borders to adjust the amount of space allocated to each area.

Outline window   Slide miniature window

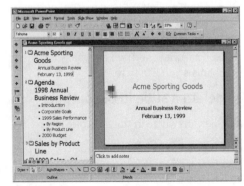

Figure 13.2 In Mac OS, Outline view displays an outline of the presentation and a slide miniature of the current slide.

Figure 13.3 Normal view also displays an outline (Windows only).

Using Outline View

While you are working in Outline view, you may notice typing mistakes or other changes you want to make to a slide.

To use Outline view:

1. Click the Outline View button near the bottom of the window.

2. Use the scroll bar, if necessary, to view additional slides in your presentation.

3. To view the slide miniature (**Figures 13.4** and **13.5**), just click anywhere in the slide's text (such as in the title).

To modify a slide when you're in Outline view:

1. To edit a slide title or other text (such as bulleted items), just edit directly on the outline.

   The slide miniature instantly reflects your changes.

2. To modify an object on the slide (such as a table, chart, or organization chart):

   ◆ Click the slide title and then click the Normal View (Windows) or Slide View button (Windows and Mac OS).

   or

   ◆ Double-click the icon in front of the slide title (Mac OS, **Figure 13.5**).

   The slide now appears in Slide (or Normal) view, and you can make any changes you like to the slide.

To delete a slide in the outline:

1. Click anywhere in the slide title or text.

2. Choose Edit > Delete Slide.

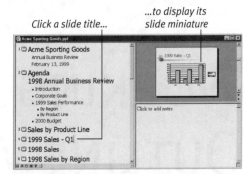

Click a slide title...   ...to display its slide miniature

Figure 13.4 It's helpful to see a miniature of the slide when you're working in Outline view (Windows).

Double-click the icon to modify the slide   Slide miniature

Figure 13.5 Click a slide title to see what the slide looks like in the slide miniature window (Mac OS).

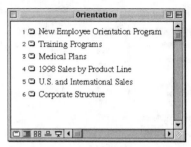

Figure 13.6 You can type your slide titles in Outline view and fill in the details later.

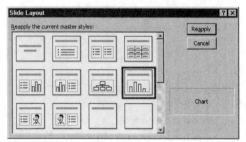

Figure 13.7 Choose a slide layout for the current slide.

Outlining a Presentation

When initially creating a presentation, you may want to focus on developing the overall content and structure rather than the detail of individual slides. You can do this by typing slide titles in Outline view (**Figure 13.6**).

Once you have typed your outline, you can go back to Slide view and complete each slide by choosing a layout type and entering the data.

To create a new outline:

1. Create a new presentation.

2. Click the Outline View button. ▤

3. For each slide, type the title and press Enter or Return.

4. When you're finished, press Ctrl+Home (Windows) or Command+Home (Mac OS) to move the cursor to the first slide.

5. Click the Slide View button. ▢

6. To change the layout for a particular slide, choose Format > Slide Layout and select the appropriate AutoLayout (**Figure 13.7**).

7. Complete the slide by entering its data.

8. Go to the next slide and repeat steps 6 and 7.

✔ Tip

- While creating your outline, you may find it convenient to type bulleted lists as you go.

  See Creating Bulleted Lists on the next page.

OUTLINING A PRESENTATION

Creating Bulleted Lists

Outline view offers a quick way to create and type bulleted lists.

To create a new bulleted list slide:

1. Click at the beginning of a slide title in the outline where you want to insert a slide.

2. Press Enter or Return.

   A new slide appears before the current one (**Figure 13.8**).

3. Press the up arrow key to place the cursor on the new slide.

4. Type the slide title and press Ctrl+Enter (Windows) or Option+Return (Mac OS).

   A blank bulleted line is inserted.

5. Type the bulleted item and press Enter or Return.

6. Continue typing bulleted items, following the same rules you do in Slide view:

   ◆ Press Enter or Return to type another line of the same level as the previous one.

   ◆ Press Tab to indent the current line (**Figure 13.9**).

   ◆ Press Shift+Tab to outdent the current line.

7. To create another slide, press Ctrl+Enter (Windows) or Option+Return (Mac OS) after the last bullet in the list.

✔ Tips

■ To create a two-line title (such as the one used in Slide 2 in **Figure 13.9**), press Shift+Enter or Shift+Return after the first line.

■ To change the level of a line, use the Promote or Demote button. ⬍

New slide

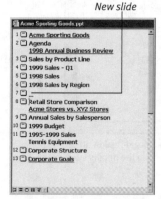

Figure 13.8 Press Enter or Return and a new slide appears.

Press Tab to insert a bullet

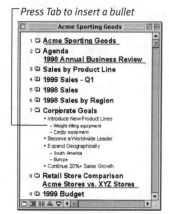

Figure 13.9 Type your bulleted lists in Outline view just as you do in Slide view.

A gray line indicates
the slide is collapsed

Figure 13.10 In this outline, only
the slide titles are displayed.

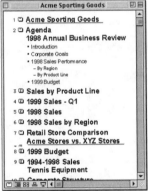

Figure 13.11 The text in slide 2 is
expanded; the text in other slides
is collapsed.

Collapsing and Expanding the Outline

You can get a better idea of your presentation's structure by hiding the main text on your slides and displaying only the slide titles (**Figure 13.10**). This way, you can see how the information flows. Furthermore, when text is hidden, you can see more slides in the window.

When you hide text, you are *collapsing* the outline. When you redisplay hidden text, you are *expanding* the outline. **Figure 13.11** shows an outline in which some text is collapsed and some is expanded.

To collapse outline text:

1. If the Outlining toolbar isn't displayed, choose View > Toolbars > Outlining.

2. To collapse the entire outline, click the Collapse All button on the Outlining toolbar.

   or

   To collapse the currently selected slide(s), click the Collapse button.

To expand outline text:

1. To expand the entire outline, click the Expand All button on the Outlining toolbar.

   or

2. To expand the currently selected slide(s), click the Expand button.

✔ Tips

■ Another way to collapse or expand the text in a single slide is to double-click the slide's icon (Windows only).

■ You can also right-click the slide text and choose Expand or Collapse from the shortcut menu (Windows only).

Reordering the Slides

Because the outline shows many slides at once, Outline view (or the outline pane in Normal view) is ideal for repositioning slides in a presentation. You can use either the Move buttons on the Outlining toolbar or the drag-and-drop technique.

To reposition a slide with the Move buttons:

1. If the Outlining toolbar isn't displayed, choose View > Toolbars > Outlining.

2. Click the Collapse All button on the Outlining toolbar so that only slide titles are displayed (**Figure 13.12**).

3. Click anywhere in the title of the slide you want to move.

4. Click the Move Up or Move Down button (**Figure 13.12**) until the slide is in the position you want.

To reposition a slide with the drag-and-drop technique:

1. Click the Collapse All button so that only slide titles are displayed.

2. Drag the slide icon for the slide you want to move (**Figure 13.13**).

   A horizontal line indicates where the slide will be inserted.

3. When the horizontal line is in position, release the mouse button.

✔ Tip

■ When the target location cannot be seen on the screen, you might find it easier to move slides by cutting and pasting them.

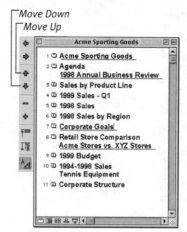

Move Down
Move Up

Figure 13.12 Reordering slides is easier if only the slide titles are displayed.

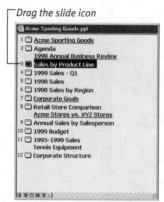

Drag the slide icon

Figure 13.13 You can move a slide with the drag-and-drop technique.

REORDERING THE SLIDES

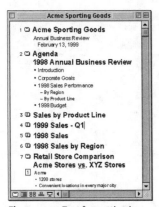

Figure 13.14 Text formatting is displayed in this outline.

Figure 13.15 Formatting is hidden in this outline.

Hiding and Displaying Formatting

As you can see in **Figure 13.14**, Outline view can show text formatting and display the actual bullet symbols for bulleted list slides. While there are times when you may want to see the formatting, at other times it may be distracting. At those times, you can choose to hide the formatting and work only with the text (**Figure 13.15**).

To hide or display text formatting:

1. If the Outlining toolbar isn't displayed along the left edge of the window, choose View > Toolbars > Outlining.

2. Click the Show Formatting button to toggle the formatting on and off.

✔ Tips

■ When formatting is hidden, you can see more slides in the outline.

■ Another way to hide and display formatting is by pressing the slash key (/) on the numeric keypad.

HIDING AND DISPLAYING FORMATTING

Importing an Outline

If you have created an outline in your word processor (**Figure 13.16**), you can bring it into PowerPoint by importing the outline into an existing presentation or by opening the outline as its own stand-alone presentation.

If you intend to create an outline in your word processor and then import it into PowerPoint, make sure it conforms to the following rules:

◆ Each title must be in its own paragraph.

◆ Two-line slide titles must have a new line character (not a new paragraph) between the lines.

◆ Bulleted items must be indented with the Tab key (don't insert bullet symbols).

To insert an outline into an existing presentation:

1. Choose Insert > Slides from Outline.
The Insert Outline dialog box appears (**Figure 13.17**).

2. Navigate to the folder in which your outline is stored.

3. Double-click the name of the outline file.

To create a new presentation by opening an outline:

1. Choose File > Open.

2. In the Files of Type field, choose All Outlines (**Figure 13.18**).

3. Navigate to the folder in which your outline is stored.

4. Double-click the name of the outline file.

✔ Tip

■ PowerPoint can import outlines from a variety of programs; your choices depend on which import filters you selected during installation.

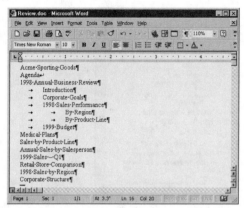

Figure 13.16 You can type an outline in your word processor and then import or open it in PowerPoint.

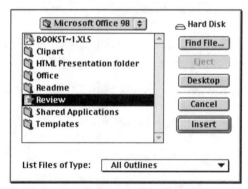

Figure 13.17 Use the Insert > Slides from Outline command and choose an outline to insert into a presentation. (A Mac OS dialog box is shown here.)

Figure 13.18 By opening an outline file, PowerPoint automatically creates a new presentation from the outline. (A Windows dialog box is shown here.)

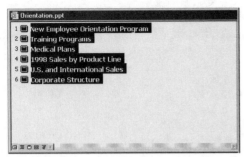

Figure 13.19 To create a summary slide, select all the slides and then click the Summary Slide button.

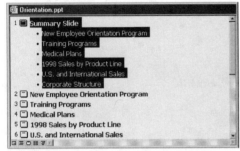

Figure 13.20 The summary slide lists the titles of all the slides in the presentation.

Creating a Summary Slide (Windows Only)

You can quickly summarize the slides in your presentation by creating a *summary slide*. A summary slide is a bulleted list that PowerPoint automatically creates from your slide titles.

To create a summary slide:

1. Select all the slides in the outline (**Figure 13.19**).

2. If the Outlining toolbar isn't displayed, choose View > Toolbars > Outlining.

3. Click the Summary Slide button on the Outlining toolbar.

   The summary slide appears at the beginning of the outline (**Figure 13.20**). Depending on the number of slides you selected, the summary may be continued on additional slides.

4. Select and delete any bulleted lines you don't want in the summary.

5. If PowerPoint created a second summary slide and you want to consolidate the summary on a single slide, select the bullets on the second slide and click the Move Up button.

6. Change the title of the summary slide, if desired.

7. Move the summary slide where you want it to appear in the presentation.

✔ Tips

- You can also create a summary slide in Slide Sorter view. The advantage to using this view is that you can choose which slides you want to include in the summary.

- To fit more items on your summary slide, you may need to choose a smaller font size. (But make sure that the text is still legible.)

WORKING IN
SLIDE SORTER VIEW

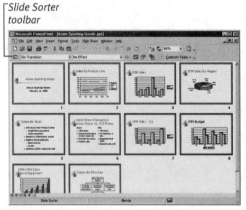

Figure 14.1 In Slide Sorter view, you can see many slides at once.

Slide Sorter view shows miniatures of each slide in your presentation (**Figure 14.1**). It's similar to Outline view in that you see many slides at once, but in Slide Sorter view you have the advantage of seeing the images of all the slides, including objects (charts, tables, and so forth).

Slide Sorter view lets you observe the flow of your presentation and reorder your slides, if necessary. You can easily copy and delete slides as well. This view is also useful for copying and moving slides to other presentations and for instantly viewing the effects of global changes to your presentation (applying a template, changing the color scheme, etc.). See Chapter 12 for information on making global changes.

Slide Sorter view is also useful when adding slide show effects; see Chapter 15 for further details.

Using Slide Sorter View

Slide Sorter view gives you the best overall look at the flow of your presentation and its graphical elements. It's simple to delete and reorder slides in this view, and if you decide to modify a particular slide, you can easily switch to a view that allows editing.

To use Slide Sorter view:

1. Click the Slide Sorter View button near the bottom of the window. ⊞

2. If necessary, use the scroll bar or zoom in to view additional slides.

See Zooming In and Out on the next page.

To modify a slide while in Slide Sorter view:

◆ Click the slide and then click the Slide View or Normal View button (Windows).

   or

   Double-click the slide (Mac OS).

   The slide now appears in Slide (or Normal) view, and you can make any changes you like to the slide.

To delete a slide:

1. Click the slide you want to delete.

   or

   To select multiple slides, hold down Ctrl (Windows) or Shift (Mac OS) as you click each one (**Figure 14.2**).

2. Press Delete or choose Edit > Delete Slide.

✔ Tips

■ Double-clicking a slide in Slide Sorter view returns you to the last view you were in (Windows only).

■ If you accidentally delete slides, immediately choose Edit > Undo.

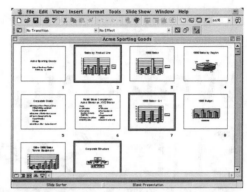

Figure 14.2 Three slides are selected for deletion.

Zoom field

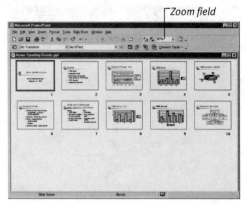

Figure 14.3 When you zoom out to 50%, you can see more slides.

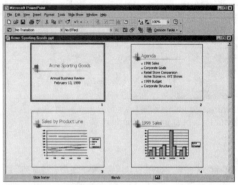

Figure 14.4 When you zoom in to 100%, you can see more detail on each slide.

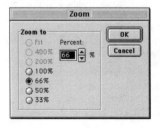

Figure 14.5 Choose a zoom percentage, or enter any value between 20 and 100 in the Percent field.

Zooming In and Out

You can control the number of slides you see in Slide Sorter view, as well as the level of detail, by zooming in and out. To see more slides, zoom out (**Figure 14.3**). To see more detail, zoom in (**Figure 14.4**).

To zoom in and out:

◆ Click the arrow in the Zoom field in the Standard toolbar (**Figure 14.3**) to display a list of zoom percentages. Then click the desired number.

or

Click the percentage in the Zoom field, type a number between 20 and 100, and press Enter or Return.

or

Choose View > Zoom and choose the desired zoom percentage in the Zoom dialog box (**Figure 14.5**).

ZOOMING IN AND OUT

Creating a Summary Slide (Windows Only)

As mentioned in Chapter 13, a *summary slide* lists the topics covered in your presentation (**Figure 14.6**). Creating a summary slide in Slide Sorter view offers one main advantage over Outline view: you can pick and choose which slides to include in the summary.

See also Creating a Summary Slide in Chapter 13.

To create a summary slide:

1. Hold down Ctrl and click each slide you want in the summary (**Figure 14.7**).

2. Click the Summary Slide button on the Slide Sorter toolbar.

   The summary slide appears before the first slide in your selection (**Figure 14.6**). (Depending on the number of slides you selected, the summary may be continued on additional slides.)

3. To edit the summary slide, click the slide and switch to Normal or Outline view.

✔ Tips

- After you have created a summary slide, you can move it to any location in the presentation.

  See Reordering the Slides on the next page.

- If PowerPoint creates your summary on several slides (**Figure 14.8**) and you prefer to fit it on one, you may need to choose a smaller font size (but make sure that the text is still legible). You can then move the text onto the first slide to consolidate it.

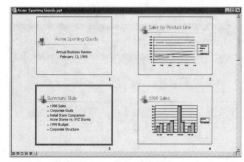

Figure 14.6 Slide 3 is a summary slide.

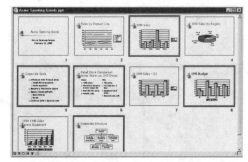

Figure 14.7 Select only the slides whose titles you want to appear on the summary slide.

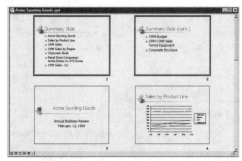

Figure 14.8 PowerPoint creates multiple summary slides if all the topics can't fit on one slide.

The slide will be moved here

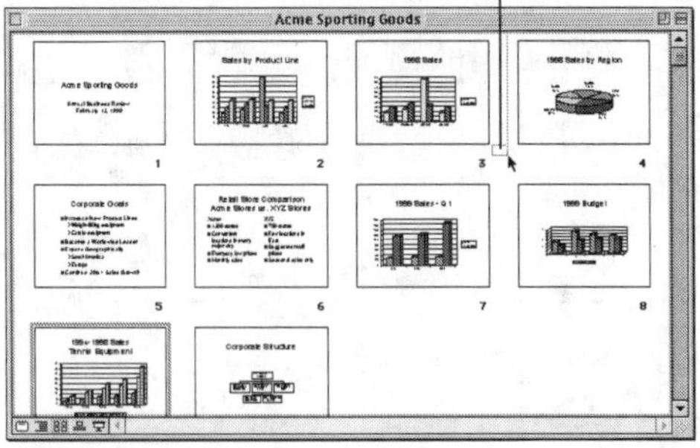

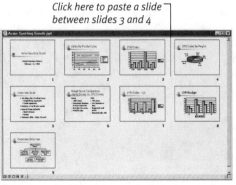

Figure 14.9 When you are dragging a slide, a vertical line indicates where PowerPoint will insert the slide when you release the mouse button.

Slide 9 is selected

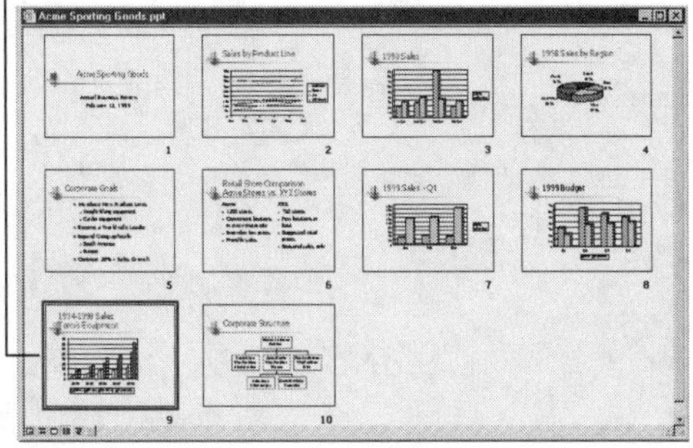

Figure 14.10 Select a slide before you cut it.

Click here to paste a slide between slides 3 and 4

Figure 14.11 Position the cursor before you paste it.

Reordering the Slides

Because you can see many slides at once in Slide Sorter view, it is the ideal view for rearranging your presentation. PowerPoint offers two ways to move slides in this view.

To move slides with the drag-and-drop technique:

1. Zoom out until you can see the slide you want to move as well as the destination (if possible).

2. Drag the slide you want to move.

   A vertical line follows the mouse pointer to indicate where the slide will be inserted (**Figure 14.9**).

3. When the vertical line is in the correct position, release the mouse button.

To move slides with the cut-and-paste technique:

1. Click the slide you want to move (**Figure 14.10**) to select it.

2. Click the Cut button on the Standard toolbar. ✂

   The slide disappears.

3. Click the space after the slide where you want to move the cut slide (**Figure 14.11**).

   A vertical line indicates where the slide will be inserted.

4. Click the Paste button to insert the slide. 📋

✔ Tip

- When you rearrange slides, they are renumbered automatically.

REORDERING THE SLIDES

Copying Slides

Sometimes you may want to create a slide that is similar to an existing one. Rather than creating the new slide from scratch, you can create a copy of the existing slide and then make any necessary revisions.

PowerPoint offers three ways to copy a slide: you can duplicate it as you drag it (sometimes known as "drag-and-dupe"), use the Duplicate command, or copy and paste it.

To copy a slide with the "drag-and-dupe" technique:

1. Zoom out until you can see the slide you want to copy as well as the destination (if possible).

2. Hold down Ctrl (Windows) or Option (Mac OS) and drag the slide you want to copy (**Figure 14.12**).

   A vertical line follows the pointer to indicate where the copy will be inserted.

3. When the vertical line is in the correct position, release the mouse button.

   The duplicate slide appears.

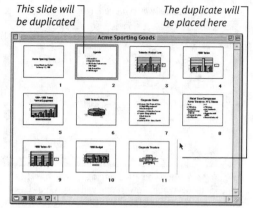

This slide will be duplicated

The duplicate will be placed here

Figure 14.12 To "drag and dupe" (duplicate) a slide, hold down Ctrl (Windows) or Option (Mac OS) as you drag.

Original ⌐   ⌐ Copy

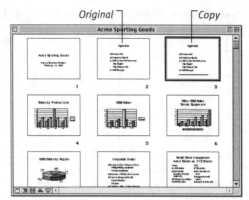

Figure 14.13 When you use the Edit > Duplicate command, the duplicate appears to the right of the original.

Select the slide ⌐
and copy it...

...then click the
destination and
paste the slide

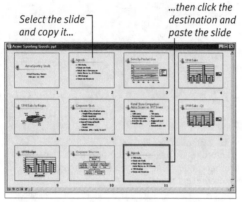

Figure 14.14 The third way to copy a slide is with the Copy and Paste commands.

To duplicate a slide:

1. Select the slide to be copied.

2. Choose Edit > Duplicate.

   A copy appears to the right of the original (**Figure 14.13**).

3. Drag the copy into place, if necessary.

To copy and paste a slide:

1. Click the slide to be copied (**Figure 14.14**).

2. Click the Copy button on the Standard toolbar.

3. Click where you want to insert the copy.

4. Click the Paste button to insert a copy of the slide (**Figure 14.14**).

COPYING SLIDES

Moving Slides Between Presentations

If a presentation gets so large that it becomes unwieldy, you may want to divide it into two or more files. You can do this by moving some of the slides into a new presentation. Or, you may need to rearrange slides between two existing presentations.

To move slides into another presentation:

1. Open the presentation that contains the slides to be moved.

2. To move slides into an existing presentation, open it also.

   or

   To move slides into a new presentation, use the File > New command.

3. Switch each presentation to Slide Sorter view and then choose Window > Arrange All (**Figure 14.15**).

4. Hold down Ctrl (Windows) or Shift (Mac OS) as you click each slide to be moved.

5. **Windows:** Drag one of the selected slides to the other presentation (**Figure 14.16**).

   Mac OS: Press Option and Command as you drag one of the selected slides to the other presentation.

6. When the vertical line is positioned where you want to insert the slides, release the mouse button.

7. **Mac OS only:** Choose Move Here from the shortcut menu.

✔ Tip

■ To format the new presentation the same as the original one, choose Format > Apply Design and select the original presentation file (**Figure 14.17**).

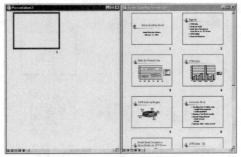

Figure 14.15 It's easy to move slides between presentations when you can see both of them on the screen.

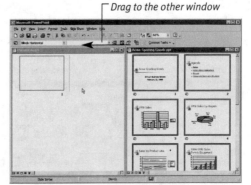

Figure 14.16 Drag any of the selected slides to the other window, and all the slides will move into the new presentation.

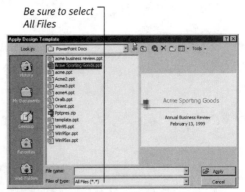

Figure 14.17 To format the new presentation the same as the original, apply the design of the original file.

Click Browse to select a file

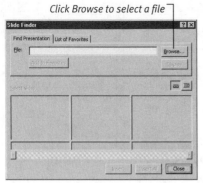

Figure 14.18 The Slide Finder dialog box helps you find the slide you want to copy to another presentation.

Figure 14.19 In the Browse dialog box, select the file containing the slides you want to copy.

Click the scroll bar to view more slides

Selected slide

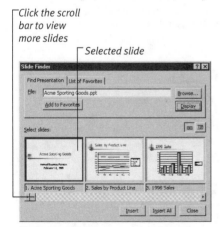

Figure 14.20 You can now select the slides you want to insert into the current presentation.

Copying Slides Between Presentations (Windows)

Using the Insert > Slides from Files command, you can copy slides from any presentation into the one that is currently open.

To insert slides from another presentation:

1. Open the presentation into which you want to insert the slides.

2. In Slide Sorter view, click after the slide where you want the slides to be inserted.

3. Choose Insert > Slides from Files to open the Slide Finder dialog box (**Figure 14.18**).

4. Click Browse to display the Browse dialog box (**Figure 14.19**).

5. Navigate to the folder containing the file with the slides you want to copy.

6. Select the filename and click Open.

7. To see the slides, click Display. Miniatures of the first three slides appear (**Figure 14.20**).

8. Hold down Ctrl as you click each slide you want to insert.

9. When you're finished selecting slides from this file, click Insert.

10. To insert slides from another presentation, repeat steps 4 through 9 above.

11. Click Close.

✔ Tips

■ You can also copy slides between presentations by opening both files, arranging the windows, and holding down Ctrl as you drag.

■ The copied slides use the Slide Master and color scheme of the target presentation.

Copying Slides Between Presentations (Mac OS)

Sometimes while working on a presentation you'll realize that you want to use slides in another presentation. By having both presentations open at the same time (**Figure 14.21**), you can copy slides from one to the other.

To copy slides between presentations:

1. Open both presentations, and switch to Slide Sorter view in each one.

2. Choose Window > Arrange All to display the two presentations side by side.

3. Click the slide to be copied.

   or

   To copy more than one slide, hold down Shift as you click each one.

   A thick border appears around each selected slide (**Figure 14.22**).

4. Hold down Option and drag one of the slides to the other presentation window.

   When the pointer is between slides, a vertical line indicates where the copies will be inserted.

5. When the vertical line is in position, release the mouse button.

✔ Tip

- The copied slides will adopt the Slide Master and color scheme of the target presentation.

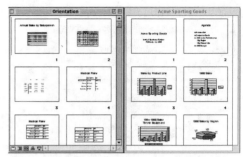

Figure 14.21 Use side-by-side windows to copy slides between presentations.

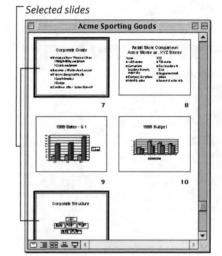

Figure 14.22 To select multiple slides, hold down Shift as you click each slide.

COPYING SLIDES BETWEEN PRESENTATIONS

Click Browse to select a file

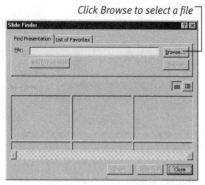

Figure 14.23 Choose Insert > Slides from Files to open the Slide Finder dialog box.

Figure 14.24 In the Browse dialog box, select the file containing the slides you want to copy.

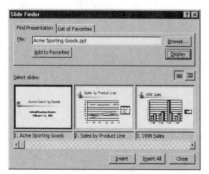

Figure 14.25 Click Insert All to copy all the slides in the file.

Inserting an Entire Presentation (Windows)

PowerPoint for Windows offers an easy way to consolidate presentations when you want to copy all the slides from one presentation into another. This is useful when you need to combine the slides created by several individuals into a single presentation.

To insert an entire presentation:

1. Open the presentation into which you want to copy the slides.

2. In Slide Sorter view, click after the slide where you want the slides to be inserted. A vertical line appears.

3. Choose Insert > Slides from Files. The Slide Finder dialog box appears (**Figure 14.23**).

4. Click Browse. The Browse dialog box appears (**Figure 14.24**).

5. Navigate to the folder containing the file to be consolidated.

6. Select the filename and click Open.

7. To see the slides in this presentation, click Display. Miniatures of the first three slides appear (**Figure 14.25**).

8. Click Insert All to copy the slides into the presentation.

9. Click Close.

All the slides from the selected presentation are inserted into the current one.

✔ Tip

- All the slides adopt the Slide Master and color scheme of the current presentation.

Inserting an Entire Presentation (Mac OS)

PowerPoint offers an easy way to consolidate presentations when you want to copy all the slides from one presentation into another. This is useful when you need to combine the slides created by several individuals into a single presentation.

To insert an entire presentation:

1. Open the presentation into which you want to copy the slides.

2. In Slide Sorter view, click after the slide where you want the slides to be inserted. A vertical line appears.

3. Choose Insert > Slides from File.

4. Navigate to the folder containing the presentation file you want to insert (**Figure 14.26**).

5. Select the file and click Insert.

   All the slides from the selected presentation file are inserted into the current presentation.

✔ Tip

■ The slides adopt the Slide Master and color scheme of the presentation into which they are inserted.

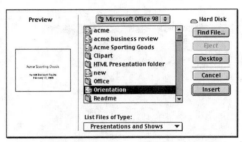

Figure 14.26 Select the file containing the slides you want to copy.

PRODUCING A SLIDE SHOW

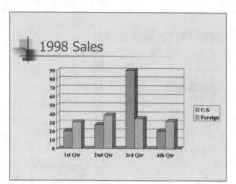

Figure 15.1 Slides are presented full screen during a slide show.

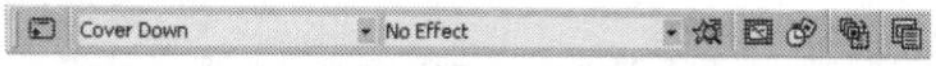

Figure 15.2 The Slide Sorter toolbar includes several tools specific to slide shows.

PowerPoint's *slide show* feature displays one slide at a time, full screen (**Figure 15.1**). You can use this feature to show your presentation to an audience or merely to preview it yourself. Since your computer becomes the equivalent of a slide projector, you can see how your presentation will look to your audience. In this full-screen view, you can concentrate on individual slides and perhaps spot mistakes you may have missed in the other views. However, you cannot edit slides during a slide show.

When you're ready for an audience, you can present your slide show directly on your monitor with one or two people looking over your shoulder; or, for a larger audience, you can project the show onto a big screen. Projection requires special equipment; you will need either an LCD (Liquid Crystal Display) panel and an overhead projector or an RGB (Red Green Blue) projector. Projecting a slide show in this manner saves you the time and expense of producing 35mm slides and also allows you to make last-minute changes.

Because the Slide Sorter toolbar (**Figure 15.2**) contains options for slide shows, you will frequently want to be in Slide Sorter view when working on your slide show.

See Chapter 14 for more information on Slide Sorter view.

Organizing a Slide Show

During a slide show, slides are displayed in the order they appear in your presentation. Therefore, before presenting your slide show, you should give some thought to the order of your slides and rearrange them if necessary.

To change the slide order, move the slides in Slide Sorter view (**Figure 15.3**) or Outline view (**Figure 15.4**).

See Reordering the Slides in Chapters 13 and 14.

You can omit a slide from a slide show by *hiding* it. Note that hidden slides remain in your presentation and appear in all other views.

To hide a slide:

1. In Slide Sorter view, click the slide you want to hide.

   or

   To select more than one slide, hold down Ctrl (Windows) or Shift (Mac OS) as you click each slide.

2. Click the Hide Slide button on the Slide Sorter toolbar (**Figure 15.5**).

   The number of the hidden slide is displayed with a slash (**Figure 15.6**).

✔ Tips

- To redisplay a hidden slide, select the slide, and click the Hide Slide button.

- You can hide slides in any view using the Slide Show > Hide Slide command. However, only Slide Sorter view has a visual indication that a slide is hidden.

- Another way to hide a slide is to right-click (Windows) or Control+click (Mac OS) the slide in Slide Sorter view and choose Hide Slide from the shortcut menu.

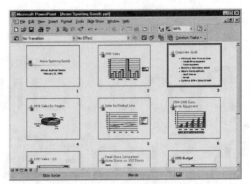

Figure 15.3 Slide Sorter view offers a convenient way to organize your slides for a slide show.

Figure 15.4 You can also organize your slides in Outline view.

⌐Hide Slide

Figure 15.5 Use the Hide Slide button to keep a slide from appearing in a slide show.

⌐ The slash across the slide number indicates the slide will be hidden during a slide show

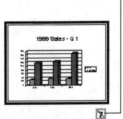

Figure 15.6 Slide 7 will be hidden during a slide show.

Slide Show

Figure 15.7 Use the Slide Show button to begin a slide show.

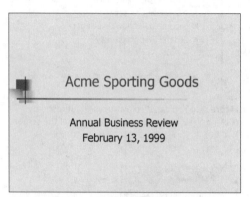

Acme Sporting Goods

Annual Business Review
February 13, 1999

Figure 15.8 When you click the Slide Show button, the current slide is displayed full screen.

Table 15.1

Navigating a Slide Show	
TO GO TO THE...	PRESS...
Next slide	Page Down
	Down Arrow
	Right Arrow
	Spacebar
	Enter or Return
Previous slide	Page Up
	Up Arrow
	Left Arrow
	Backspace (Windows)
	Delete (Mac OS)
First slide	Home
Last slide	End
Specific slide	Slide number and Enter or Return

Displaying a Slide Show

It's easy to display an onscreen slide show in PowerPoint.

To display a slide show:

1. In any view, press Ctrl+Home (Windows) or Command+Home (Mac OS) to go to the first slide in the presentation.

2. Click the Slide Show button (**Figure 15.7**).

   The slide appears full screen (**Figure 15.8**).

3. Press Page Down to view the next slide.

4. Press Page Down until you have viewed all the slides.

   or

   Press Esc to cancel the slide show.

✔ Tips

- Pressing F5 displays the slide show starting at the beginning of the presentation (Windows only).

- You can also display the next slide in the show by pressing the mouse button (the left button on a two-button mouse). See **Table 15.1** for other ways to navigate a slide show.

Navigating to a Slide

PowerPoint comes with a way to jump to any slide during a slide show by choosing the slide title from a list.

To navigate to a slide:

1. Start the slide show.

2. Display the shortcut menu using one of the following techniques:
   ◆ Right-click (Windows) or Control + click (Mac OS).
   ◆ Move the mouse pointer around, and click the icon that appears in the lower-left corner of the screen (**Figure 15.9**).

3. Choose Go > By Title (**Figure 15.10**). A list of slide titles appears (**Figure 15.11**).

4. Click the title of the slide you want to view.

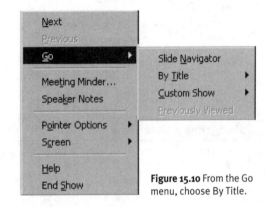

⌐ This icon doesn't appear until you start moving the mouse

Corporate Goals

- Introduce New Product Lines
  - ➤ Weight-lifting equipment
  - ➤ Cardio equipment
- Become a Worldwide Leader
- Expand Geographically
  - ➤ South America
  - ➤ Europe
- Continue 20%+ Sales Growth

Figure 15.9 You can display the shortcut menu by clicking the icon in the lower-left corner of the screen.

| Next |
| Previous |
| Go ▶ |
| Meeting Minder... |
| Speaker Notes |
| Pointer Options ▶ |
| Screen ▶ |
| Help |
| End Show |

| Slide Navigator |
| By Title ▶ |
| Custom Show ▶ |
| Previously Viewed |

Figure 15.10 From the Go menu, choose By Title.

1 Acme Sporting Goods
2 Agenda
3 1998 Sales
4 1998 Sales by Region
5 Sales by Product Line
6 1994-1998 Sales Tennis Equipment
7 1999 Sales - Q1
✓ 8 Retail Store Comparison Acme Sto
9 1999 Budget
10 Corporate Goals
11 Corporate Structure
Slide Navigator

Figure 15.11 Select the slide title from the list.

Custom

Figure 15.12 Select an action button.

Click here to display the list

Figure 15.13 To branch to a specific slide, choose Slide in the Hyperlink To list.

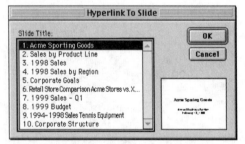

Figure 15.14 After selecting Slide in the Hyperlink To list, PowerPoint offers a list of slide titles to branch to.

To add more dimension to the button, drag the diamond handle down and to the right

Figure 15.15 This action button was formatted.

To resize, drag any square handle

To label the button, select it and type the desired text

Creating Action Buttons

In addition to keyboard shortcuts and navigating by title, PowerPoint offers another way to jump to a slide in a slide show. You can create an *action button* on any slide, and program it to jump to another specific slide during a show. This branching is faster and more seamless than navigating by title, since the audience sees no menus on-screen.

To create an action button:

1. In Slide view, go to the slide on which you want to create the action button.

2. Click AutoShapes on the Drawing toolbar.

3. Choose Action Buttons.

4. Choose the Custom button (**Figure 15.12**).

5. Drag a rectangular shape on the slide where you want the button to go.

   When you release the mouse button, the Action Settings dialog box appears.

6. Click the Hyperlink To radio button, select Slide (**Figure 15.13**), and choose the destination slide for your jump (**Figure 15.14**).

7. Click OK to close the dialog box.

   The action button appears on the slide.

8. Format and resize the button as needed (**Figure 15.15**).

9. To make sure the button works properly, start the slide show and then click the action button. The presentation should jump directly to the slide you selected.

✔ Tips

- Action buttons function only in a slide show.

- You can create an action button with the Slide Show > Action Buttons command.

Creating a Return Button

If you create an action button that branches to another slide, you will probably want an easy way to return. You can create a return button that allows you to resume your presentation at the point where you were before your detour.

To create a return button:

1. In Slide view, go to the slide on which you want to create the return button.

2. Click AutoShapes on the Drawing toolbar.

3. Choose Action Buttons.

4. Choose the Return (Windows) or Last Slide Viewed (Mac OS) button type (**Figure 15.16**).

5. Drag a rectangular shape on the slide where you want the button to go.

   When you release the mouse button, the Action Settings dialog box appears. The Hyperlink To field defaults to Last Slide Viewed (**Figure 15.17**).

6. Click OK to close the dialog box.

   The return button appears on the slide (**Figure 15.18**).

7. Format and resize the button as needed.

✔ Tips

- You can also create action buttons that go to the first or last slide, open other files, jump to Web sites, or launch multimedia events.

- To modify an action button, select the button and then choose Slide Show > Action Settings.

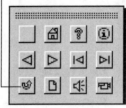

Figure 15.16 Select the Return (Windows) or Last Slide Viewed (Mac OS) action button.

Figure 15.17 The hyperlink is automatically set to Last Slide Viewed.

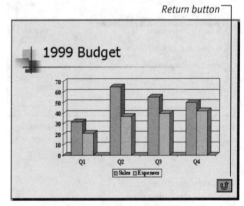

Figure 15.18 Clicking the return button in a slide show will branch to the previously-viewed location.

These slides are selected *Slide Show Name field*

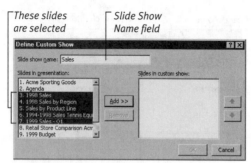

Figure 15.19 Select the slides you want to include in the custom show.

After you click Add... *...the slides are added to the custom show*

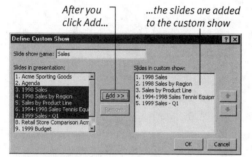

Figure 15.20 Click the Add button to add the selected slides to the current custom show.

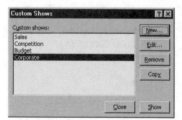

Figure 15.21 This presentation has four custom shows.

Creating Custom Shows

Think of a *custom show* as a "show within a show." You can assign names to the different parts of your presentation and then quickly go to these areas during a slide show.

To create a custom show:

1. Choose Slide Show > Custom Shows.
   The Custom Shows dialog box appears.

2. Click New.
   The Define Custom Show dialog box appears.

3. In the Slide Show Name field, type a descriptive name for the custom show.

4. In the Slides in Presentation list, hold down Ctrl (Windows) or Shift (Mac OS) and click each slide title that is to be part of the custom show (**Figure 15.19**).

5. Click Add.
   The selected slide titles now appear in the Slides in Custom Show list (**Figure 15.20**).

6. Click OK.
   The Custom Shows dialog box lists the custom shows you have created (**Figure 15.21**).

7. Repeat steps 2 through 6 to define additional custom shows.

8. When you're finished, click Close.

✔ Tip

■ To modify a custom show, choose Slide Show > Custom Shows, select the show's name, and click Edit.

CREATING CUSTOM SHOWS

Viewing a Custom Show

You can start a custom slide show from any PowerPoint view, or you can jump to the different custom shows while you are giving a presentation.

To view a custom show:

1. Choose Slide Show > Custom Shows.

2. Click the name of the show you want to view (**Figure 15.22**).

3. Click Show.

   The first slide in the custom show is displayed.

4. Press Page Down until you have viewed all the slides in the custom show.

To jump to a custom show:

1. During a slide show, right-click (Windows) or Control+click (Mac OS) to display the shortcut menu.

2. Choose Go > Custom Show (**Figure 15.23**).

3. Select the name of the custom show you want to see (**Figure 15.24**).

   The first slide in the custom show is displayed.

4. Press Page Down to view other slides in the custom show.

✔ Tip

- It's helpful to display an empty black slide after the last slide in a show so that you have the opportunity to immediately select another custom show. To display an empty black slide at the end of a show, choose Tools > Options (Windows) or Tools > Preferences (Mac OS), select the View tab, and then click the End With Black Slide checkbox.

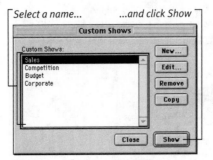
Select a name...   ...and click Show

Figure 15.22 To view a custom show, choose its name in the Custom Shows dialog box.

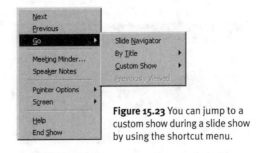

Figure 15.23 You can jump to a custom show during a slide show by using the shortcut menu.

Figure 15.24 Select the name of the custom show.

The underlining indicates a hyperlink

Figure 15.25 An agenda slide offers hyperlinks to custom shows.

Click here to display the list

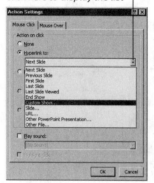

Figure 15.26 Create a hyperlink to a custom show in the Action Settings dialog box.

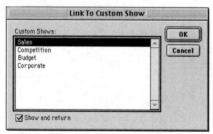

Figure 15.27 Select the name of the custom show you want to link to.

Creating an Agenda Slide

An *agenda slide* (**Figure 15.25**) is a slide with a simple list of hyperlinked topics. Each topic is linked to a custom show pertaining to one area of your presentation. When you click an item on the agenda slide during a slide show, PowerPoint displays the custom show and then returns to the agenda slide.

Agenda slides are useful for dividing your presentation into logical areas and keeping the audience tuned in to where you are in the presentation.

To create an agenda slide:

1. Create a custom show for each of the sections in your presentation.

   See Creating Custom Shows earlier in this chapter.

2. Create a new slide with the Bulleted List layout.

3. Enter a title (such as *Agenda*) and type bulleted items to describe each of the sections in your presentation.

4. Select all the text in a bulleted item.

5. Choose Slide Show > Action Settings.

6. Click the Hyperlink To radio button and choose Custom Show (**Figure 15.26**).

7. From the Link to Custom Show dialog box, select the show to which you want to jump (**Figure 15.27**).

8. Select the Show and Return checkbox.

9. Click OK twice to close both dialog boxes.

   The bulleted item is now underlined, indicating a hyperlink (**Figure 15.25**).

10. Repeat steps 4 through 9 for each item.

✔ Tip

- Hyperlinks function only in a slide show.

Annotating a Slide

During a slide show, you may want to mark a slide to emphasize a point. Using your mouse like a marking pen, you can draw circles, lines, arrows, and so forth (**Figure 15.28**). These annotations are temporary, and as soon as you move on to the next slide in the show, your freehand drawings disappear.

To annotate a slide:

1. During a slide show, press Ctrl+P (Windows) or Command+P (Mac OS) to display the pen. (If you don't see the pen right away, move the mouse slightly.)

2. Position the pen where you want to make an annotation and click and drag the mouse.

3. To turn off Annotation mode, you have several alternatives:
   - Press Esc, Ctrl+A (Windows) or Command+A (Mac OS) to exit and display the mouse pointer.
   - Press Ctrl+H (Windows) or Command+H (Mac OS) to exit and hide both the pen and the pointer.

✔ Tips

- To erase all annotations on a slide, press E.

- To draw straight lines, hold down Shift as you drag.

- While in Annotation mode, you can't use the mouse button to advance slides. Keyboard navigation keys such as the arrow keys, however, will still operate. Note that once you leave a slide, all its annotations disappear.

- To choose a different pen color, right-click (Windows) or Control+click (Mac OS) during the show, choose Pointer Options > Pen Color, and choose a color (**Figure 15.29**).

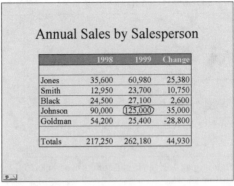

Annual Sales by Salesperson

	1998	1999	Change
Jones	35,600	60,980	25,380
Smith	12,950	23,700	10,750
Black	24,500	27,100	2,600
Johnson	90,000	125,000	35,000
Goldman	54,200	25,400	-28,800
Totals	217,250	262,180	44,930

Figure 15.28 The number 125,000 was circled during a slide show.

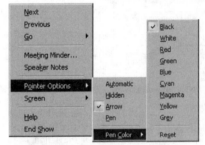

Figure 15.29 To change the annotation pen color, right-click or Control + click to bring up the shortcut menu.

Slide Transition Effects field ⌐*Selected slide*

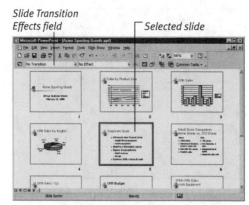

Figure 15.30 In Slide Sorter view, select the slide(s) and then choose a transition effect.

Figure 15.31 Choose an effect from the list.

Figure 15.32 To preview the effect, click the transition icon.

— *Transition icon*

Adding a Transition Effect to a Slide

Transition effects control how slides are displayed on the screen during a slide show. Transition effects not only hold the attention of your audience, but they also add a professional touch.

To apply slide transition effects:

1. Switch to Slide Sorter view.

2. Select the slide for which you want to add a transition effect (**Figure 15.30**).

   or

   To apply the same transition effect to multiple slides, hold down Ctrl (Windows) or Shift (Mac OS) as you click each slide.

3. On the Slide Sorter toolbar, click the Slide Transition Effects field (**Figure 15.30**) to display the list of effects (**Figure 15.31**).

4. Click the desired transition effect.

   Immediately after you choose an effect, the first selected slide is drawn with that effect to show you what it looks like.

5. Repeat steps 2-4 to apply transition effects to other slides.

6. To see the effects during a slide show, press Ctrl+Home (Windows) or Option+Home (Mac OS) and then click the Slide Show button. ⌐

✔ Tips

- To preview the effect chosen for a slide, click the transition icon beneath the slide in Slide Sorter view (**Figure 15.32**).

- For consistency, don't use too many different transition effects in one show. Stick with a conservative transition effect for most slides, and, if you like, emphasize only a select few with a special effect.

Adding a Transition Effect to a Slide (cont'd)

You can also choose a transition effect in the Slide Transition dialog box (**Figure 15.33**). The dialog box offers two advantages: You can access it from any view (not just Slide Sorter), and you can designate a speed at which the effect is drawn on the screen.

To select a speed for a transition:

1. In any view, select the slide(s) to which you want to add a transition effect.

2. Choose Slide Show > Slide Transition, or in Slide Sorter view, click the Slide Transition button on the toolbar (**Figure 15.34**).

3. Click the Effect field arrow to display a list of effects (**Figure 15.35**).

4. Click the desired transition effect.

   The preview box immediately demonstrates the effect.

5. You can click the preview box to see the effect again. If you don't like this effect, pick another one.

6. Choose a speed: Slow, Medium, or Fast.

7. Click Apply to apply to the current selection, or choose Apply to All to apply to the entire presentation.

8. Repeat steps 1-7 to apply transition effects to other slides.

9. To see the effects during a slide show, press Ctrl+Home (Windows) or Option+Home (Mac OS) and then click the Slide Show button. ⬚

✔ Tip

- Because some effects draw more slowly than others, it's helpful to control the rate at which slides are drawn on the screen during a slide show.

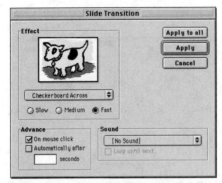

Figure 15.33 In the Slide Transition dialog box, you can select a transition effect and set a speed for the effect.

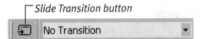

Figure 15.34 To display the Slide Transition dialog box, click the Slide Transition button on the Slide Sorter toolbar.

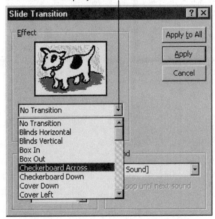

Figure 15.35 Choose an effect from the list.

Figure 15.36 Use the Animation toolbar to apply preset animations.

Animation Preview

Figure 15.37 Choose Slide Show > Preset Animation to see additional animation choices.

Applying Preset Animations

While a transition effect controls how the entire slide is displayed on the screen during the slide show, an *animation* controls how a particular object or piece of text appears on a slide. For example, you can have a slide title "type" on the screen one character at a time, complete with typewriter sound effects.

The *preset animations* included with PowerPoint offer a quick and easy way to apply animations that include transitions and sounds.

To apply a preset animation:

1. In Slide view, click the text or object you want to animate.

2. Click the Animation Effects button on the Formatting toolbar. 📝

   The Animation toolbar appears (**Figure 15.36**).

3. Select one of the animations.

4. To see what the animation looks like, click the Animation Preview button on the Animation toolbar (Windows). The animation appears in the Slide Miniature window.

   or

   Click the Slide Show button (Mac OS) and then click the mouse to see the animation. Press Esc to cancel the show.

✔ Tips

- You can find even more preset animations by choosing Slide Show > Preset Animation (**Figure 15.37**).

- To modify the settings of a preset animation, click the Custom Animation button on the Animation toolbar. 🦘

Animating a Bulleted List

During a slide show, you can create an animation that progressively reveals the bulleted items on a slide. By animating your bulleted lists, you can display each successive bulleted item when you are ready to discuss it. In addition, you can dim previous items so the current item stands out. **Figures 15.38** through **15.40** show an animated bulleted list in progress.

To animate a bulleted list:

1. In Slide view, select the bullet placeholder.

2. Choose Slide Show > Custom Animation.
   or
   If the Animation toolbar is displayed, click the Custom Animation button.

3. Select the Effects tab.

4. **Windows only:** Select the Text checkbox that is currently highlighted.

5. In the Entry Animation and Sound area, choose an effect, direction for the effect, and a sound if desired (**Figures 15.41** and **15.42**).

Figure 15.38 Press Page Down (or click the mouse) to see the first set of bulleted items.

Figure 15.39 When you press Page Down again, the first set of items is dimmed and the second bullet appears.

Figure 15.40 Press Page Down a third time to see the third set of bulleted items.

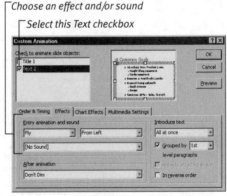

Figure 15.41 Choose an animation effect for bulleted items (Windows).

Choose an effect and/or sound

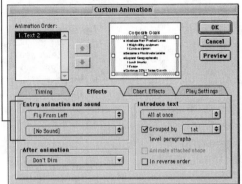

Figure 15.42 Choose an animation effect for bulleted items (Mac OS).

For additional color choices, click here   *Click here to choose a color for dimmed text*

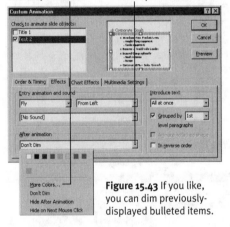

Figure 15.43 If you like, you can dim previously-displayed bulleted items.

6. If you would like previous text to dim when new text appears, choose a color for dimmed text in the After Animation field (**Figure 15.43**).

7. In the Grouped By field, choose 1st to display each first-level bullet along with its subtext.

   or

   Choose 2nd to display first- and second-level bullets separately.

8. Click OK.

9. To see the bullet animation in action, click the Slide Show button.

   Only the slide title is displayed.

10. Press Page Down or click the mouse to display the bulleted items one at a time.

✔ Tip

- Click Preview in the Custom Animation dialog box to preview the animation.

Animating Charts

Charts are ideal for animation effects—you can progressively display different chart elements, such as categories or series. **Figures 15.44** through **15.46** show an animated chart in progress.

To animate a chart:

1. In Slide view, select the chart placeholder.

2. Choose Slide Show > Custom Animation.

   or

   If the Animation toolbar is displayed, click the Custom Animation button.

3. Make sure the Chart Effects tab is selected.

4. **Windows only:** Select the Chart checkbox that is currently highlighted (**Figure 15.47**).

5. Click the Introduce Chart Elements field arrow and choose how you want to display chart elements (**Figures 15.47** and **15.48**).

Figure 15.44 Press Page Down (or click the mouse) to see the chart grid and legend.

Figure 15.45 When you press Page Down again, the first data series (Other) is displayed.

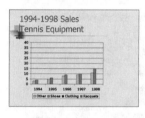

Figure 15.46 One more Page Down displays the next data series (Shoes).

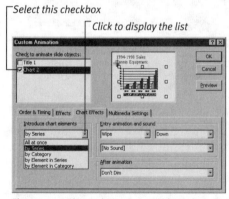

Figure 15.47 Choose how you want chart elements to be displayed (Windows).

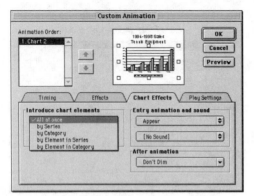

Figure 15.48 In the Chart Effects tab, you can choose how you want chart elements to be displayed (Mac OS).

Choose an effect and/or sound ⌐

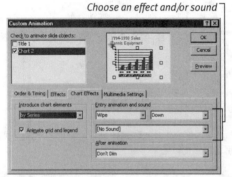

Figure 15.49 Choose an animation effect for chart elements (Windows).

Choose an effect and/or sound ⌐

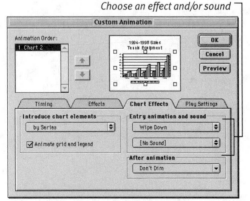

Figure 15.50 Choose an animation effect for chart elements (Mac OS).

6. In the Entry Animation and Sound area, choose an effect, direction for the effect, and a sound if desired (**Figures 15.49** and **15.50**).

7. Click OK.

8. To see the chart animation in action, click the Slide Show button.

   Only the slide title is displayed.

9. Press Page Down or click the mouse to display the chart elements one at a time.

✔ Tip

■ Click Preview in the Custom Animation dialog box to preview the animation.

Inserting Movie Clips

PowerPoint can insert and play movies that were recorded in a variety of formats, such as Audio Video Interleave (AVI), QuickTime, and Moving Picture Expert Group (MPEG) videos.

To insert a movie clip (Windows):

1. In Slide view, go to the slide on which you want to insert a movie (or insert a blank slide).

2. Choose Insert > Movies and Sounds > Movie from File.

   The Insert Movie dialog box appears (**Figure 15.51**).

3. Navigate to the drive and folder containing your movie file.

4. Select the movie file and click OK.

   PowerPoint asks if you want the movie to play automatically during a slide show.

5. Choose Yes if you want the movie to play automatically when the slide appears.

   or

   Choose No if you want to start the movie by clicking it.

   The first frame of the movie appears in the center of the slide (**Figure 15.52**).

6. To see the movie play during a slide show, click the Slide Show button.

7. If you didn't set the movie to play automatically, click anywhere on the movie frame.

To locate movie files, click Tools and choose Find

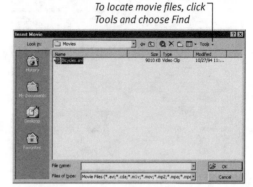

Figure 15.51 Select the name of the movie file in the Insert Movie dialog box.

Drag a corner selection handle to resize the movie

Figure 15.52 After you insert a movie file, the first frame of the movie appears on the slide.

Figure 15.53 Select the name of the movie file.

First frame of movie

Figure 15.54 After you insert a movie file, the first frame of the movie appears on the slide; when the frame is selected, the Movie toolbar is displayed.

Play   Movie toolbar

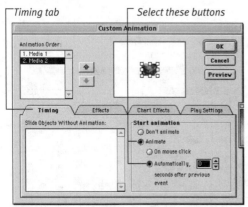

Timing tab   Select these buttons

Figure 15.55 In the Timing tab of the Custom Animation dialog box, you can choose to have the movie play automatically during a slide show.

To insert a movie clip (Mac OS):

1. In Slide view, go to the slide on which you want to insert a movie (or insert a blank slide).

2. Choose Insert > Movies and Sounds > Movie from File.

   The movie dialog box appears (**Figure 15.53**).

3. Navigate to the drive and folder containing your movie file.

4. Select the movie file and click Open.

   The first frame of the movie appears in the center of the slide (**Figure 15.54**).

5. To see the movie play during a slide show, click the Slide Show button.

6. Click anywhere on the movie frame to play the movie.

To automatically play the movie during a slide show (Mac OS):

1. In Slide view, make sure the movie frame is selected, and choose Slide Show > Custom Animation.

   The Custom Animation dialog box appears (**Figure 15.55**).

2. Select the Timing tab.

3. In the Start Animation area, choose Animate.

4. Choose Automatically.

5. Click OK.

✔ Tip

■ To play the movie in Slide view, click the Play button on the Movie toolbar (**Figure 15.54**, Mac OS only) or double-click the embedded movie object.

Adding Sounds

You can liven up your PowerPoint slide shows by adding sound effects (such as ringing bells or applause recorded in WAV files), playing songs (recorded in MIDI files), or even playing tracks from a music CD in your CD-ROM drive.

To insert a sound (Windows):

1. In Slide view, go to the slide to which you want to add a sound.

2. Choose Insert > Movies and Sounds > Sound from File.

   The Insert Sound dialog box appears (**Figure 15.56**).

3. Navigate to the drive and folder containing your sound file.

4. Select the sound file and click OK.

   You are asked if you want the sound to play automatically during a slide show.

5. Choose Yes if you want the sound to play automatically when the slide appears.

   or

   Choose No if you want to play the sound by clicking its icon.

   A sound icon appears on the slide (**Figure 15.57**).

6. Drag the sound icon to an empty area of the slide (such as a corner).

To hide the sound icon during a slide show:

1. In Slide view, select the sound icon, and choose Slide Show > Custom Animation.

2. Select the Hide While Not Playing checkbox (**Figure 15.58**).

3. Click OK.

To locate sound files, click Tools and choose Find

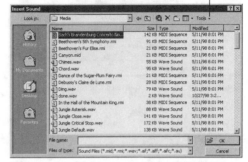

Figure 15.56 Select the name of the sound file in the Insert Sound dialog box.

MIDI sound icon

WAV sound icon

Figure 15.57 After you insert a sound file, a sound icon appears on the slide.

Select this checkbox to hide the icon

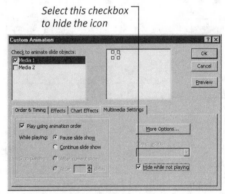

Figure 15.58 You can hide the sound icon during a slide show.

ADDING SOUNDS (WINDOWS)

To locate sound files, click here

Figure 15.59 Select the name of the sound file.

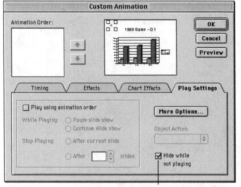

Select this checkbox to hide the icon

Figure 15.60 You can hide the sound icon during a slide show.

Timing tab   Select these buttons

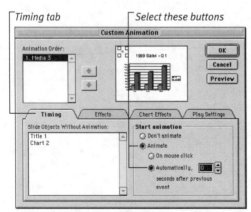

Figure 15.61 In the Timing tab of the Custom Animation dialog box, you can choose to have the sound play automatically during a slide show.

To insert a sound (Mac OS):

1. In Slide view, go to the slide to which you want to add a sound.

2. Choose Insert > Movies and Sounds > Sound from File.

   The Insert Sound dialog box appears (**Figure 15.59**).

3. Navigate to the drive and folder containing your sound file.

4. Select the sound file and click Insert.

   A sound icon appears on the slide (**Figure 15.57**).

5. Drag the sound icon to an empty area of the slide (such as a corner).

To hide the sound icon during a slide show:

1. In Slide view, select the sound icon, and choose Slide Show > Custom Animation.

   The Custom Animation dialog box appears.

2. Select the Hide While Not Playing checkbox (**Figure 15.60**).

3. Select the Timing tab (**Figure 15.61**).

4. In the Start Animation area, choose Animate.

5. Choose Automatically.

6. Click OK.

When you run the slide show, the sound will automatically play when the slide appears.

Playing CD Sound Tracks (Windows)

During a slide show, you can play tracks from a music CD in your computer's CD-ROM drive. You can have the music play while one slide is displayed, for the entire show, or for any range of slides.

To play CD sound tracks (Windows):

1. In Slide view, go to the slide in which you want the CD to start playing.

2. Choose Insert > Movies and Sounds > Play CD Audio Track.

   The Movie and Sound Options dialog box appears (**Figure 15.62**).

3. Fill in the starting and ending track numbers you want to play.

   Note: Track numbers correspond to the order in which songs play on the CD.

4. Click OK.

   You are asked if you want the sound to play automatically during a slide show.

5. Choose Yes if you want the CD to play automatically when the slide appears.

   or

   Choose No if you want to start playing the CD by clicking the sound icon.

   A CD sound icon appears in the center of the slide (**Figure 15.63**).

6. Drag the sound icon to an empty area of the slide (such as a corner).

Enter the range of track numbers

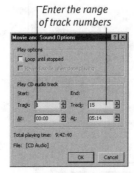

Figure 15.62 Specify the track numbers you want to play.

Figure 15.63 After you select the track numbers, a CD sound icon appears on the slide.

Select Continue Slide Show...

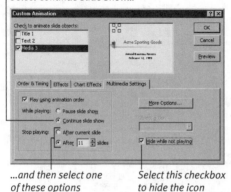

...and then select one of these options

Select this checkbox to hide the icon

Figure 15.64 In the Multimedia Settings tab, you can hide the CD sound icon, indicate how long you want the CD to play, or set other options.

Select the Order & Timing tab

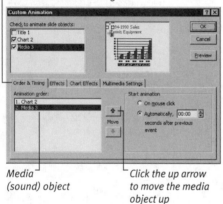

Media (sound) object

Click the up arrow to move the media object up

Figure 15.65 To play the CD before any animations on the slide begin, move the media object to the top of the animation order.

To set sound options (Windows):

1. In Slide view, select the sound icon, and choose Slide Show > Custom Animation.

   The Multimedia Settings tab in the Custom Animation dialog box appears (**Figure 15.64**).

2. To hide the icon during the slide show, select the Hide While Not Playing checkbox.

3. To have the music continue while you display other slides, choose Continue Slide Show in the While Playing area.

4. To play the CD during the current slide only, choose After Current Slide in the Stop Playing area.

   or

   To play the CD during a range of slides, choose After ____ Slides and fill in a number.

5. Click OK.

✔ Tip

- If the slide contains other animated objects, you'll probably want to change the animation order so that the music begins playing before the animation starts. You can do this from the Order & Timing tab in the Custom Animation dialog box (**Figure 15.65**).

PLAYING CD SOUND TRACKS (WINDOWS)

Playing CD Sound Tracks (Mac OS)

During a slide show, you can play tracks from a music CD in your computer's CD-ROM drive. You can have the music play while one slide is displayed, for the entire show, or for any range of slides.

To play CD sound tracks (Mac OS):

1. In Slide view, go to the slide in which you want the CD to start playing.

2. Choose Insert > Movies and Sounds > Play CD Audio Track.

   The Play Options dialog box appears (**Figure 15.66**).

3. Fill in the starting and ending track numbers you want to play.

   Note: Track numbers correspond to the order in which songs play on the CD.

4. Click OK.

   A CD sound icon appears on the slide (**Figure 15.67**).

5. Drag the sound icon to an empty area of the slide (such as a corner).

6. If you want to hide the sound icon or if you want the CD to play while the slide show continues, you can set sound options as described on the following page.

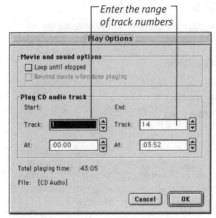

Enter the range of track numbers

Figure 15.66 Specify the track numbers you want to play.

Figure 15.67 After you select the track numbers, a CD sound icon appears on the slide.

Select Continue Slide Show...

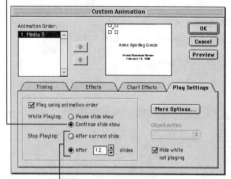

...and then select one of these options

Figure 15.68 Select play settings here.

Select the Timing tab   *Select Automatically*

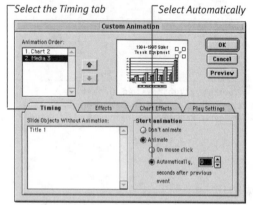

Figure 15.69 In the Timing tab, you can automate the playing of a CD during a slide show.

Media (sound) object   *Click the up arrow*

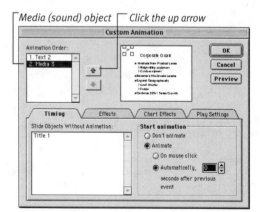

Figure 15.70 Move "Media 3" to the top of the list to play the CD first.

To set sound options (Mac OS):

1. In Slide view, select the sound icon and choose Slide Show > Custom Animation.

   The Play Settings tab in the Custom Animation dialog box appears (**Figure 15.68**).

2. To hide the icon during the slide show, select the Hide While Not Playing checkbox.

3. Select the Play Using Animation Order checkbox.

4. To have the music continue while you display other slides, choose Continue Slide Show in the While Playing area.

5. To play the CD during the current slide only, choose After Current Slide in the Stop Playing area.

   or

   To play the CD during a range of slides, choose After ___ Slides and fill in a number.

6. Select the Timing tab (**Figure 15.69**).

7. Choose Automatically.

8. Click OK.

✔ Tip

- If the slide contains other animated objects, you'll need to change the animation order so that the music begins playing before the animation starts. To do this, select the Timing tab in the Custom Animation dialog box (**Figure 15.70**). Click the up arrow to move the media (sound) object to the top of the Animation Order list.

PLAYING CD SOUND TRACKS (MAC OS)

Creating a Self-Running Slide Show

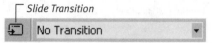

Slide Transition

Figure 15.71 Click the Slide Transition button on the Slide Sorter toolbar to display the Slide Transition dialog box.

If you want to sit back and watch your slide show without having to click the mouse or press any keys, you can tell PowerPoint to advance each slide automatically after a certain number of seconds. Self-running slide shows are often used during trade shows or at sales kiosks.

To create a self-running slide show:

1. In Slide Sorter view, click the Slide Transition button on the toolbar (**Figure 15.71**).

   The Slide Transition dialog box appears (**Figure 15.72**).

2. In the Automatically After field, enter the number of seconds you want each slide to remain on the screen.

3. Click Apply to All.

   The number of seconds that the slide will remain onscreen is indicated beneath each slide.

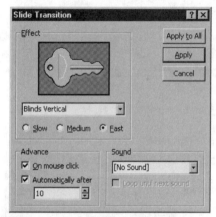

Figure 15.72 With these transition settings, slides will advance automatically every 10 seconds unless you click the mouse.

✔ Tips

- To temporarily suspend a self-running slide show, press S or +. To continue with the show, press Page Down or click the mouse button.

- You can always advance a slide before the specified time has passed, by pressing Page Down, clicking the mouse, etc. (Note: Mouse-clicking will work only if the On Mouse Click checkbox is selected in the Slide Transition dialog box.)

- If you want a particular slide to remain on screen for a longer or shorter time than the rest of the slides, select the slide, specify the time in the Slide Transition dialog box, and choose Apply.

Pause ┐ ┌ Time on
timing   current slide

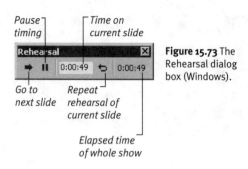

Figure 15.73 The Rehearsal dialog box (Windows).

Go to   Repeat
next slide rehearsal of
            current slide

Elapsed time
of whole show

Figure 15.74 The Rehearsal dialog box (Mac OS) shows the elapsed time of the current slide.

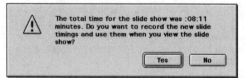

Figure 15.75 Choosing Yes saves the rehearsal timings to be used for a self-running slide show.

Rehearsing the Slide Show

You may have only a specific length of time in which to make your presentation. To make sure your slide show fits in the allotted time, you can rehearse your slide show and have PowerPoint record the timing.

To time your slide show:

1. In Slide Sorter view, click the Rehearse Timings button.

    The first slide in the show appears, and the Rehearsal dialog box displays in the corner of the screen (**Figure 15.73** and **15.74**).

2. Rehearse out loud whatever you want to say when the slide is displayed.

3. When you are ready to advance to the next slide, press Page Down (Windows or Mac OS) or click the Next button in the Rehearsal dialog box (Windows only).

4. Repeat steps 2 and 3 for each slide.

    When you're finished, PowerPoint displays the total time for the slide show (**Figure 15.75**) and asks if you want to record the slide times and use them when viewing a slide show.

5. Choose Yes to record the slide times and create a self-running slide show.

    or

    Choose No if you don't want to record the slide times.

    If you record the times, they display underneath each slide.

✔ Tip

- To run a slide show manually but still preserve the timings, choose Slide Show > Set Up Show and under Advance Slides, select Manually.

Creating Meeting Minutes

During a slide show, you can record minutes of your meeting and then print them out.

To record meeting minutes:

1. During a slide show, display the shortcut menu (**Figure 15.76**) by right-clicking (Windows) or Control+clicking (Mac OS).

2. Choose Meeting Minder.

3. In the Meeting Minutes tab (**Figure 15.77**), enter your comments and click OK.

4. Repeat the above steps whenever you need to type additional minutes. (Note that the Meeting Minder does not associate your notes with the slide that was onscreen.)

If you like, you can export the minutes to a Microsoft Word file and then print them out.

To print meeting minutes:

1. In Slide view, choose Tools > Meeting Minder.

   or

   During a slide show, go to Meeting Minder.

2. Click the Export (Windows) or Export to Word (Mac OS) button in the Meeting Minder dialog box.

   Note: If the Export button is dimmed, you may need to type something (such as a space) in the Meeting Minutes tab.

3. **Windows only:** In the Meeting Minder Export dialog box, make sure the option Send Meeting Minutes and Action Items to Microsoft Word is selected, and click Export Now. You'll see your minutes formatted in Word (**Figure 15.78**).

4. To print, choose File > Print.

Figure 15.76 Display the shortcut menu during a slide show and choose Meeting Minder.

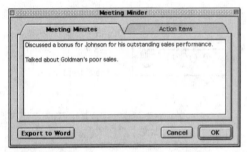

Figure 15.77 Enter your minutes in the Meeting Minutes tab.

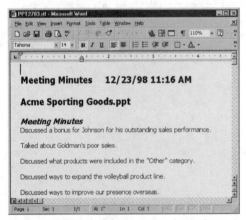

Figure 15.78 Once the minutes appear in Word, use the File > Print command to print them out.

CREATING MEETING MINUTES

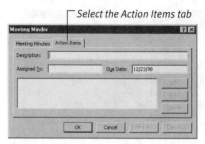

⌐Select the Action Items tab

Figure 15.79 To enter an action item, fill in the Description, Assigned To, and Due Date fields.

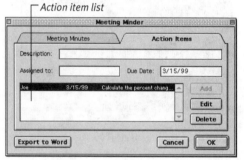

⌐Action item list

Figure 15.80 After you click the Add button, the item appears on the list.

Action Items

Owner	Due Date	Description
Joe	3/15/99	Calculate the percent change between 1998 and 1999
Mary Ann	3/21/99	Compile a complete list of overseas markets
Georgia	3/26/99	Project sales for 1999 Q2

Figure 15.81 Action items are listed on a slide at the end of the presentation.

Creating an Action Item List

As you are giving a slide show, you and your audience may come up with ideas that need follow-up. Using PowerPoint's action item feature, you can create a to-do list during a show and then print it out along with your meeting minutes.

To record action items:

1. During a slide show, display the shortcut menu by right-clicking (Windows) or Control+clicking (Mac OS).

2. Choose Meeting Minder.
   The Meeting Minder dialog box appears.

3. Select the Action Items tab (**Figure 15.79**).

4. Fill in the description of the item, name of the person who is assigned to act on it, and a due date.

5. Click Add.
   The item is entered into the box (**Figure 15.80**).

6. Repeat steps 4 and 5 to enter additional action items.

7. Click OK.

8. PowerPoint creates a slide of your action items and puts it at the end of the presentation (**Figure 15.81**). This slide is continually updated as you add to your action item list.

✔ Tip

- You can edit the action item list before, during, or after the slide show.

Packaging Your Presentation (Windows Only)

Using PowerPoint's Pack and Go Wizard, you can easily copy to a diskette all the files that you need to run a slide show on another computer. Specifically, Pack and Go Wizard copies your presentation and offers the option to copy PowerPoint Viewer, a handy utility for viewing slide shows on computers that don't have PowerPoint installed.

To package a presentation:

1. Open the presentation you want to package.

2. Insert a blank, formatted diskette into the drive. (Note: you may need several diskettes.)

3. Choose File > Pack And Go and click Next.

4. Make sure Active Presentation is chosen, and click Next.

5. Choose the correct letter for your diskette drive (**Figure 15.82**) and click Next.

6. If your presentation includes linked files or TrueType fonts and the destination computer does not have them, ask Pack and Go to include them in your package (**Figure 15.83**) and then click Next.

7. If you plan to show the presentation on a computer that doesn't have PowerPoint, choose to include the Viewer and then click Next.

   Note: To include the Viewer, you must have installed it when you originally installed Microsoft Office.

8. Read the final screen, and click Finish.

   See the next page for details on showing the packaged presentation on another computer.

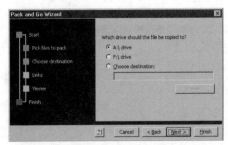

Figure 15.82 The Pack and Go Wizard first asks you to choose a drive to copy the files to.

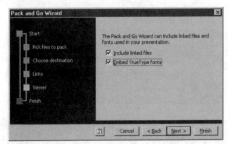

Figure 15.83 The Wizard gives you an opportunity to include linked files and TrueType fonts in the package.

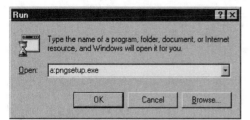

Figure 15.84 Run the PNGSETUP.EXE program to copy your presentation onto the new computer.

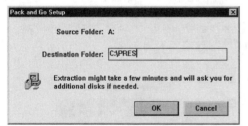

Figure 15.85 The Pack and Go Setup program prompts you for a destination folder for the copied files.

Figure 15.86 Select the presentation filename in the Viewer dialog box.

Showing Your Presentation on Another Computer

The Pack and Go Wizard creates a file called PNGSETUP.EXE on the first diskette. Executing this file will copy the necessary files onto the computer you will be using to give the presentation and will give you the opportunity to run the slide show immediately.

To show the packaged presentation:

1. Insert the first diskette into the drive.

2. In Windows, click the Start button and choose Run (**Figure 15.84**).

3. Assuming the diskette drive is drive A:, type *A:pngsetup.exe* and click OK.

4. Enter a destination folder for your presentation files—it can be a new one, if you prefer (**Figure 15.85**).

5. Click OK.
   After the files have been "unpackaged," you'll see a message asking if you want to run the slide show now.

6. Click Yes to run the slide show.

✔ Tips

- To make sure things run smoothly in front of your audience, it's a good idea to unpackage and run the slide show before you present it.

- To run a slide show after the files have been unpackaged, go to the destination folder and double-click the file named PPVIEW32.EXE—this is the PowerPoint Viewer program (**Figure 15.86**). Then double-click the presentation filename to begin the show.

Viewing a Show Outside of PowerPoint

How would you like to give a slide show without having to launch PowerPoint and open your presentation? One way to do this is to save the presentation as a PowerPoint slide show; you can then run this file from Windows Explorer or the Mac OS Finder. Note that this technique works only on computers that have PowerPoint installed.

To save a presentation as a slide show:

1. With the presentation open, choose File > Save As.

   The Save As dialog box appears (**Figure 15.87**).

2. Change the filename if you want.

3. In the Save As Type (Windows) or Save File as Type (Mac OS) field, choose PowerPoint Show.

4. Click OK (Windows) or Save (Mac OS).

To begin the slide show without opening PowerPoint:

1. Make sure you have created a PowerPoint Show file as described above.

2. In My Computer or Windows Explorer (Windows) or the Finder (Mac OS), navigate to the folder containing the PowerPoint show file (**Figures 15.88** and **15.89**).

3. Find the icon for your slide show and double-click it.

   The first slide in the show displays full screen.

4. Press Page Down (or any of the other slide show navigation keys) to advance to the next slide.

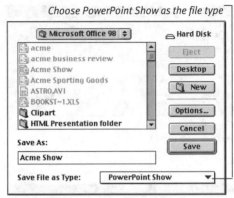

Choose PowerPoint Show as the file type

Figure 15.87 Save the presentation as a PowerPoint Show (Mac OS).

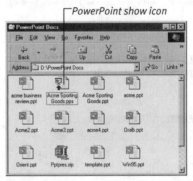

PowerPoint show icon

Figure 15.88 PowerPoint show files have a different icon from presentation files; they also have a .PPS file extension (Windows).

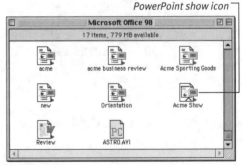

PowerPoint show icon

Figure 15.89 You can recognize PowerPoint show files by their unique icon (Mac OS).

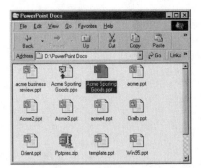

Figure 15.90 In Windows, you can show presentation files without having to start PowerPoint.

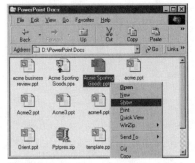

Figure 15.91 To view a presentation, right-click the presentation filename and choose Show.

Viewing a Slide Show from Windows

Windows offers another way to give a slide show from Explorer or My Computer. Unlike the technique described on the previous page, this method doesn't require you to create a special PowerPoint show (.PPS) file.

To show a PowerPoint presentation file (Windows only):

1. In My Computer or Windows Explorer, navigate to the folder containing the PowerPoint presentation (.PPT) file (**Figure 15.90**).

2. Right-click the PowerPoint presentation file and choose Show from the shortcut menu (**Figure 15.91**).

   The first slide in the show displays full screen.

3. Press Page Down (or any of the other slide show navigation keys) to advance to the next slide.

✔ Tip

- This technique works only on computers that have PowerPoint installed.

PRESENTATION OUTPUT 16

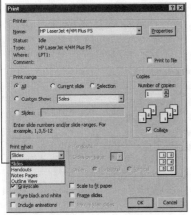

Figure 16.1 Indicate the type of output in the Print dialog box.

Once you've completed your presentation, you can output it in several ways: to the screen (in the form of a slide show), to a printer (on paper or on overhead transparencies), or to a file (to produce 35mm slides or high-resolution output). While Chapter 15 covered running a slide show, this chapter covers sending a presentation to a printer or file. You can also create Web pages out of your presentation; this topic is covered in Chapter 17.

The Print dialog box (**Figure 16.1**), used for outputting to a printer or file, allows you to select what to print: slides, handouts, speaker notes, or an outline of the presentation. These four types of output are covered in this chapter.

Selecting a Printer

The Print dialog box (**Figures 16.2** and **16.3**) indicates the current printer. If you are connected to more than one printer and would like to specify a different one, follow these steps.

To select a different printer (Windows):

1. Choose File > Print or press Ctrl+P.

2. In the Name field, choose the printer you want to use.

3. Choose other options as desired and click OK to begin printing.

To select a different printer (Mac OS):

1. Click the Apple icon in the upper-left corner of the screen.

2. Choose Chooser.

3. In the left window pane, click the icon of the printer you want to use (**Figure 16.4**).

4. If prompted, choose a printer port and change other options if necessary.

5. Close the Chooser window.

6. Choose File > Print or press Command+P.

   The top of the dialog box displays the printer name you just selected in the Chooser (**Figure 16.3**). Note that this dialog box is customized to the selected printer, so yours may have different settings than those shown here.

7. If desired, click Print to begin printing.

✔ Tip

■ To set printer-specific options, click Properties in the Print dialog box (Windows). In Mac OS, click Options, or for a PostScript printer, click General and choose Layout and/or Imaging Options.

⌐ Current printer

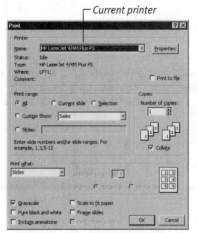

Figure 16.2 The name of the current printer is listed in the Name field in the Print dialog box (Windows).

⌐ Current printer

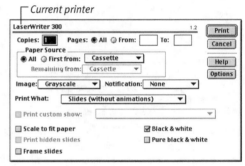

Figure 16.3 The name of the current printer appears at the top of the print dialog box (Mac OS).

⌐ Click the printer you want to use

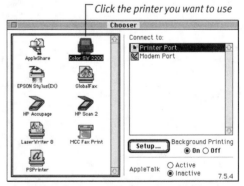

Figure 16.4 Use the Chooser to select a different printer (Mac OS).

SELECTING A PRINTER

Figure 16.5 Use this button to switch between color and grayscale (black-and-white) preview.

Figure 16.6 Black-and-white preview is currently enabled (as indicated by the checkmark next to Black and White).

Figure 16.7 A colored slide miniature appears when you are in black-and-white view.

Previewing Slides in Black and White

If you plan to print your slides on a monochrome printer, you may want to preview them in black and white beforehand. PowerPoint offers an easy way to do this.

To preview slides in black and white:

◆ Choose View > Black and White.

   or

   Click the Grayscale Preview (Windows) or Black and White View (Mac OS) button on the Standard toolbar (**Figure 16.5**).

A checkmark next to Black and White on the View menu indicates this view is currently turned on (**Figure 16.6**).

✔ Tips

■ To return to viewing in color, choose View > Black and White or click the Grayscale Preview button again.

■ Unless you manually closed the slide miniature in the past, a colored miniature of the current slide (**Figure 16.7**) automatically appears when you turn on black-and-white view. (If you don't see the miniature, choose View > Slide Miniature.)

Printing Slides

Undoubtedly the most common type of printing is to produce full-page slides on either paper or overhead transparencies.

Before printing, make sure to select the appropriate paper size.

To select the paper size:

1. Choose File > Page Setup.

   The Page Setup dialog box appears (**Figure 16.8**).

2. In the Slides Sized For list, select Letter Paper, A4 Paper, Overhead, Banner, or Custom (for other paper sizes).

3. If necessary, adjust the dimensions of the printed size in the Width and Height boxes. (Be sure to leave room for the margins on the paper.)

4. Click OK.

To print slides (Windows):

1. Choose File > Print or press Ctrl+P to display the Print dialog box (**Figure 16.9**).

   To choose a different printer, see Selecting a Printer earlier in this chapter.

2. Under Print Range, choose All to print the entire presentation.

   or

   To print specific slides, click Slides and enter the range of slides you want to print. Use a dash to indicate a range of slides (such as 1-5), and a comma to indicate non-consecutive slides (1-5, 7, 10).

3. In the Print What field, choose Slides.

4. Make sure your paper or overhead transparencies are loaded in the printer and then click OK.

Choose the paper size here

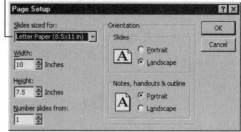

Figure 16.8 In the Page Setup dialog box, specify the size of the paper on which you will be printing the slides.

Choose All... ...Current Slide...

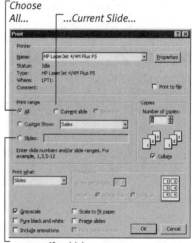

...or specify which slide numbers to print

Figure 16.9 In the Print dialog box, you can choose to print all slides, the current slide on-screen, or a specific range of slides (Windows).

Choose All... ──┐   ...or enter a range of
                     slide numbers to print

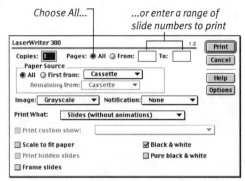

Figure 16.10 A LaserWriter printer dialog box is shown here (Mac OS).

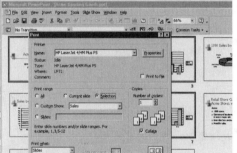

Figure 16.11 The General settings for a PostScript printer are shown here (Mac OS).

⌐ *To set PowerPoint options, click here*
  and choose Microsoft PowerPoint

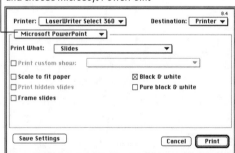

Figure 16.12 In this PostScript printer dialog box, PowerPoint printing options are displayed (Mac OS).

To print slides (Mac OS):

To choose a different printer, see Selecting a Printer earlier in this chapter.

1. Choose File > Print or press Command+P.

   Note that the Print dialog box (**Figures 16.10** and **16.11**) is customized to the type of printer you have selected, so yours may look different than the one shown in the figures.

2. Choose All to print the entire presentation.

   or

   To print a range of slides, enter the starting and ending slide numbers in the From and To fields.

3. If you have a PostScript printer, click General and then choose Microsoft PowerPoint.

   The dialog box now displays the options that are specific to PowerPoint (**Figure 16.12**).

4. In the Print What field, choose Slides.

   or

   If your presentation contains animations, choose Slides (Without Animations).

5. Make sure your paper or transparencies are loaded in the printer and click Print.

✔ Tips

- Another way to specify a range of slides is by first selecting them in Slide Sorter view. Then, in the Print dialog box, choose Selection as the Print Range (Windows only).

- The Print button on the Standard toolbar does not display the Print dialog box—it immediately prints the range last specified.

- When you print a color presentation on a black-and-white printer, PowerPoint automatically converts the colors to shades of gray.

265

Stopping a Print Job (Windows)

If you choose the Print command and then decide you want to cancel the print job, you can delete it from the print queue.

To stop a print job (Windows):

1. Double-click the printer icon on the Windows taskbar (**Figure 16.13**).

   The print queue displays.

2. Click the document name.

3. Press Delete.

   or

   Choose Document > Cancel Printing.

4. Close the print queue window.

✔ Tip

- For small print jobs, the printer icon may come and go very quickly. If the icon isn't there, the print job has already been spooled to the printer and it's too late to cancel the print job.

*Double-click
the Printer icon*

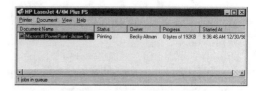

Figure 16.13 To display the print queue, double-click the printer icon on the Windows taskbar.

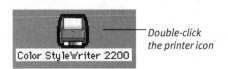

*Double-click
the printer icon*

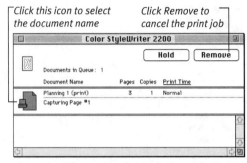

*Click this icon to select
the document name*

*Click Remove to
cancel the print job*

Figure 16.14 When you're using the Desktop PrintMonitor, you display the print queue by double-clicking the printer icon on the desktop.

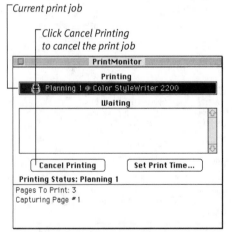

Current print job

*Click Cancel Printing
to cancel the print job*

Figure 16.15 When you're not using the Desktop PrintMonitor, you display the print queue by selecting PrintMonitor on the application menu.

Stopping a Print Job (Mac OS)

How you stop a print job depends on whether the Desktop PrintMonitor extension is enabled. Refer to the instructions below that are applicable to your situation.

To stop a print job using the Desktop PrintMonitor:

1. Double-click the printer icon on the desktop (**Figure 16.14**).

2. In the printer queue window, click the icon next to the document name and then click Remove.

3. Close the print queue window.

To stop a print job if Desktop PrintMonitor is disabled:

1. Click the application icon on the upper-right corner of the screen and choose PrintMonitor.

2. In the PrintMonitor window, click Cancel Printing (**Figure 16.15**).

3. Close the PrintMonitor window.

Printing the Outline

You can print an outline of the presentation exactly as it appears in Outline view. For instance, if only the slide titles are displayed in Outline view, only the slide titles are printed (**Figure 16.16**). Or, if the outline is completely expanded, all the slide titles and bulleted items are printed (**Figure 16.17**). In addition, if formatting is hidden, the text and bullets are not formatted.

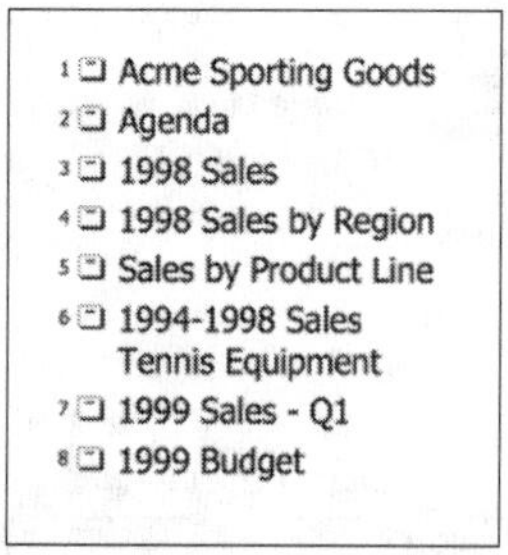

To get the results you want, go into Outline view and set your options—before printing your outline.

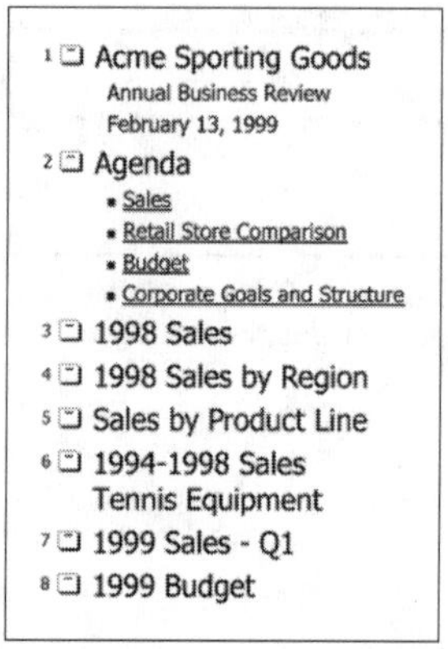

To print the outline:

1. Switch to Outline view. ▦

2. Make any of the following changes:

    ◆ To hide or display formatting, click the Show Formatting button. ᴬ▵

    ◆ To display only the slide titles, click the Collapse All button. ▤

    or

    ◆ To display the entire outline, click the Expand All button. ▦

3. Choose File > Print.

    Mac OS only: If you have a PostScript printer, click General and choose Microsoft PowerPoint. The dialog box now displays the options that are specific to PowerPoint.

4. In the Print What field, choose Outline View (**Figure 16.18**).

5. Click OK (Windows) or Print (Mac OS) to begin printing.

1 ▭ Acme Sporting Goods
2 ▭ Agenda
3 ▭ 1998 Sales
4 ▭ 1998 Sales by Region
5 ▭ Sales by Product Line
6 ▭ 1994-1998 Sales
 Tennis Equipment
7 ▭ 1999 Sales - Q1
8 ▭ 1999 Budget

Figure 16.16 This printed outline shows only the slide titles.

1 ▭ Acme Sporting Goods
 Annual Business Review
 February 13, 1999
2 ▭ Agenda
    • Sales
    • Retail Store Comparison
    • Budget
    • Corporate Goals and Structure
3 ▭ 1998 Sales
4 ▭ 1998 Sales by Region
5 ▭ Sales by Product Line
6 ▭ 1994-1998 Sales
 Tennis Equipment
7 ▭ 1999 Sales - Q1
8 ▭ 1999 Budget

Figure 16.17 This printed outline shows slide titles and expanded text.

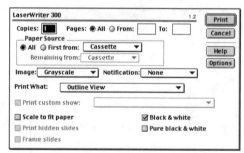

Figure 16.18 Choose Outline View in the Print What field to print the outline.

Slide placeholder ⌐   Text placeholder for notes

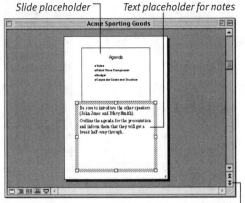

Next Slide
button

Figure 16.19 Use Notes Page view to enter speaker notes (Windows or Mac OS).

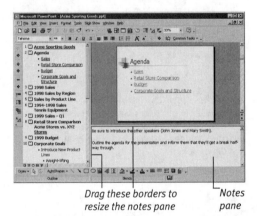

Drag these borders to   *Notes*
resize the notes pane   *pane*

Figure 16.20 In Windows, you can also enter speaker notes in the notes pane of Normal view (shown here) or Outline view.

Adding Speaker Notes

To help remind yourself what to say when you present each slide during a slide show, you can refer to *speaker notes* saved on *notes pages*. When printed, each page of notes consists of the slide on the top half, with any speaker notes you have for that slide on the bottom half.

You can enter your speaker notes in Notes Page view (**Figure 16.19**). In Windows, you can also enter notes in Normal (**Figure 16.20**) or Outline view.

To enter speaker notes (Windows or Mac OS):

1. Choose View > Notes Page to switch to Notes Page view (**Figure 16.19**).

2. Zoom in if necessary.

3. Click the text placeholder, and type your notes.

4. To go to the next slide, click the Next Slide button.

5. Repeat steps 3 and 4 for each slide.

To enter speaker notes (Windows only):

1. Switch to Normal or Outline view.

2. Adjust the size of the notes pane (**Figure 16.20**), if desired.

3. Click inside the notes pane and type your notes.

4. To go to the next slide, click the Next Slide button.

5. Repeat steps 3 and 4 for each slide.

✔ Tip

■ Another way to switch to Notes Page view is to click the Notes Page View button (Mac OS only). 🖳

Editing the Notes Master

You can perform global formatting of your notes pages on the Notes Master. (It works just like the Slide Master discussed in Chapter 12.) For instance, by adding bullet symbols to the Notes Master, bullets will automatically appear when you enter text on all notes pages. You might also want to add a page number, format the text in a different font, or resize the slide or text placeholders.

To edit the Notes Master:

1. Choose View > Master > Notes Master. The Notes Master appears (**Figure 16.21**).

2. Zoom in if necessary.

3. Make any of the following changes:
   - ◆ Adjust the size and position of the slide or text placeholders.
   - ◆ Format the text as desired—add bullet symbols, adjust indents, change the font, and so forth. **Figure 16.22** shows the text placeholder after formatting.
   - ◆ To add text that you want to appear on each page (such as the page number or presentation title), use the View > Header and Footer command.

4. When finished, click Close on the Master toolbar (**Figure 16.23**). Note: If you don't see this toolbar, choose View > Toolbars > Master.

✔ Tips

- ■ Another way to edit the Notes Master is to hold down Shift as you click the Notes Page View button (Mac OS only).

- ■ Any headers or footers you add do not display on the Notes Master; however, you will see them in Notes Page view.

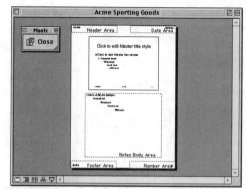

Figure 16.21 To globally format notes pages, make changes to the Notes Master.

Figure 16.22 In this Notes Master, bullets were added to the first and second level items, the indents were adjusted, and the text was formatted to a larger size and different font.

Figure 16.23 Click Close when you're finished editing the Notes Master.

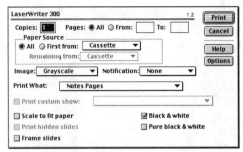

Figure 16.24 Choose Notes Pages in the Print What field to print speaker notes.

Printing Speaker Notes

Once you have typed your notes and format-ted the Notes Master, you are ready to print the notes pages.

To print speaker notes:

1. Choose File > Print (**Figure 16.24**).

2. Choose a print range.

3. **Mac OS only:** If you have a PostScript printer, click General and choose Microsoft PowerPoint.

   The dialog box now displays the options that are specific to PowerPoint.

4. In the Print What list box, choose Notes Pages.

5. Click OK (Windows) or Print (Mac OS).

✔ Tips

- If appropriate, you may want to pro-vide copies of your notes pages to your audience.

- You can view your notes pages during a slide show using Meeting Minder.

  See Creating Meeting Minutes in Chapter 15.

Formatting Handout Pages

Handout pages are smaller, printed versions of your slides, used to help the audience follow along in your presentation. In Windows, they can consist of 2, 3, 4, 6, or 9 slides per page; in Mac OS, handouts can have 2, 3, or 6 slides per page. Before printing, you may want to add titles, page numbers, or borders. You can perform all these tasks on the Handout Master.

To format handout pages:

1. Choose View > Master > Handout Master or hold down Shift as you click the Slide Sorter View button.

   The Handout Master appears (**Figure 16.25**).

2. On the Handout Master toolbar (**Figures 16.26** and **16.27**), choose the icon representing the number of slides you want to appear on each handout page.

3. Make any of the following changes:
   - ◆ To add text that you want to appear on each page (such as the presentation title or page number), choose the View > Header and Footer command.
   - ◆ Add any desired background graphics.

4. When finished, click Close on the Master toolbar (**Figure 16.28**). Note: If you don't see this toolbar, choose View > Toolbars > Master.

✔ Tips

- ■ The 3-per-page layout includes lines on the right half of the page for the audience to take notes next to each slide.

- ■ Any headers or footers you add do not display on the Handout Master; you see them only on the printed handout page.

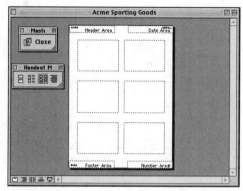

Figure 16.25 To format and lay out your handout pages, edit the Handout Master.

Figure 16.26 Choose the desired number of slides per handout page on the Handout Master toolbar (Windows).

Figure 16.27 Choose the desired number of slides per handout page on the Handout Master toolbar (Mac OS).

Figure 16.28 Click Close when you're finished editing the Handout Master.

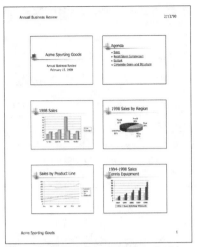

Figure 16.29 This handout page has six slides.

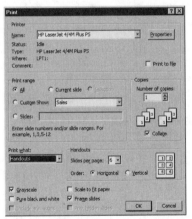

Figure 16.30 Choose Handouts in the Print What field to print handout pages (Windows).

Figure 16.31 In the Print What field, choose a Handouts option (Mac OS).

Printing Handouts

After formatting the Handout Master (described on the previous page), you are ready to print your handouts. **Figure 16.29** shows an example of a printed handout page.

To print handout pages (Windows):

1. Choose File > Print.

   The Print dialog box appears (**Figure 16.30**).

2. Choose a print range.

3. In the Print What list box, choose Handouts.

4. In the Slides Per Page field, change the number if desired.

5. If you've chosen 4 or more per page, select Horizontal or Vertical.

6. Click OK.

To print handouts (Mac OS):

1. Choose File > Print.

   The Print dialog box appears (**Figure 16.31**).

2. Choose a print range.

3. If you have a PostScript printer, click General and choose Microsoft PowerPoint. The dialog box now displays the options that are specific to PowerPoint.

4. In the Print What list box, choose one of the Handouts options.

5. Click Print.

✔ Tip

- PowerPoint automatically places borders around each slide on the printed handout. To eliminate borders, unselect the Frame Slides checkbox in the Print dialog box.

Producing 35mm Slides Using Genigraphics

Included with PowerPoint is a wizard that allows you to send a presentation by modem to Genigraphics, a company that produces 35mm slides from PowerPoint presentation files. The Genigraphics Wizard not only sends your file to the company via modem, but it also displays order forms for your print job and sends these along with your presentation.

The Genigraphics Wizard offers an easy, one-step procedure for producing 35mm slides. If you don't have a modem or you prefer to use a local service bureau, see Producing 35mm Slides Using a Service Bureau on the next page.

To send slides to Genigraphics:

1. Open the presentation you want to send to Genigraphics.

2. Choose File > Send To > Genigraphics. The Genigraphics Wizard begins.

3. Follow the Genigraphics Wizard instructions, clicking Next after each step (**Figures 16.32** and **16.33**).

✔ Tip

- Your presentation is transmitted using the GraphicsLink program (**Figure 16.34**). If you encounter trouble during data transmission, you can adjust your communication settings (COM port, baud rate, etc.) and then use the Connect button to retransmit.

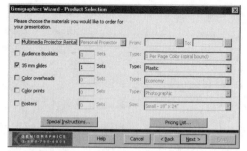

Figure 16.32 To get 35mm color slides of your presentation, you can use the Genigraphics Wizard included with PowerPoint (Windows).

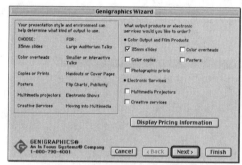

Figure 16.33 The Mac version of the Genigraphics Wizard looks a little different, but its basic functionality is the same.

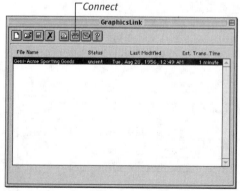

Figure 16.34 The GraphicsLink program manages the transmission of your presentation to Genigraphics.

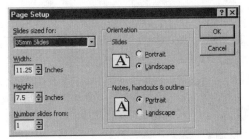

Figure 16.35 Size your slides for 35mm Slides in the Page Setup dialog box.

Select this option

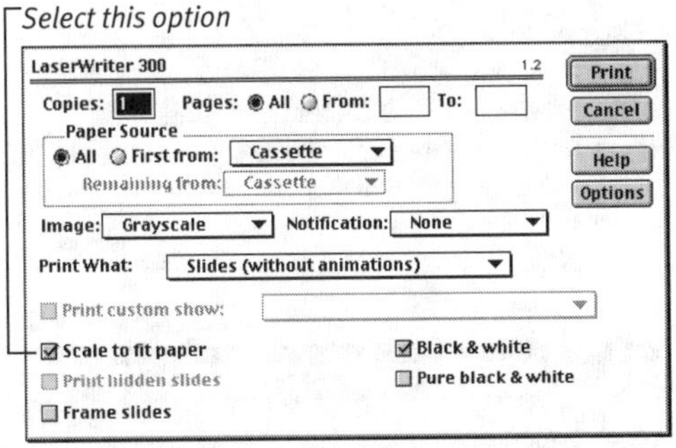

Figure 16.36 To print a presentation that was previously sized for 35mm slides, select the Scale to Fit Paper checkbox in the Print dialog box.

Producing 35mm Slides Using a Service Bureau

If you want to produce 35mm slides using a *service bureau* (a business that specializes in high-resolution production work), you can create a special output file (called a *PostScript file*) to bring to the bureau.

Since 35mm slides have slightly different dimensions than printed or onscreen slides, you'll need to change the slide size.

To set the size for 35mm slides:

1. Choose File > Page Setup.

   The Page Setup dialog box appears (**Figure 16.35**).

2. In the Slides Sized For list, select 35mm Slides.

3. Click OK.

   PowerPoint automatically scales your slides to fit the new format.

✔ Tips

- For the best legibility on 35mm slides, choose a dark background with a contrasting color for text.

  See Changing the Default Colors in Chapter 12.

- If you want to print the slides on paper, you don't need to change the setup again. Just select the Scale to Fit Paper checkbox in the Print dialog box (**Figure 16.36**).

  Refer to the next page to learn how to prepare slides for a service bureau.

Creating a PostScript File

The service bureau will require that a file be formatted in PostScript format. You don't need a PostScript printer to create a PostScript file—you just need a color PostScript driver. Your service bureau may give you a driver you can use, or you can use one of the drivers included with your operating system.

After you have located a driver and installed it in your computer (see your operating system's manual), you can use the Print dialog box to create a PostScript file.

To create a PostScript file (Windows):

1. Choose File > Print.

2. In the Name list, click the name of your PostScript driver (**Figure 16.37**).

3. Select the Print to File checkbox.

4. In the Print What field, choose Slides.

5. To produce color slides, unselect the Grayscale checkbox.

6. Click OK.

   You are then prompted to enter a filename.

7. Enter a filename (**Figure 16.38**).

   PowerPoint automatically adds PRN as the file extension.

8. Click Save.

   You can then copy this file to a diskette or to a high capacity storage disk and take it to your local service bureau.

Choose a color ⌐   Select Print ⌐
PostScript driver   to File

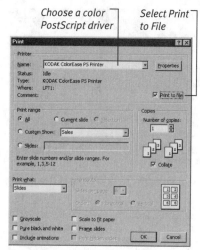

Figure 16.37 To create a color PostScript file, make sure the Print dialog box has the proper settings.

Figure 16.38 Enter a name for the PostScript file.

Click in the Destination field and choose File

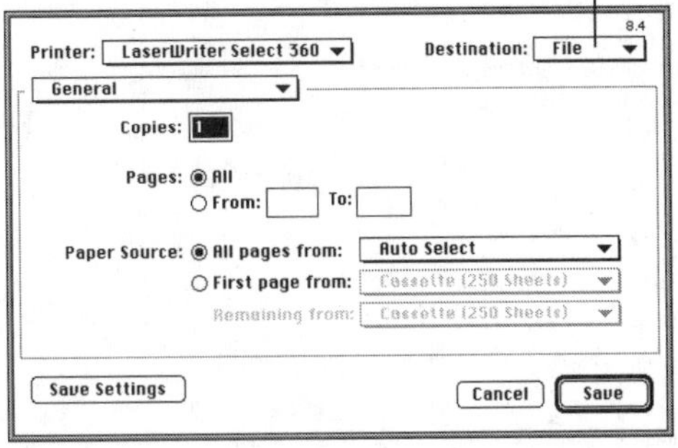

Figure 16.39 To create a PostScript file, choose File for the destination. (The General settings are shown here.)

Choose Microsoft PowerPoint to see PowerPoint printing options

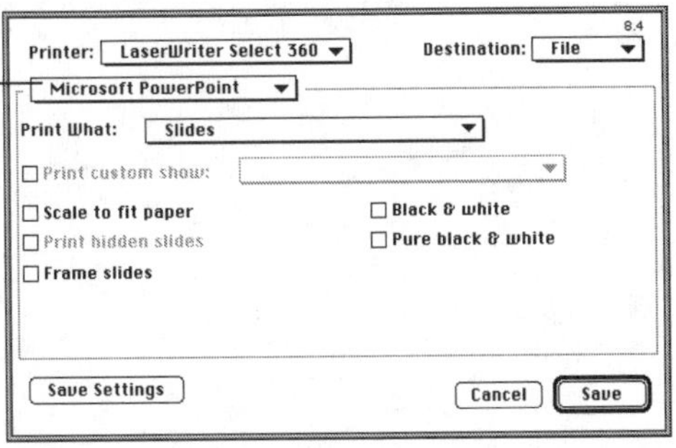

Figure 16.40 Select PowerPoint printing options.

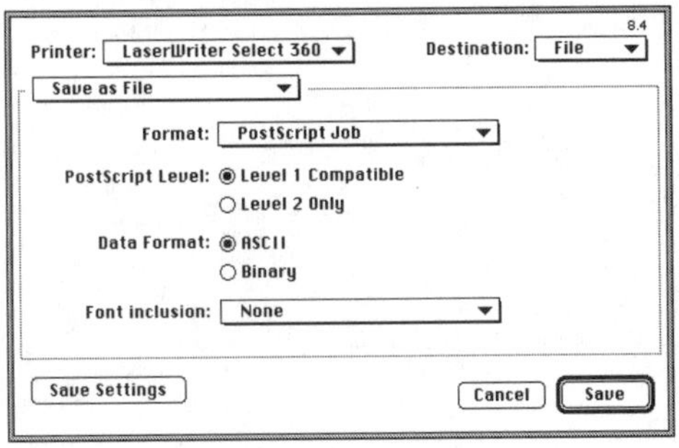

Figure 16.41 Check (and change, if necessary) PostScript file options before you save the file.

To create a PostScript file (Mac OS):

Before you begin, choose a color PostScript driver in the Chooser. See Selecting a Printer earlier in this chapter.

1. Choose File > Print.

2. In the Destination field, choose File (**Figure 16.39**).

3. In the Pages area, select All to create a file of the entire presentation.

   or

   For a range of slides, enter the starting and ending slide numbers in the From and To fields.

4. Click General and choose Microsoft PowerPoint from the list.

   The dialog box displays the options specific to PowerPoint (**Figure 16.40**).

5. Unselect the Black & White checkbox so that your slides will appear in color.

6. Change other PowerPoint printing options, if necessary.

7. To set PostScript file options, choose the Microsoft PowerPoint field and then choose Save as File.

   The dialog box now displays options that are specific to PostScript files (**Figure 16.41**).

8. Set the desired options.

9. Click Save.

10. In the Create File field, type a filename and include *.ps* at the end of the name.

11. Navigate to the drive and folder in which you want to save the file.

12. Click Save.

   You can then copy this file to a diskette or to a high capacity storage disk.

CREATING A POSTSCRIPT FILE (MAC OS)

PRESENTING ON THE INTERNET

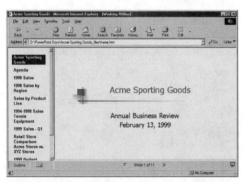

Figure 17.1 You can produce an HTML file of your PowerPoint presentation so that anyone with a Web browser can view your slide show.

PowerPoint includes a number of built-in features and wizards that use the Internet. For example, you can insert hyperlinks to Web sites, save a PowerPoint presentation directly to an FTP (File Transfer Protocol) site, and produce Web pages of your presentations.

The Web version of your presentation can be viewed in any browser (**Figure 17.1**), such as Internet Explorer or Netscape Navigator. The browser displays the slides one at a time, just as PowerPoint's slide show feature does. And if you like, you can publish your Web page on the Internet or on your company's intranet. Anyone who has a Web browser can view your slide show even if PowerPoint is not installed on the local computer.

You can also give a slide show remotely by broadcasting the show over an intranet (Windows only).

Linking to a Web Site

In your presentations, you can create a hyperlink to any Web site so that your audience can view a particular Web page during a slide show. Links to Web sites are useful for slide shows that are published on the Internet as well as those that are presented live to an audience. The hyperlink can be hypertext (such as *Acme Web Site*), a URL (Universal Resource Locator, such as *www.acme.com*), or an action button (**Figure 17.2**)

To create a link to a Web site:

1. In Slide view, enter the text that will become a hyperlink, and then select it.

2. Click the Insert Hyperlink button on the Standard toolbar.

   or

   Choose Insert > Hyperlink.

   The Insert Hyperlink dialog box appears (**Figures 17.3** and **17.4**).

3. Enter the URL of the Web page to which you want to link. (The prefix *http://* is not necessary.)

4. Click OK.

   The text is underlined and in a different color to show that it's a hyperlink.

✔ Tips

- Hypertext links to Web sites work only during a slide show.

- An easy way to create hypertext is to type the URL, such as *www.acme.com*, directly on the slide (Windows only). PowerPoint immediately recognizes the URL as a hyperlink. Note that you may need to press the spacebar or Enter after the text.

- To edit or remove a link, select the hypertext and click the Insert Hyperlink button.

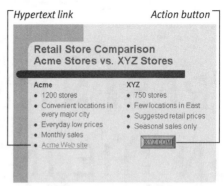

Figure 17.2 This slide shows two ways to insert a hyperlink to a Web site: using hypertext or an action button.

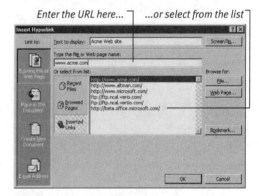

Figure 17.3 Enter the address of the Web page to which you want to link (Windows).

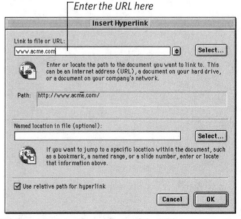

Figure 17.4 Enter the address of the Web page to which you want to link (Mac OS).

Custom button

Figure 17.5 To create an action button in Windows, choose Slide Show > Action Buttons and then select the Custom button.

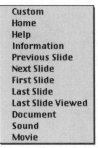

Figure 17.6 To create an action button in Mac OS, choose Slide Show > Action Buttons and then select Custom.

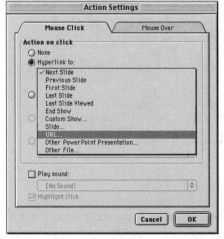

Figure 17.7 Choose URL on the Hyperlink To list.

Drag the diamond handle to add dimension

Select the button and type a label

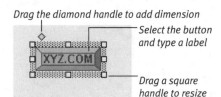

Drag a square handle to resize

Figure 17.8 You can format your action button however you like.

To create an action button that links to a Web site:

1. In Slide view, go to the slide on which you want to create the button.

2. Choose Slide Show > Action Buttons.

   or

   On the Drawing toolbar, click AutoShapes and then choose Action Buttons.

3. Choose the Custom button (**Figures 17.5** and **17.6**).

4. Drag a rectangular shape where you want to insert the button.

   When you release the mouse button, the Action Settings dialog box appears.

5. Click Hyperlink To.

6. In the Hyperlink To list, select URL (**Figure 17.7**).

7. In the Hyperlink to URL dialog box, type the URL (such as *www.acme.com*) and click OK. (Note that the prefix *http://* is not necessary.)

8. Click OK to close the dialog box.

   The action button appears on the slide.

9. Format and resize the button as needed (**Figure 17.8**).

✔ Tip

■ Action buttons link to Web sites only during a slide show.

LINKING TO A WEB SITE

Saving a Presentation to an FTP Site (Windows)

SAVING A PRESENTATION TO AN FTP SITE

In PowerPoint for Windows, you can save a presentation directly to an FTP site using the File > Save As command. After you have done this, anyone with access to the FTP site can copy the file and/or open it in PowerPoint.

Before you start, you may need to contact your Internet Service Provider to get the address of your FTP site, the location where you can store files, and a user name and password.

To save a presentation to an FTP site (Windows only):

1. Connect to the Internet.

2. In PowerPoint, choose File > Save As.

3. Change the filename, if desired.

4. Click the arrow in the Save In field and choose FTP Locations (**Figure 17.9**).

5. If you haven't yet created any FTP locations, double-click Add/Modify FTP Locations.

   or

   If you have already set up an FTP location, skip to step 9.

6. In the Add/Modify FTP Locations dialog box (**Figure 17.10**), enter the address of the FTP site.

7. If a password is required, enter your user name and password.

8. Click Add and then click OK.

   The FTP location now appears in the Save As dialog box (**Figure 17.11**).

9. Double-click the name of the FTP site.

10. After PowerPoint has found the site, navigate to the folder to which you want to save the presentation.

11. Click Save.

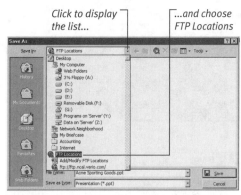

Click to display the list... ...and choose FTP Locations

Figure 17.9 In Windows, you can save directly to an FTP site.

Figure 17.10 To create an FTP location where you can save your presentation, enter the address of the FTP site and click Add.

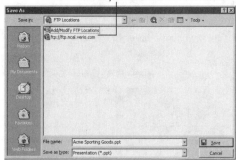

Names of FTP locations are listed here

Figure 17.11 You can save your presentation to an FTP site in the Save As dialog box.

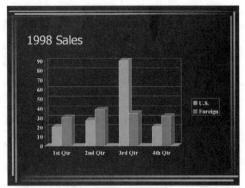

Figure 17.12 This slide has good contrast between the background and slide elements.

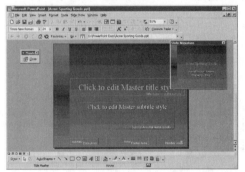

Figure 17.13 Edit the Slide Master to give your Web page consistent formatting.

Designing a Web Page

Designing a Web page is similar to designing a presentation for onscreen slide shows. Here are some important considerations:

◆ Give a lot of thought to your color scheme. You want to make sure there is sufficient contrast between the slide background and the text and other objects on the slide (**Figure 17.12**).

◆ Whenever possible, format the Slide Master instead of individual slides (**Figure 17.13**). This way, your presentation will be formatted consistently throughout.

See Chapter 12 for information on editing the Slide Master.

◆ Try to resist the temptation to get too fancy; for best viewability, be conservative with your typefaces, background fills, and special effects.

Many of the templates included with PowerPoint will produce attractive and consistently formatted Web pages.

See Applying a Template in Chapter 12 for more information about applying templates.

DESIGNING A WEB PAGE

Creating a Web Page (Windows)

If you would like to post a PowerPoint presentation on the Internet, or e-mail a slide show to someone who doesn't have PowerPoint, you can easily create an HTML file of your presentation. When PowerPoint converts your presentation, the HTML file will use the same color scheme, fonts, background, transition effects, animations, and links as your PowerPoint presentation.

To save a presentation as a Web page:

1. Choose File > Save as Web Page.

2. Use the Create New Folder tool (**Figure 17.14**) to create a folder for the Web page and its supporting files.

3. Click Publish.

   The Publish as Web Page dialog box appears (**Figure 17.15**).

4. In the Publish What area, choose what you want to publish.

5. In the Browser Support area, select the browsers that will be used to view your presentation.

6. In the File Name field, confirm the path to your new folder and change the filename if desired.

7. Change other settings, if necessary.

8. Click Web Options, and select the General tab (**Figure 17.16**).

9. If your show requires the viewer to manually advance the slides, make sure the Add Slide Navigation Controls checkbox is selected. This gives the user a navigation pane on the left side of the window (**Figure 17.17**). If your presentation is self-running, unselect this checkbox.

Create New Folder tool ⌐

Figure 17.14 Create a new folder for your HTML files.

⌐Select this option if you don't know which browser will be used to view the Web page

⌐Unselect this checkbox if you don't want a notes pane on the Web page

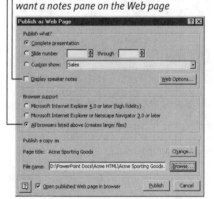

Figure 17.15 Select your options in the Publish as Web Page dialog box.

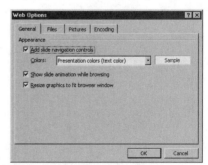

Figure 17.16 The General tab is one of four tabs used for setting Web options.

Navigation pane

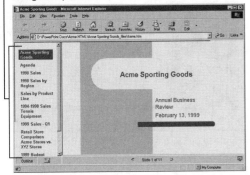

Figure 17.17 Clicking slide titles in a navigation pane helps the user to navigate your presentation.

Unselect this checkbox to place supporting files and the Web page in a single folder

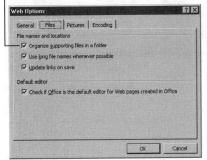

Figure 17.18 In the Files tab, you can indicate whether you want to place all supporting files in the same folder as the Web page or separate them into a subfolder.

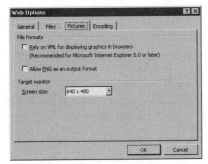

Figure 17.19 In the Pictures tab, select the screen size for the target monitor.

10. If you want your slide transitions and animations to work, make sure the Show Slide Animation While Browsing checkbox is selected.

11. Select the Files tab (**Figure 17.18**).

12. To place the Web page and its supporting files in the same folder, unselect the Organize Supporting Files in a Folder checkbox.

or

To place the image files (such as bullets, background textures, graphics, and navigational buttons) in a subfolder, select this checkbox.

13. Select the Pictures tab (**Figure 17.19**).

14. In the Screen Size field, select the desired resolution. (640×480 or 800×600 both work well on a majority of systems.)

15. Change other settings, if desired, and then click OK.

16. To see the Web page in your default browser, select the Open Published Web Page in Browser checkbox.

17. To create the Web page, click Publish.

After the file is created, the first slide in the show will appear in your default browser (**Figure 17.17**).

✔ Tips

■ To get an idea of what your presentation looks like as a Web page before you actually create the page, use the File > Web Page Preview command.

■ View your Web page in a variety of browsers (and different versions of each browser) to make sure it looks and functions as you intended.

See Viewing a Slide Show in a Web Browser (Windows) later in this chapter.

Creating a Web Page (Mac OS)

If you want to post a PowerPoint presentation on the Internet, or e-mail a slide show to someone who doesn't have PowerPoint, you can easily create an HTML file of your presentation. When PowerPoint converts your presentation, the HTML file will use the same color scheme, fonts, background, and links as your PowerPoint presentation.

To save a presentation as an HTML file:

1. Choose File > Save as HTML.
   The Save as HTML Wizard opening window appears.

2. Click Next to begin.

3. Select the page style (**Figure 17.20**):
   - ◆ Choose Standard for a style that will work in all browsers.
     or
   - ◆ Choose Browser Frames for a style that will work in browsers that support HTML frames.

4. Click Next.

5. For the graphic type, choose GIF (for the best quality images) or JPEG (for the smallest file sizes), and then click Next.

6. Select the desired monitor resolution (640 by 480 or 800 by 600 both work well on a majority of systems).

7. For the Width of Graphics (**Figure 17.21**), choose ½ or ¾ width of screen to fit the entire slide in the browser window.

8. Click Next.

9. Define the information page options; this information will appear on the slide show's opening page.

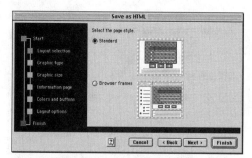

Figure 17.20 The Save as HTML Wizard first asks you to select a page style.

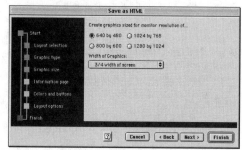

Figure 17.21 Select a monitor resolution and size your graphics.

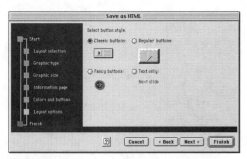

Figure 17.22 Select a style for navigation buttons.

Unselect this checkbox if you don't want a notes pane on the Web page

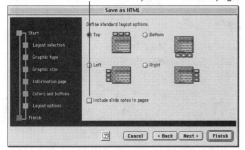

Figure 17.23 For the standard page layout, indicate where you want navigation buttons to appear.

Default folder name

Figure 17.24 The Web page and supporting files will be saved in the folder name you specify.

10. Click Next.

11. Select the colors for the introductory page and navigation bars and click Next.

12. Select a style for the navigation buttons (**Figure 17.22**) and click Next.

13. If you selected the Standard layout in step 3 above, you can select where you want the navigation buttons to appear on the layout (**Figure 17.23**).

14. Click Next.

You now need to select the name and location for the folder that will hold your Web page and supporting files.

15. Click Select, type a name for the folder (**Figure 17.24**), navigate to the location for the new folder, and then click Save.

16. Click Next.

17. To create the HTML file, click Finish.

✔ Tip

- View your Web page in a variety of browsers (and different versions of each browser) to make sure it looks and functions as you intended.

  See Viewing a Slide Show in a Web Browser (Mac OS) later in this chapter.

CREATING A WEB PAGE (MAC OS)

Viewing a Slide Show in a Web Browser (Windows)

After you save your PowerPoint presentation as a Web page, you can view it as a slide show in any browser to see what it will look like on the Web. (At this point you don't need to be connected to the Internet since your Web page is stored on your hard disk.)

To view a slide show in your default Web browser:

1. Choose View > Toolbars > Web to display the Web toolbar (**Figure 17.25**).

2. In the Address field on the Web toolbar, type the complete pathname and file-name of the Web page and then press Enter.

   or

   Choose Go > Open on the Web toolbar and browse to the Web page file (**Figure 17.26**).

   The presentation's first slide appears in your browser window (**Figure 17.27**).

3. Use the navigation pane on the left to jump to other slides. (This pane appears if you selected the Add Slide Navigation Controls checkbox when creating the Web page.)

   or

   If the slide show is self-running, your browser will automatically advance the slides in your presentation.

To view a show in other browsers:

1. Launch the browser.

2. Choose File > Open, navigate to the folder in which you saved your Web page, and select the filename.

3. To view other slides, click the slide title in the navigation pane on the left.

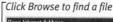
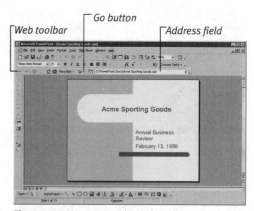

Figure 17.25 You can use the Web toolbar to open Web pages.

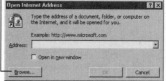

Figure 17.26 Use the Go button on the Web toolbar to browse to a Web page.

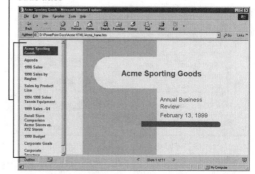

Figure 17.27 Click a slide title to display the slide in the browser window.

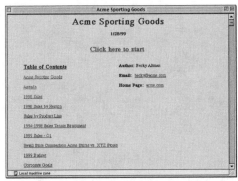

Figure 17.28 The introductory screen of the Web page (Index.htm).

Navigation buttons

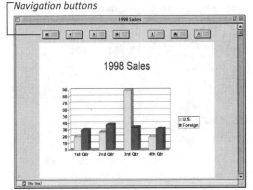

Figure 17.29 This Web page uses the Standard layout.

Click a slide title...   *...or use the navigation buttons*

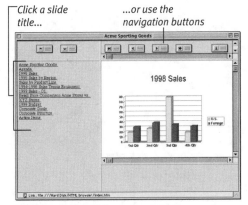

Figure 17.30 This Web page uses the Browser Frames layout.

Viewing a Slide Show in a Web Browser (Mac OS)

After you save your PowerPoint presentation as an HTML file, you can view it as a slide show in any browser to see what it will look like on the Web. (At this point you don't need to be connected to the Internet since your Web page is stored on your hard disk.)

To view a slide show in your default Web browser:

1. In Finder, open the folder containing your HTML files.

2. Double-click INDEX.HTM.

   The introductory page appears in your browser window (**Figure 17.28**).

3. Click the hypertext *Click here to start*.

   The first slide in your presentation appears.

4. To view other slides, click the navigation buttons (**Figure 17.29**) or click a slide title in the outline on the left (**Figure 17.30**).

To view a show in other browsers:

1. Launch the browser.

2. Choose File > Open, navigate to the folder containing your HTML files, and select INDEX.HTM.

   The introductory page appears in your browser window.

Publishing a Presentation on the Internet

When your presentation is ready for public viewing, you can publish it on the Internet. One way to do this is to use FTP software to transfer the files to your Web site.

Windows users have an alternative way to copy HTML files to a Web site: the Web Publishing Wizard. This Wizard comes with the Windows version of Internet Explorer 4.0 or later and is an easy way to post your Web pages to a Web site.

Before you begin, contact your Internet Service Provider and ascertain the following information:

- ◆ The host or server name (such as *ftp://webshell.ncal.verio.com*)
- ◆ The remote directory (such as *www.acme.com/files*)
- ◆ Your user name and password

To use the Web Publishing Wizard (Windows only):

1. Click the Start button on the taskbar.

2. Choose Programs > Communications > Internet Explorer > Web Publishing Wizard.

   The Web Publishing Wizard window appears (**Figure 17.31**).

3. Click Next to begin.

4. Specify the name of the folder containing your Web page and supporting files (**Figure 17.32**) and click Next.

5. Enter a descriptive name for your server and click Next.

Figure 17.31 The Web Publishing Wizard is one way to copy HTML files to a Web site.

Click here to find the folder

Figure 17.32 Enter the name of the folder on your hard drive containing your HTML files.

Enter the URL here

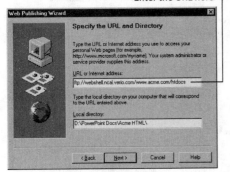

Figure 17.33 Enter the Internet address where you want to copy the HTML files.

6. Enter the URL where you will post your files (**Figure 17.33**).

7. Make sure the Local Directory field contains the folder name you specified in step 4 above, and then click Next.

8. Click Finish.

   You may be asked to enter authentication information. If you are, enter your user name and password, and click OK.

   Assuming you specified all the above information correctly, the files will be copied to the Internet address you indicated.

✔ Tip

■ After you publish your presentation on the Internet, open the Web page and test each hyperlink to make sure it is working properly.

Scheduling a Broadcast (Windows)

With PowerPoint's Broadcast feature, you can present a slide show over an intranet to a designated group of people in real time and include live audio or video. (For audiences of 15 people or more, you'll need to use a NetShow server on a local area network.) The participants (except for the presenter) don't need PowerPoint—they just need a Web browser and access to the network server where you stored the presentation.

To schedule a broadcast:

1. Open the presentation you want to broadcast.

2. Choose Slide Show > Online Broadcast > Set Up and Schedule.

   The Broadcast Schedule dialog box opens.

3. Choose Setup Up and Schedule a New Broadcast and click OK.

   The Description tab (**Figure 17.34**) is used to create your *lobby page*. (A lobby page is displayed in the participant's browser before the broadcast begins.)

4. Fill in the fields on the Description tab.

5. Select the Broadcast Settings tab (**Figure 17.35**).

6. If you plan to narrate the presentation, select the appropriate options in the Audio and Video section.

7. If you want participants to be able to e-mail questions and comments to you during the broadcast, select the Viewers Can Email checkbox and enter an e-mail address (or choose one from the Address Book).

8. Click Server Options.

   The Server Options dialog box appears (**Figure 17.36**).

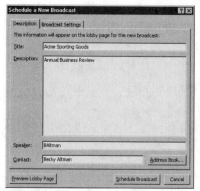

Figure 17.34 The information in the Description tab will appear on the lobby page.

Select one or both of these checkboxes if you will be narrating the broadcast

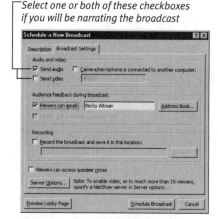

Figure 17.35 Use the Broadcast Settings tab to specify options for your broadcast.

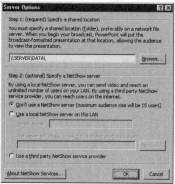

Figure 17.36 Enter a location accessible to all broadcast participants.

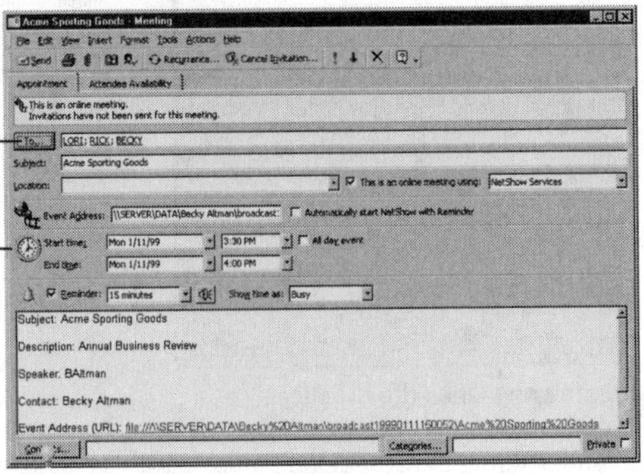

*Enter the e-mail
addresses of invitees*

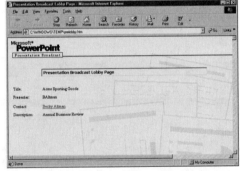

Set the broadcast date and time

Figure 17.37 After you set your broadcast options, enter the names of the invitees and set the date and time for the broadcast.

Figure 17.38 Your browser displays a preview of the lobby page.

9. Enter the location of the shared folder (preferably on a network server) in which you want PowerPoint to place the broadcast-formatted presentation.

10. Click OK.

11. Click Schedule Broadcast.

   You are notified that a maximum of 15 users will be able to watch the live broadcast unless you specify a NetShow server.

12. Click Yes to continue.

   Your e-mail program, such as Microsoft Outlook (**Figure 17.37**), opens so that you can send out invitations to your broadcast.

13. If you are using an e-mail program other than Outlook 2000, enter the broadcast date and time in the message. The URL of the broadcast site will be included in the message.

   or

   If you are using Outlook, enter the e-mail addresses of those to whom you want to send invitations, and in the Start Time field, select the date and time for your broadcast.

14. Click the Send button on the toolbar to send the invitations.

✔ Tips

■ In the Schedule a New Broadcast dialog box, click Preview Lobby Page to see how the lobby page looks in your default browser (**Figure 17.38**).

■ To send another invitation or to change the broadcast time after you have scheduled a broadcast, choose Slide Show > Online Broadcast > Set Up and Schedule, select Change Settings or Reschedule a Broadcast, and then click Reschedule.

Broadcasting a Presentation (Windows)

Before you can broadcast a presentation, make sure you have set up and scheduled the broadcast as described on the preceding pages. Then, about 30 minutes before your broadcast is scheduled to begin, start the procedure below to get everything ready for the broadcast. If you plan to provide live narration, you'll need to connect a microphone to your computer.

To broadcast a presentation:

1. Open the presentation you want to broadcast.

2. Choose Slide Show > Online Broadcast > Begin Broadcast.

   The Broadcast Presentation dialog box appears (**Figure 17.39**). Your presentation is saved as an HTML file in the server location, and PowerPoint checks audio and video connections (if applicable) to make sure they are working properly.

3. To send your participants late-breaking information, click Audience Message (**Figure 17.40**), type your message, and click Update. (This information will appear on the lobby page.)

4. When you're ready to begin broadcasting, click Start.

   The first slide in your presentation appears full screen (as in a PowerPoint slide show). The viewers of your broadcast will see this same slide in their browsers (**Figure 17.41**).

5. Press Page Down to display the next slide in your show; if you enabled audio or video, you can narrate your presentation.

✔ Tip

■ The same techniques you use to navigate a slide show will work during a broadcast.

Figure 17.39 Open the Broadcast Presentation dialog box about 30 minutes before the scheduled time to prepare for your broadcast.

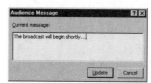

Figure 17.40 Enter last-minute updates to your audience in the Audience Message dialog box.

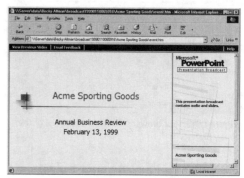

Figure 17.41 During a broadcast, participants see the presentation in their browsers.

INDEX

B

D

INDEX

M

O

INDEX

Q R

INDEX